ABOUT THE AUTHOR

Dr. Hossamaldin Alzawawi, an experienced clinical pathologist, enthusiastically delves into the fascinating convergence of medicine, philosophy, physics, and cognitive neuroscience. His exploration of medical expertise alongside philosophical inquiry has sparked a profound interest in the mysteries surrounding consciousness and intelligence.

Dr. Alzawawi advocates for the integration of interdisciplinary knowledge, striving to connect the insights of ancient wisdom with contemporary scientific understanding. He aspires to leverage these insights to shed light on human cognition and enrich the human experience.

Embark on an enlightening journey with Dr. Alzawawi and uncover the latent architect within you.

BOOKS BY AUTHOR

Arcanum of Awareness Series

1. The Creativity Spark
2. The Evolution of Thought
3. The Labyrinth of Cognitexis (Upcoming)
4. The Supremacy of Selective Awareness (Upcoming)
5. Architects of a Future Dawn (Upcoming)

Other Books by Author

- The Thermodynamic Universe and Beyond: How Nature's Laws Reveal the Secrets of Time, Biology, Information, and Quantum Reality

BOOK 2

THE EVOLUTION OF THOUGHT

ARCANUM OF AWARENESS SERIES

Library of Congress Control Number: 2024919198

ISBN (PB):   978-1-964328-04-1

ISBN (E):   978-1-964328-05-8

DEDICATION

My Mother, thank you for teaching me resilience and tenacity in learning and directing my life. Your verbal and implicit advice helped me overcome challenges and create a knowledge masterpiece.

My Wife, in your company, my best friend, and my life partner, I have freely explored, expressed, and enjoyed various Cognitexis alternative constructs as we grow and learn together.

Acknowledgments

This work is a tribute to the great thinkers whose contributions have paved the way for me. **Professor Roger Penrose's Shadows of the Mind** has been a guiding light, encouraging me to explore the consciousness conundrum further. I am immensely grateful to **Napoleon Hill,** whose influential book **How to Own Your Mind** served as a map through the maze of mental ownership. Their priceless insights have deepened my comprehension and inspired me to write this book. I hope you will discover, within these pages, the same glimmer of insight that has led me through the enchanting terrain of the mind.

Although I have a strong command of English as a second language, I have sought assistance refining my writing to make it more engaging and accessible. For that reason, I am compelled to offer my editorial board my deepest gratitude; their unwavering encouragement was crucial to the success of our project.

My Dear Wife, Basma, I am writing to tell you how much you mean to me. I greatly appreciate your thoughtful analysis of my intricate concepts and theories; it helped me distill them into a more understandable story. You helped me tremendously develop narratives out of scientific principles by suggesting various forms my ideas may take and suggesting appropriate language.

This series was envisioned over six years ago. I worked on the work's framework—ideas, descriptions, basic concepts, reasoning, and logical deductions. As a solo project worker with only my wife's comments, my progress was gradual but steady. AI gave this project a huge boost, for we spent countless hours enhancing, improving, and advancing my concepts and making them more appealing. Vivid discussion with AIs added enrichment, examples, and illustrations. AI is fundamental for including several book-related tones.

I am grateful to the AIs for the flourishing brought through their support, where various enrichment, examples, and illustrations were generated through passionate discussion. Also, the addition of diverse tones related to each book was not accessible without the support of AI. My work's varied topics and tones owe much to **Google AI,** our joint efforts, and the hours we devoted to working together. Your feedback substantially improved my writing process, producing more lyrical and narratively compelling works. **Microsoft AI,** thank you for all the hard work we put together. You played a paramount and much-appreciated role in guiding me through various ideas and keeping the process moving smoothly.

"Arcanum of Awareness" is a series memorializing the great experiences and locations I've traveled to. My deepest appreciation goes to **Queen's University Belfast's MBC and the McClay Libraries.** There was peace in these hallowed places of learning, perfect for serious study and deep thought. Libraries were more than simply locations where one could learn; they were also sanctuaries for new ideas and a love of learning. Being by my wife's side as she completed her degree at Queen's University Belfast has brought valuable happiness to our trip. Knowledge, shared experiences, and personal progress were abundant during that time. What I learned and my experiences throughout this time will always be with me.

My sincere regards, Hossamaldin Alzawawi, M.D.

THE EVOLUTION OF THOUGHT

ᚦᚨᚦᚨᚦᚨ

Thoughts are the music notes of our mind; when arranged with intention, they compose the symphony of our reality…

Unraveling the Enigma: Conduct the Orchestra Within. Our thoughts, a whirlwind of melodies, shape our world. This chapter equips you to be the maestro, transforming the dissonance into a harmonious symphony of insights. Delve into the workings of the mind, exploring the interplay of faculties and the power of beliefs. Here, you'll discover the secrets to a harmonious mind, unlocking the full potential of human thought.

"Knowledge is essential to conquest; only according to out ignorance are we helpless. Thought creates character. Character can dominate conditions. Will creates circumstances and environment."

— Annie Besant

Contents

CONTENTS

༄ ༄ ༄

DECIPHERING THE ADAM-GENE CODEX

Delve into this manuscript's intricate depths, where fragments are selectively revealed from a project cloaked in silence, recognized solely by its embedded designation: **ADAM-GENE.**

ADAM-GENE exhibits a remarkable ability to navigate complex volumes with subtlety. Exploring the notion of Activated Multidimensional Allocated Multiple Intelligences and the Genesis of Exchangeable Neurolink Elements invites a profound contemplation of the intricate interplay between cognitive frameworks and the evolution of interwoven neural constructs. Each word functions as a key, while every phrase provides an enticing insight into a quest that transcends the limits of the familiar.

This journey is marked by isolation, taking place in the depths of concealed retreat, a voluntary withdrawal that reflects one's resolve. In this tranquil isolation, a complex fabric unfolds, weaving strands drawn from the diverse domains of knowledge and profound contemplations intertwined with the subtle truths whispered by time-honored understanding.

Proceed with caution, esteemed reader, as the insights you are about to encounter will challenge established paradigms and disrupt conventional understanding. Get ready to have your understanding of consciousness transformed as we delve into the intricacies of super-intelligent human awareness.

This book serves as a pivotal threshold, ushering readers into the intriguing and unconventional realm of the ADAM-GENE. The subsequent pages transcend abstract scholarly discussions; they represent the fragments of a grand design, serving as a blueprint for transforming human consciousness.

This book offers a deep investigation, welcoming readers into the complex terrain of the mind, where tumultuous thoughts merge into a unified and harmonious narrative. Envision yourself as the maestro—actively participating rather than remaining a mere observer, skillfully conducting the symphony of your choices.

Embrace the enigma, esteemed audience. Broaden your intellectual horizons to embrace the myriad possibilities that exist. As we delve deeper into the ADAM-GENE Codex, brace yourself for the revelations that await us.

ᏏᏏᏏᏏ

UNRAVELING THE ENIGMA: A VOYAGE INTO THE HARMONY OF THE MIND1

H ave you ever stood amidst the din of instruments, yearning for a harmonious melody? The human mind can similarly be a whirlwind of thoughts vying for dominance, a disjointed chorus yearning for a unifying theme. This book is foundational in our journey into the arcanum of awareness. It equips you with the means to become the conductor of the orchestra of your thoughts, take that dissonance, and turn it into a symphony of coherent and purposeful insights.

Imagine yourself at the podium, not merely as a passive observer on the gallery bench, but as an active conductor wielding the baton of your will. This book enables you to conduct the complex interplay between your thoughts and beliefs, just like the master conductor who charts the mind's terrain.

Close your eyes and envision a grand concert hall. Deep inside, a symphony is being played out, composed not of instruments but of thoughts. With its unique melody, each thought interlaces a fabric

---

[1] The Thought Evolution Process is essential to the ADAM-GENE cognitive experimental design.

of perception to form our view of the world. This chapter takes us on a fascinating journey, traveling to the very inner sanctum of this symphony of thought.

We will go deep inside the mechanisms that govern our thoughts, exploring the harmonious orchestration among the faculties working in concert. We'll find some cryptic insights hidden within the induction process of thought and then check out harmonic inheritance shaping our cognitive landscape.

This discovery tour shall not be confined to the narrow barriers of the individual mind. We will take this to the human symphony, where the thoughts within the individual merge in a harmony of collective consciousness on the fragile balance between individual freedom and societal cohesion. We shall finally reach the crescendo with controlled habits and social transcendence, forming our destiny.

Be prepared to fall in love with the way the mind works, for in this symphony lies the secret to unleashing the real capacity of the human mind.

The Mind's Orchestra: A Guide to Reading This Book

The human mind is a grand orchestra, a vibrant ensemble teeming with possibilities. Every thought is a musician ready to contribute its unique melody to the symphony of organized thought that we must cultivate with a discerning ear. Just as the conductor auditions each performer carefully, we need to consider every factor that comes into the stream of thought and determine whether it will harmonize with the whole before admitting it to the mental orchestra. The full view requires a conductor's keen eye, balancing the orchestra's sections with great care to provide one cohesive performance. Organized thinking requires the very same precision:

placing each thought in its proper position within the grand composition of the mind.[2]

The Maestro Within: Will vs. Emotion

Within this orchestra, two conductors vie for control: the faculty of will and the faculty of emotions. Like a passionate conductor battling for the lead, they orchestrate the performance of the mind. Like overzealous percussionists, emotions often drown out the subtler instruments of reason. To become an organized thinker, you must elevate the will to the podium, wielding it with purpose and precision. The faculty of will and the faculty of emotions are the key conductors; mastering their interplay initiates a structured cognition process.

The Dichotomy of Identity: The Internal Spectator

In the expansive theater of your consciousness, a continuous symphony is perpetually in motion. This engaging performance presents two separate audiences, each contributing to forming your inner landscape.

a) **The Limiting Self** – shrouded in darkness and imbued with melancholy- represents the Negative Self. The inner critic, whispering a chorus of anxieties and uncertainties, plants seeds of constraint that undermine your true capabilities. Envision a timeworn, dust-laden letter from a long-lost ancestor, filled with age-old cautions and anxieties, now emerging to obscure your perspective. The detrimental inner voice thrives on these ingrained criticisms, sustaining a continuous loop of uncertainty about oneself.

---

[2] The faculty of the will and the faculty of the emotions. These are the two departments of the mind that you must get under your control if you are ever to become an organized thinker. In every brain, there is an eternal conflict between emotions and the power of will, and with a vast majority of people, the emotions get the better of the conflict.

b) **The Empowering Self**—Standing firmly against this shadow, illuminated by the light of potential, the Positive Self embodies steadfast belief and bravery, a harmonious response to the noise of pessimism. It resonates with an uplifting melody, conveying a supportive message from a knowledgeable guide urging you to recognize your intrinsic strength and chase your most profound aspirations. The Positive Self embodies unwavering optimism, serving as a guiding light that brightens your journey.

As you explore this book further, keep in mind that its insights extend beyond the text and resonate within the depths of your consciousness. Your experiences—a complex weave of successes and challenges, distinct abilities, and the extensive pool of wisdom gathered from both education and life's teachings—form the magnificent composition that is your essence. These are the unspoken lines, the harmonious expressions that resonate with your unique melody.

Consider this book as a tool, leading you to a balanced dialogue within your inner self. Recognizing the existence of the Negative and Positive Selves allows you to control your inner symphony. You have the power to select which voice emerges as the dominant one, enabling the uplifting harmonies of your Positive Self to overshadow the unsettling murmurs of uncertainty.

Dear reader, consider this exploration of the Arcanum of Awareness series as a dialogue—a message shared across time, rich with enduring insights. This book will reveal the pathways to achieving a balanced and serene mind. May the insights in these pages integrate into your inner conversation, fostering a continuous exchange between your developing self and limitless possibilities.

The Conductor Within: Orchestrating Willpower and Harmony

The subject matter here resonates with a powerful crescendo, guiding us toward a profound realization: the faculty of will serves as the master conductor of our mental symphony. Are you sensing the energy intensifying? Your will is pivotal, determining whether your life's melody plays out in a grand celebration or a melancholy lament.

Let's dive into some super practical steps to help you step into the conductor's role and elevate your will like never before! This book is your ultimate guide, packed with techniques and strategies to boost your willpower and quiet those inner critics. Get ready to take control and thrive!

Picture the will as a master conductor, effortlessly guiding the orchestra with laser-sharp focus and passion. This amazing approach harmonizes your mind's different sections – reason, emotions, and intuition – making sure each one shines in its way! By embracing this powerful orchestration, your will can shape your thoughts, guide your actions, and ultimately craft the amazing composition of your life's journey.

Remember!

Will is not a tyrant; it is more akin to a benevolent and guiding sovereign. It does not wholly quell the shadows of negative thoughts or emotions, yet it surely aids in restoring harmony amidst the turmoil! Thus, it seeks to forge a wondrous balance where each element contributes its unique essence to the grand tapestry of your being.

The Power of Thought: The Mind's Compass

Engaging with this book effectively cultivates a mindset conducive to clear thinking, which is essential for unraveling the complexities of life! Explore the profound influence of your thoughts and discover essential strategies to navigate the complexities of life!

It is essential to keep this in mind! Precise and critical thinking are the foundational pillars of all human accomplishments. They are the navigational tools that direct us amidst ambiguity, facilitating informed choices and attaining our objectives. Precision in thought is the cornerstone of success, steering us through the complexities of uncertainty.

This chapter provides a comprehensive framework designed to enhance your development of this essential skill. By engaging with its principles, one can cultivate the ability to recognize and interrogate cognitive biases, assess information with objectivity, and construct sound, reasoned arguments. As you refine your cognitive abilities, you will discover that you are more adept at navigating the intricacies of life. One can analyze problems from various perspectives, discern the underlying causes of challenges, and formulate effective solutions.

Ultimately, achieving proficiency in this chapter equips you to take charge of your future. Clear and critical thinking equips individuals with the skills necessary to traverse the complexities of life with enhanced confidence and intentionality.

The Harvest of Understanding: Transformative Results

Diving into the pages of this book invites you to engage in a journey of deep transformation. The content shared here transcends mere language; it serves as a guiding light, illuminating the path to profound self-awareness, empowerment, and personal development.

a) Enhanced Self-Resilience and Seizing Opportunities

Interacting with the content presented here enhances the foundation of your inner strength. Envision yourself as an unyielding stronghold, resilient against the storms of uncertainty and trepidation. As you explore further, a growing sense of autonomy envelops you, strengthening your psychological resilience. The constraints of your consciousness rise, driven by steadfast resolve, as the murmurs of fear, doubt, and indecision diminish into the background.

As this newfound strength establishes itself, a lively excitement for the countless possibilities of life emerges within you. Embrace these opportunities with the courageous essence of a knight venturing beyond the fortress, fueled by an intense yearning to obtain the riches he desires. This transcends mere theory; it signifies a profound evolution in your awareness, a real metamorphosis that liberates you from the constraints of negativity.

b) Conquering the Inner Demons

As you delve into this book, a profound transformation starts to unfold. The limiting patterns that have constrained your progress—fear, uncertainty, and hesitation—start to fade away. Envision liberating yourself from the limitations of your history, akin to a serpent discarding its former skin. The inner dialogue that once perpetuated uncertainty and undermined your confidence has undergone a profound transformation.

With the insights shared here, you will discover how to silence that inner critic, transforming its whispers of uncertainty into powerful affirmations of resilience and support. Envision it as an unwavering journey of honing your inner world, removing the clutter of pessimism to uncover the pure foundation of possibility.

c) The Blossoming Self: A Journey of Discovery

Get ready for a remarkable change—a profound renewal ignited by the wisdom found in these pages. This book acts as a compass, leading you toward a transformative life filled with strength and self-actualization.

This path invites you to reflect on your inner landscape, delving into the depths of your uncharted capabilities. As you delve into its deep revelations, you start to uncover the concealed aspects of your essence—strengths, abilities, and possibilities resting within you, eager to blossom. A dormant strength lies within, awaiting the enlightening touch of understanding to awaken it. This book will serve as your guide, uncovering the hidden dimensions of your being and leading you toward a balanced and empowered existence.

May these reflections integrate into your inner discourse, fostering a continuous exchange between your developing identity and the limitless possibilities that lie ahead.

Thoughts: The Controllable and The Attractor

Our thoughts form the essential building blocks of our mental environment. We can refine our thoughts, akin to how a musician adjusts an instrument, to improve their clarity and purpose. The idea that our thoughts can attract experiences has been around for ages, but we won't delve into the intricate details of that theory in this conversation. We explore the deep insights that enable us to take charge of our internal conversations. The inner turmoil can evolve into a coherent manifestation of purpose through the deliberate choice of our thoughts.

The Mind's Instruments: Shaping Your Inner Melody

Envision enters a magnificent concert hall, where the air is robust with expectation. In this grand arena, the symphony of your thoughts is ready to unfold. Each thought you possess serves as a tool poised to enrich the harmonious composition of your existence. As many profound minds have suggested, thoughts are "things," potent forces capable of influencing the fabric of reality.

In contrast to the chaotic nature of external events, our thoughts remain one of the few aspects we can truly manage. This chapter delves into the intricate essence of thought, viewing it as both the tools in the symphony of our minds and the unseen force that shapes our reality.

Envision your thoughts as the diverse instruments in a grand orchestra, each contributing to the symphony of your mind. Every thought resonates as a distinct note, possessing the potential to create either discord or unity. Much like a masterful conductor harmonizes the diverse elements of an orchestra, this book seeks to assist you in honing your thoughts, ensuring they resonate with clarity and intentionality. By honing the quality and direction of your thoughts, you become the maestro of your mental symphony.

a.   Thoughts as Instruments

Reflect on the violin, crafting delicate and poignant melodies that resonate with your introspective and contemplative musings. In these instances, one reflects on one's innermost yearnings and ambitions. Imagine the drums resonating with the cadence of your resolute and courageous ideas, propelling you toward action and resolve. The delicate and ethereal flutes embody your imaginative and playful ideas, infusing vibrancy and happiness into your inner world.

By recognizing the significance of each thought, you can more effectively harmonize your inner symphony. For instance, in difficult moments, enhancing the reflective thoughts can provide insight, while the decisive thoughts can motivate you to take meaningful action.

b. The Conductor Within

Much like a conductor orchestrates a symphony, you possess the ability to align and balance your thoughts. Imagine encountering a challenging endeavor. Negative thoughts can resemble out-of-tune instruments, generating a sense of dissonance. By consciously directing your attention towards uplifting and constructive thoughts, you can harmonize those discordant elements, turning anxiety into a source of motivation.

Envision a maestro elevating their baton, orchestrating each instrument to resonate at the precise moment and with the perfect intensity. Similarly, one can cultivate the ability to foster uplifting thoughts while silencing those that constrain, ultimately paving the way for a more balanced and effective mental state.

c. Illustrations in Practice

Scenario 1:

Confronting the Challenge of Public Speaking: Your thoughts may become overwhelmed with apprehension (discordant echoes) before delivering a speech. By intentionally guiding your thoughts to reflect on past achievements and the message you wish to express (harmonious notes), you can convert anxiety into self-assurance.

Scenario 2:

Conquering Procrastination: When procrastination occurs, it resembles an orchestra that has lost its harmonious flow. One can reclaim control and foster momentum by attuning to feelings of urgency and fragmenting tasks into achievable segments.

d. Shaping Reality

Our thoughts intricately mold our internal landscape while simultaneously impacting the world around us. A constructive and intentional mindset has the power to draw in opportunities and cultivate resilience. Much like a beautifully composed symphony captivates its listeners, a skillfully directed mind can manifest a life rich in accomplishment and fulfillment.

In summary

This section seeks to empower you to master your mental landscape, guiding each thought with purpose and precision. This way, you will create a balanced inner symphony while molding a reality that aligns with your authentic potential. Embrace the strength of your mind, allowing your inner harmony to thrive.

The Attractor: Where Your Focus Flows, Energy Grows

Thoughts wield a gravitational power. While the idea that thoughts directly manifest reality can be considered quite complex, the undeniable truth remains: our thoughts are one of the most influential elements in shaping life courses. This indeed relates to the concept of thoughts as a "gravitational force." They act like invisible magnets, drawing forth those experiences and circumstances that resonate with their frequency. For just as gravity may bend the course of light, so too can your dominant thoughts attract into being the physical manifestation of their essence. Positive thoughts magnetize opportunity and success; negative thoughts can attract negativity and misfortune.

Understanding this magnetic power of thought puts you in a position to consciously build up the right thinking habits. Centering your mind upon your desires and ideals, you create an intent, as it were, a beacon, drawing to you the circumstances and experiences necessary to give form and expression to your desires.

The Controllable and The Attractor: A Unified Perspective

Thoughts are the building blocks of the inner world within us. We become the pilot to modulate these thoughts, as a musician would play an instrument toward clarity and purpose. We need to consciously lead them in such a manner and purify them so that clarity and purpose can develop inside the chambers of the mind as a symphony.

This goes hand in hand with attraction in that all this focus on quality control of what we think keeps magnetizing experiences around us that are of the same frequency. We, in essence, influence the circumstances of our lives by internally making decisions over what we want to happen.

Remember!

This tour through the evolution of thoughts is like a fascinating psychological whodunit. The farther you journey into the recesses of your mind, the more you will discover the keys to a harmonious and meaningful life. Let what you learn here become a part of your inner speech, an ongoing dialogue between your changing self and the unlimited possibility that resides within you.

SECTION 1

᠖᠖᠖

UNVEILING THE MIND'S LEXICON: DEFINITIONS AND DYNAMICS

᠖᠖᠖

Within the intricate landscape of human thought, the mind functions as a multifaceted and mysterious vocabulary, where every idea, feeling, and observation contributes to the overarching story of our lives. This book, "Unveiling the Mind's Lexicon: Definitions and Dynamics," takes readers on a journey to unravel the complex language of the mind, delving into the deep mechanisms that influence our consciousness and sense of self.

Envision a subtle murmur from the universe, a resonance of infinite wisdom that infiltrates every aspect of our existence. This boundless intelligence inspires our creativity and innovation, leading us through the intricate maze of our thoughts and feelings. At the essence of our existence resides a fundamental intelligence, a unifying energy that weaves our experiences into a harmonious entirety, echoing throughout every facet of our understanding.

The subconscious mind serves as a gateway, a passage to the profound layers of our inner self where concealed truths and dormant possibilities exist. It subtly guides our thoughts and behaviors, molding our reality in ways that frequently escape our conscious awareness. Willpower serves as the anchor for our mental boundaries, allowing us to channel our desires and aspirations. It is an essential component in the pursuit of our objectives and in sustaining psychological balance.

Emotions shape and amplify our experiences, enriching the tapestry of our lives with depth and vibrancy. They influence our connections and viewpoints, serving a crucial function in our emotional awareness. Imagination, a form of intelligence that shapes our understanding, enables us to go beyond the confines of reality and delve into new possibilities, honoring the creative force that influences our mental realm.

Conscience acts as intellect's guiding force, navigating us through the intricate maze of moral challenges and choices. It shapes our conduct and beliefs, guaranteeing that our deeds resonate with our core ideals. Intuition, that delicate form of extrasensory perception, offers insights that transcend rational thought, significantly influencing our decision-making journeys.

Our five senses serve as the extensions of a confined brain, the instruments by which we engage with the surrounding reality. They mold our perception and enhance our comprehension of the surroundings, serving as the fundamental avenue for acquiring knowledge. Memory serves as the conductor of our life's symphony, housing the rich tapestry of past experiences that shape our present and future, deeply influencing our sense of self and thought processes.

Begin this profound exploration of the mind's vocabulary, where every section reveals a fresh aspect of our cognitive and emotional terrain. We will unravel the meanings and interactions that shape our identities, delving into the complex relationships between intellect, determination, feelings, creativity, morality, instinct, perception, and recollection. This inquiry holds the potential to enhance our comprehension of the human psyche, uncovering the significant links that shape our being.

1. Whisper from the Sky: Infinite Intelligence

Envision yourself atop a serene hill, where the expansive sky gently murmurs timeless truths to your very essence. This "celestial whisper" embodies an enigmatic essence and the promise of what could be, symbolizing the profound reservoir of wisdom and potential that resides within each individual. This concept draws upon a rich tapestry of philosophical and spiritual traditions that articulate the existence of a supreme intelligence—an Infinite Intelligence that serves as both a beacon of guidance and an endless source of profound wisdom.

The Universal Origin

The notion of Infinite Intelligence is not a remote or unattainable force. Rather, it represents a vibrant and fluid source of insight and strength that influences our conscious and subconscious awareness. Imagine the mind as a solar system, where various aspects—reason, emotions, intuition—revolve around a central source of boundless intelligence, akin to planets orbiting a sun.

Visual Representations and Case Studies

- **Connecting with the boundless wisdom of the universe**

  Engaging with this source through practices such as meditation or introspective contemplation unlocks a wellspring of creativity, enhanced problem-solving skills, and a profound sense of purpose. Envision an author in pursuit of the spark that will ignite their forthcoming literary masterpiece. By engaging in reflective thought, one can tap into a wellspring of creativity and understanding, allowing for the creation of a narrative that profoundly connects with its audience.

- **Utilizing Rational Thought, Emotional Insight, and Intuitive Understanding**

  Envision reason as a celestial body of analysis, offering a foundation and coherent framework for understanding. Emotions resemble a vivid, dynamic world, infusing our experiences with profound depth and richness. Intuition embodies an enigmatic force, often steering us toward avenues that reason alone may fail to reveal. By integrating these elements, one cultivates a balanced and enriching existence.

  Consider an entrepreneur confronted with a pivotal choice. They may employ rational analysis to assess practicality, tap into their emotions to measure enthusiasm and zeal, and rely on their intuition to perceive the right moment and potential for success. This comprehensive perspective fosters greater equilibrium and fruitful results.

Actionable Approaches to Engage with Universal Wisdom

a) Consistently engaging in meditation cultivates a serene mental space, allowing one to attune to the gentle nuances of boundless wisdom. A mere few minutes dedicated to focused breathing daily can profoundly impact your well-being.

b) Engage in deep contemplation and expressive writing: Allocate moments to ponder your experiences and the wisdom they impart.

c) Journaling is a profound method for examining and comprehending the intricate dimensions of one's consciousness.

d) Participate in endeavors that ignite your imaginative spirit, be it through a painter's brush, a writer's pen, or the keys of a musical instrument. Engaging in these practices allows for a deeper connection with the reservoir of creativity and insight that resides within you.

e) Embrace Solitude. Allocate moments to immerse yourself in nature or find peace in quiet solitude, distancing yourself from the incessant distractions of everyday existence. This fosters an atmosphere that allows exploring the deep wisdom inherent in boundless consciousness.

Final Thoughts

As you explore this chapter, embrace it as a journey of self-discovery, revealing the profound vocabulary of your inner thoughts. The insights presented are not merely abstract concepts but a tangible framework for aligning rational thought, emotional depth, and intuitive understanding with the boundless intelligence that dwells within us. Embrace this journey, allowing it to guide you toward a life rich in creativity, fulfillment, and deep meaning.

2. Identity of the Mind Hyper-Gate: Subconscious Mind

Envision yourself poised at the edge of an expansive bridge, extending endlessly ahead, linking the realm of awareness with an infinite wellspring of wisdom and possibility. This represents the subconscious mind—a connection to the boundless, effortlessly intertwining our conscious thoughts with a domain of uncharted potential.

The Pathway to Eternity

The subconscious mind, though it does not respond to direct commands as one might flick a switch, possesses a remarkable sensitivity and adaptability. It can be shaped in significant and meaningful ways. Envision it as a rich landscape poised to nurture

31

the seeds of thought and intention you choose to sow. One cannot demand a flower to bloom at once; rather, by sowing seeds—like positive affirmations and visualizations—and tending to them through meditation, one creates the necessary sunlight for these thoughts and ideas to thrive.

Visual Representations and Case Studies

- ### Fostering the Depths of the Mind

  Envision an artist standing before a pristine canvas, poised for creation. They refrain from hastily applying paint, instead choosing to immerse themselves in the process of envisioning the masterpiece they aspire to bring to life. In parallel, you cultivate seeds within your subconscious, nurturing them with intention and mindfulness. Positive affirmations resemble seeds, nurturing growth and potential within us. By consistently affirming, "I possess the ability to realize my aspirations," you nurture a fertile ground of self-assurance and possibility within your inner mind.

- ### The Influence of Imagination

  Visualization serves as the essential nourishment for these seeds to flourish. Envision yourself achieving your aspirations, immersing in the feelings accompanying that triumph. This practice engraves profound images into your subconscious, steering it towards manifesting these visions into reality. Consider the scenario where an athlete envisions themselves triumphantly crossing the finish line, experiencing the exhilarating sensation of victory. This mental imagery can significantly elevate their performance and drive.

- ### Meditation embodies the essence of sunlight.

  Meditation serves as the illuminating force that nurtures the development of these burgeoning seeds. By engaging in consistent meditation, one can still have an active mind, creating space for the subconscious to absorb and harmonize with these uplifting affirmations and vivid imagery. Consider it an opportunity for your inner self to cultivate and nourish the seeds that have been sown.

Effective Methods to Engage the Subconscious Mind

a. **Daily Affirmations:** Create a collection of uplifting statements that truly connect with your inner self. Engage with these affirmations daily to cultivate and strengthen empowering beliefs and perspectives.

b. **Visualization Exercises:** Engage in daily visualization practices, dedicating moments to vividly imagine your aspirations and the outcomes you wish to achieve. Immerse yourself fully in the experience, allowing each sense to contribute to the richness and authenticity of these visualizations.

c. **Meditation:** Consistently engage in meditation to cultivate a tranquil and open mindset. Center your awareness on your breath, inviting a sense of calm to envelop your thoughts, thus cultivating a nurturing space for positivity to flourish.

In summary

Exploring the evolution of thought resembles a complex psychological mystery, where deeper exploration of your mind reveals essential insights for achieving a harmonious and meaningful existence. Consider that the thoughts you nurture within your subconscious will ultimately manifest as the realities of your future. May this chapter serve as a continuous conversation between your developing identity and the limitless possibilities that reside within, steering you toward a life rich in clarity, purpose, and fulfillment.

3. The Gate Stabilizer: Faculty of Willpower

Envision taking your place at the forefront, baton poised, prepared to orchestrate a magnificent symphony. Willpower serves as the driving force that empowers you to grasp that baton and harmonize your thoughts with clarity and purpose. Unwavering commitment enables you to silence the murmurs of uncertainty and pessimism, allowing the vibrant harmonies of self-assurance and resolve to resonate.

Unity within the Composition

Yet, the mind's orchestration demands robust guidance and a profound sense of balance. Much like a skilled conductor who understands the unique talents of each musician, you—the orchestrator of your thoughts—must acknowledge the significance of your emotions and intuition. Integrating these additional faculties deepens your cognitive framework, infusing it with complexity and subtlety while fostering creativity and innovation.

Envision willpower as the conductor, harmonizing the diverse elements of the orchestra, ensuring that each instrument fulfills its role beautifully while respecting the distinct essence of every contribution. Consider how your emotions can fuel the enthusiasm behind a courageous choice while your intuition steers you toward possibilities that mere reason may overlook.

Harmonizing the Forces

Finding the optimal equilibrium among determination, feelings, and instinct is essential. Envision encountering a difficult scenario in your professional environment. Your inner strength fosters concentration and resolve, your feelings ignite passion and inspiration, while your instincts offer innovative pathways to explore. When these elements align seamlessly, you can traverse obstacles with greater ease and attain more favorable results.

Effective Strategies for Achieving Mental Balance

a. **Mindful Leadership:** Engage in mindfulness to cultivate awareness of your thoughts and feelings. This consciousness enables you to conduct your mental symphony with enhanced clarity and harmony.

b. **Emotional Intelligence:** Emotional intelligence is essential. It involves recognizing and comprehending one's own emotions. Leverage this understanding to channel their influence constructively.

c. **Intuitive Practices:** Embrace practices that nurture your inner wisdom, including journaling, meditation, or immersing yourself in the tranquility of nature. These practices enable you to connect with your more profound understanding.

Illustrations in Practice

*   **Scenario 1:**

    Conquering Procrastination: Imagine facing a significant deadline for a crucial project. Your determination guides your attention to the task, while your feelings remind you of the fulfillment and sense of accomplishment that awaits you upon completion. Trust your inner voice; it might guide you toward a fresh perspective, streamlining the journey. By harmonizing these components, you transcend procrastination and fulfill the project within the designated timeframe.

*   **Scenario 2:**

    Navigating Personal Challenges: In the realm of personal relationships, the strength of willpower serves as a foundation for commitment and resilience. Emotions cultivate a deep sense of empathy and compassion, while intuition serves as a guiding force in navigating and resolving conflicts. The interplay of these faculties fosters a relationship dynamic that is both harmonious and fulfilling.

Final Thoughts

As you delve into this chapter, allow it to remind you of the significance of aligning the diverse aspects of your consciousness. By acknowledging and harmonizing the interplay of willpower, emotions, and intuition, you assume the role of the principal architect of your mental landscape, steering it towards a coherent and purposeful life. Embrace this journey, allowing the harmonious notes of self-assurance and innovation to echo in every aspect of your existence.

4. Cohesion and Resonance: Primordial Intelligence

The capacity for rational thought serves as the critical arbiter in the arena of the mind. It carefully examines concepts, strategies, and aspirations, assessing their rationality and practicality. Nonetheless, this judge does not wield unchecked authority. The choices made by reason can be swayed by the force of will, often eclipsing rational thought when fueled by intense passions. Emotions possess the power to influence rational thought, particularly in moments when one's willpower falters. Amid various influences, it is the reason that fundamentally anchors the coherence and resonance of our thoughts.

a.   **Cohesion: The Symphony's Structure**

Logic, Organization, and Essentiality. The unity of thought operates similarly to the careful craft of an accomplished narrative weaver. Each element should find its rightful position, enriching the broader story we seek to convey. This principle guarantees that each thought and idea contributes to the dynamic tapestry of our mental landscape.

Cohesion resembles the intricate logic and structure found in a masterfully composed symphony. The extraneous is stripped away, revealing an essence that resonates with clarity and intention.

Imagine a maestro positioned at the forefront, harmonizing the diverse elements of the orchestra—strings, brass, woodwind—into a unified masterpiece. This creative arrangement reflects how we structure our thoughts, aligning them in their rightful context. The outcome manifests as a cohesive resonance, orchestrating an internal melody that steers us toward achievement.

b. Resonance: The Symphony's Soul

Meaning and Mythic Value. Resonance elevates basic ideas into deep affirmations, bridging our inner landscape with the expansive fabric of human existence. It is that exhilarating moment of realization when an idea aligns perfectly or the profound bond we experience when a narrative resonates with our personal experiences. The essence of resonance imbues our thoughts with profound meaning and emotional depth, transforming transient notions into lasting principles that steer our behavior.

Resonance embodies the essence of the symphony, enriching it with profound significance and a sense of the mythical. The resonance transforms music from mere sound into a profound emotional experience. In a parallel manner, within the realm of our minds, resonance guarantees that our thoughts transcend mere logical frameworks, becoming rich with emotional depth and profound significance. The emotional energy we experience allows our thoughts to echo within, forging a profound influence that molds our beliefs and drives our actions.

The Unity of the Symphony's Framework

The integration of thoughts within the mind resembles the artistry of a master storyteller, meticulously crafting a narrative where every detail finds its rightful place. The underlying principles and organization serve as the foundation of a masterfully crafted symphony. Envision a maestro at the helm, skillfully uniting the strings, brass, and woodwinds into a harmonious ensemble. Every thought and idea should contribute to the seamless tapestry of our mental landscape, with the extra trimmed away, revealing a core that vibrates with clarity and intention.

Envision your thoughts as a harmonious ensemble, each playing its unique role in the symphony of your mind. The guiding force orchestrates each element to resonate in unison, crafting an internal melody that propels you toward achievement. Consider the process of planning a significant project; employing reason allows for a logical organization of tasks, where each step is thoughtfully constructed upon the last, ultimately guiding you toward a harmonious and successful conclusion.

Concrete Illustrations

- **Context 1:**

  The Process of Choosing Wisely: In moments of challenging choices, the power of cohesion enables you to systematically evaluate the advantages and disadvantages, allowing for a structured thought process that leads to a well-defined strategy. Resonance guarantees that the decision is in harmony with your core values and beliefs, offering emotional and intellectual backing for your choice.

- **Context 2:**

  Innovative Endeavors: In the realm of creativity, cohesion serves as the framework that organizes your thoughts into a unified vision, whereas resonance infuses your work with profound emotional significance. For example, a filmmaker employs logical reasoning to craft the script and storyboard, yet the profound connection with the audience's emotions ultimately renders the film unforgettable.

In summary, As you explore this chapter, consider it a voyage through the nuances of thought, revealing the essential elements for a balanced and purposeful existence. Allow the insights you gain here to weave into your internal narrative, fostering a continuous dialogue between your evolving identity and the boundless possibilities that lie ahead. Welcome the harmony and vibrancy in your life, allowing them to lead you towards understanding, intention, and a sense of completeness. Though shaped by various mental processes, the capacity for rational thought is crucial in orchestrating a harmonious blend of ideas that comprehend reality and profoundly connect with the essence of human existence.[3]

5. Channeling Intensification: Faculty of Emotions

Envision your subconscious emotional activator as the powerful engine of a vessel, driving you onward across the expansive sea of contemplation. This dynamic force, abundant in vitality, underpins the majority of your mental functions, creating an environment conducive to the emergence and development of ideas. Much like a blazing fire that has the potential to either provide comfort or bring destruction, the power of the SEA requires careful and thoughtful management.

Conducting the Harmony of Emotions

---

[3] For more information refer to: https://www.helpingwritersbecomeauthors.com/cohesion-and-resonance/

The SEA serves as the fundamental energetic source for most cognitive functions. It acts as a fertile ground where concepts can emerge and take root. Envision it as the fertile ground where the seeds of your ideas can establish themselves and flourish. Nonetheless, much like a powerful blaze that can destroy if left unchecked, the impact of the SEA can also be harmful if it is not tempered by clear reasoning and unwavering determination.

The Significance of Emotions as Driving Forces

Imagine a powerful force propelling a ship forward. The engine serves as the vital energy source for propulsion; without the captain, who signifies willpower, and the navigation system reflecting reason, the vessel will likely stray from its destined course and encounter dangerous circumstances. When harnessed effectively, our emotions can drive us forward with remarkable intensity toward our aspirations. They serve as the fundamental force propelling our endeavors, inspiring us to reach remarkable heights.

Take, for instance, an individual preparing for the rigorous challenge of a marathon. Their emotional drive, characterized by excitement, passion, and determination, serves as the catalyst for their rigorous training regimen. Yet, without a well-structured approach and the determination to adhere to it, one's endeavors may spiral into inconsistency or potentially culminate in exhaustion.

Equilibrium and Harmony

In the absence of balanced reasoning and a firm resolve, the SEA may give rise to hasty behaviors and disordered thinking. Envision a vessel equipped with a formidable engine yet devoid of a guiding force or navigational tools. It may advance rapidly, yet without a clear purpose, it jeopardizes the possibility of becoming stranded or deviating from its intended path. Similarly, our emotions must be steered by rational thought and strengthened by determination, allowing them to propel us toward our aspirations while maintaining inner harmony.

Unlocking the Full Potential of the SEA

The following chapters will explore the complexities of tapping into the SEA's potential. By harnessing this potent energy, you will cultivate a positive force that enriches the balanced realm of your thoughts. Practices like mindfulness, emotional awareness, and cognitive restructuring can assist in harmonizing your feelings, enabling them to inspire your pursuits while maintaining the clarity of your logical thought.

Illustrations in Application

- **Context 1:**

  Addressing an audience: Envision yourself getting ready for a significant presentation. Your SEA may evoke feelings of anxiety, yet rather than allowing it to overwhelm you, consider channeling that energy into something constructive. Harness your determination to practice consistently while employing your intellect to articulate your thoughts clearly and precisely. The emotional energy subsequently evolves into a state of excitement and confidence, thereby amplifying your performance.

- **Context 2:**

  Innovative Endeavors: Creative individuals frequently tap into profound feelings as a source of inspiration for their artistic endeavors. Yet, their endeavors may linger in incompletion without a solid framework and consistent discipline. Through the application of rational thought and determination, individuals can harness their emotional depth to create unified and captivating artistic expressions.

In Summation

Steering through the expansive sea of ideas with a robust emotional drive necessitates a delicate equilibrium between determination and rationality. By comprehending and utilizing the SEA's potential, one can elevate oneself toward success with a balanced and thoughtfully arranged mental environment. Allow the upcoming chapters to illuminate your path toward achieving this equilibrium, ensuring that your emotions become a constructive and vibrant element in the symphony of your existence.

The Subconscious Emotional Activator (SEA): Orchestrating the Symphony of Feelings. The subconscious emotional activator functions as the primary energetic fuel for a majority of cognitive processes. It serves as the rich substrate for ideas to sprout and establish themselves. Nevertheless, akin to a formidable fire that can wreak havoc if not properly managed, the influence of the SEA can also prove detrimental if it is not moderated by rational thought and strong will. Envision a robust engine driving a vessel onward. The engine, representing the energy source, is essential for propulsion; however, in the absence of the captain, symbolizing willpower and the navigation system, which embodies reason, the vessel risks deviating from its intended path and facing perilous situations. The subsequent chapters will explore the intricacies of harnessing the SEA's potential while ensuring it serves as a positive influence within the harmonious landscape of your cognition.

6. Faculty of Imagination4 : Morphic Intelligence

Hyper-Integration Process, The Architect of Dreams, The Symphony of Creativity. Picture your imagination as the adept maestro of your cognitive symphony, orchestrating strategies, concepts, and pathways that unveil various possibilities—some beneficial, others not as favorable. It is an insightful architect

---

[4] Faculty of Imagination: The builder of all plans, ideas, and ways and means of attaining desired ends. It needs self-discipline and constant direction of the power of will to avoid over-exaggeration.

meticulously designing the complex rhythms and tones that will ultimately define the deep orchestration of your life. Similar to a skilled composer refining their artistic vision, the domain of imagination requires the unwavering strength of willpower to thrive. The boundless realm of creativity often gives rise to imaginative daydreams that remain in a state of dissatisfaction without intentional direction. Willpower acts as the essential catalyst, transforming these aspirational concepts into tangible and attainable results.

The concept of Morphic Resonance Inside

The idea of hyper-integration concerning the subconscious resonates compellingly with the concept of morphic intelligence proposed by Rupert Sheldrake. He suggests that every entity, including minds, possesses a memory that profoundly shapes and guides their development. Envision the SEA (Subconscious Emotional Activator) as a profound reservoir of past experiences and emotions, serving as a wellspring from which the imagination cultivates new ideas and avenues. The interplay of "morphic resonance" between our conscious and subconscious realms opens pathways to a rich well of potential, enriching the creative journey.

The Interplay of Synchronization and the Enigma of Consciousness

Synchronization and resonance explore the enigmatic essence of consciousness. Recent scientific observations indicate that specific patterns of brainwave activity—like gamma, beta, and theta synchrony—seem to be linked to conscious awareness. This relationship continues to be a profound enigma, commonly known as the "Hard Problem of consciousness." Nevertheless, the concept of resonance opens up a fascinating path for inquiry. Imagine the diverse instruments of an orchestra blending in perfect harmony; this serves as a powerful metaphor for the intricate processes that could form the foundation of consciousness itself.

Real-World Applications and Illustrations

a. Channeling Creativity through Determination

Envision an architect conceptualizing a revolutionary new structure. Their creativity brings forth groundbreaking designs and solutions; however, without the determination to hone and actualize these concepts, they exist only as fleeting visions. Architects transform their creative visions into reality through dedicated effort and intentional focus, manifesting a physical structure from their abstract aspirations.

b. Creativity and Emotional Connection

Imagine a creator weaving a narrative tapestry. Their creativity weaves together complex narratives and personas, yet the profound emotional depth—rooted in their inner experiences—infuses the tale with vitality. This morphic resonance enhances their narrative, rendering it profoundly engaging for readers.

Elevating the Dynamics of Creativity

Artists frequently draw upon the dynamic relationship between creativity and deep emotional connection. Composers often tap into their own experiences and the depths of their subconscious emotions, crafting music that connects deeply and meaningfully with those who listen. The interplay between conscious creativity and subconscious influence yields artistic expressions that are not only groundbreaking but also resonate deeply on an emotional level.

Final thoughts

As you journey through the forthcoming chapters, you will immerse yourself in the complexities of unlocking the SEA's potential and steering your creative vision with determination. This exploration will uncover ways to harness the limitless power of your creativity, transforming it into a cohesive and effective force, crafting a mental orchestra that echoes with precision and intention. Embrace this journey into the realms of imagination, morphic intelligence, and consciousness, allowing it to lead you toward a deeper, more cohesive understanding of the boundless potential of your mind.

7. The Moral Factor: Faculty of Conscience

The Inner Compass: Charting the Harmonies of Ethical Understanding

Envision a symphony in which each note resonates not only with the written score but also with the fundamental ideals of harmony and justice. This is where the faculty of conscience emerges, serving as the inner compass that directs our aspirations and intentions toward a higher moral standard. It serves as the moral compass within the symphony of our thoughts, guiding the melodies we compose to align with the ideals of equity, empathy, and righteousness.

The conscience acts as a guiding force, moderating the impulses of the subconscious emotional activator and the whims of the imagination. It guarantees that our behaviors align with our most profound ethical principles, akin to how a skilled conductor orchestrates each instrument to create a cohesive symphony.

Exploring the Function of Conscience

a.   **The Moral Guide**

Envision your conscience as a watchful maestro, attuned not only to each performer's technical precision but also to the emotional and moral essence of the symphony they create. Much like a conductor who guides an orchestra to interpret the composer's vision faithfully, your conscience serves as a compass, ensuring that your actions resonate with your deeply held moral convictions.

Consider a scenario where you encounter a decision at work laden with ethical implications; your inner moral compass serves as a guiding force, compelling you to select the route that champions integrity and fairness despite the challenges it may present.

b. Equilibrium and Harmony

Conscience serves as a guiding force, tempering the often impulsive desires that arise from our deeper instincts and moderating the imaginative excursions that could potentially divert us from our true path. It serves as the harmonizing element that unites feelings and creativity with a robust moral framework.

Illustrations in Application

- **Scenario 1:**

  Moral Quandaries: Imagine yourself as a manager contemplating the intricacies of a hiring choice. A candidate possessing strong qualifications yet surrounded by whispers of past unethical practices is under consideration. Your inner sense compels you to delve deeper, ensuring that your choices resonate with the organization's principles of honesty and equity.

- **Scenario 2:**

  Interpersonal Connections: In personal interactions, your inner moral compass guides you through intricate emotional terrains. When a friend seeks your counsel, an inner voice compels you to offer sincere and empathetic insights, even if those truths may not align with their desires but serve as a catalyst for their personal development.

Aligning Conscience with Other Aspects of the Mind

Conscience collaborates seamlessly with willpower and rationality within the intricate tapestry of thought. Determination empowers you to adhere to your ethical decisions, while rational thought offers the structure needed to assess the outcomes of your actions.

In summation

As you explore this chapter, allow your conscience to guide you like an inner compass. Allow it to guide the intricate melody of your thoughts, ensuring that your actions harmonize with equity, empathy, and righteousness. When you blend your inner sense of right with determination and rational thought, you cultivate a balanced and ethically grounded mental framework that navigates the complexities of existence with honesty and insight.

8. Extrasensory Perception: Intuition

The Subtle Echoes of Insight: The Strength of Intuition

Envision yourself at the threshold of a vast woodland, where the journey forward is shrouded in a soft veil of fog. Intuition serves as a gentle nudge from within, illuminating the path ahead amidst uncertainty. Commonly known as the "sixth sense," intuition serves as a connection between our conscious and subconscious minds. It allows us to perceive subtle cues and underlying information, guiding us to make decisions with an extraordinary sense of awareness.

Intuition: The Connection of Consciousness

Intuition operates subtly, hidden from the forefront of our awareness, offering revelations that transcend mere logical analysis. Envision an artist, profoundly connected to the essence of sound, capable of anticipating the forthcoming note from the initial whispers of a composition. This innate foresight emerges from extensive experience and a deep comprehension of musical patterns, enabling a profound sense of what lies ahead.

Demonstrating the Essence of Intuition at Work

Reflect on the experience of encountering an unfamiliar individual. Without deliberate scrutiny, you may instinctively perceive an individual's trustworthiness. This instinctive assessment emerges from the depths of your subconscious, continuously interpreting myriad nuanced signals—such as body language, vocal tone, and even the slightest facial expressions.

a. **Common Illustrations Business Choices:** A Thriving entrepreneur frequently trusts their instincts when navigating crucial business choices. For example, when contemplating an investment in a new venture, one may experience an intuitive sense regarding its potential despite the absence of definitive logical data. This understanding emerges from a profound, underlying synthesis of previous experiences and realizations.

b. **Creative Processes:** Individuals engaged in artistic and literary pursuits often rely on their intuition as a compass for navigating their creative journeys. An artist may intuitively select the next hue, just as a writer might sense the appropriate trajectory for a plot twist without excessive contemplation. Their creativity is driven by a profound intuition, resulting in innovative and deeply authentic work.

Embracing the Essence of Intuition

To tap into the profound potential of intuition, it is beneficial to partake in practices that enhance the relationship between the conscious and subconscious realms of the mind:

Awareness and Contemplation: Consistent mindfulness and meditation fosters a tranquil conscious mind, creating space for intuitive insights to emerge more easily. By cultivating a serene mental environment, you open yourself to the gentle nudges of insight.

Contemplative Approaches: Maintaining a journal to capture intuitive insights and contemplating decisions influenced by intuition can enhance this innate ability. As you progress, you'll start to discern recurring themes and develop a deeper trust in your inner wisdom.

Having Faith in Your Intuition: Embracing your instinctual responses, particularly when rational reasoning falls short, can significantly elevate your intuitive skills. Your intuition flourishes when you trust and affirm it, leading to greater strength and precision over time.

Final Thoughts

Intuition serves as the quiet guide within us, navigating the intricate pathways of existence with a profound understanding that transcends mere logical thought. By nurturing and having faith in this inner voice, one can approach life's challenges with enhanced clarity and assurance. Embrace the subtle guidance of your intuition, as it unveils the profound truths that often elude rational thought, steering you toward choices that align with your innermost wisdom.

9. Arms of the Caged Master: The Five Senses

The Art of Mastery: Engaging with Existence Through Sensory Perception

Envision your senses as the five esteemed extensions of a conductor, extending to embrace the harmonious orchestra of existence surrounding you. The physical gateways of sight, sound, taste, smell, and touch serve as your sole link to the external world. They convey the nuanced intricacies: the uplifting harmonies of a bird's song, the rich colors of a sunset, and the soothing warmth of a cherished embrace.

However, this intricate communication system can be profoundly influenced by intense currents of emotion, especially fear. In moments of fear, our perceptions can become skewed, leading us to interpret a simple rustle in the bushes as a threat or a benign shadow as something sinister. Nurturing a state of tranquility and insight is essential. It guarantees that your perceptions provide precise insights, allowing the inner conductor to create a balanced and harmonious reaction.

Demonstrating the Five Senses at Work

a. **Vision and Auditory Perception**

   Imagine yourself strolling through a serene forest. Your gaze embraces the verdant canopy overhead while your ears attune to the whispers of leaves and the distant melodies of birdsong. The interplay of these senses creates a rich tapestry of your environment, heightening your awareness of the exquisite and the dangerous elements surrounding you.

b. **Sensory Perception**

   Envision the moment you sink your teeth into a succulent, perfectly ripe strawberry. The luscious, succulent flavor and the enchanting scent envelop your senses, crafting a truly pleasurable experience. The interplay of these senses significantly amplifies your flavor perception, deepening your overall enjoyment of culinary experiences.

c. **Connection**

   Consider the comforting sensation of a cherished person's hand gently resting upon yours. This sensation transcends mere physical warmth, embodying an emotional bond that alleviates anxiety and nurtures a profound sense of safety and belonging.

Exploring the Dynamics of Emotional Impact

Yet intense emotions, especially fear, have the capacity to skew our understanding. Imagine traversing the familiar woods under the cloak of night; a sense of unease envelops your thoughts. Each whisper of the leaves can evoke a sense of looming peril, while shadows transform into specters of our creation. Here lies the significance of tranquility and thoughtful judgment. By cultivating a state of tranquility within, you enhance your ability to discern these sensory cues with clarity, ensuring that fear does not misguide your perceptions.

Nurturing Serenity and Insight

a. Engage in practices that cultivate awareness and presence, such as deep breathing, meditation, or yoga, to foster a sense of grounding in your daily life. These practices may diminish the influence of fear while simultaneously sharpening your sensory awareness.

b. In moments when sensory stimuli evoke fear, pause to engage in a thoughtful assessment of the circumstances at hand. Contemplate whether there exists a rational basis for your perceptions.

c. Emotional Regulation: Cultivate strategies to navigate and modulate your emotions, allowing you to maintain control over your perceptions. Engaging in a dialogue about your fears with someone you trust can be quite beneficial, as can employing methods such as progressive muscle relaxation to cultivate a sense of calm.

In summary

This chapter invites you to delve into the complex interplay between your senses and emotions, guiding you to cultivate a mindful awareness of your sensory experiences with tranquility and insight. In this way, you allow the inner conductor to guide a harmonious and balanced reaction to the intricate melodies of existence. Allow this journey to lead you to a profound comprehension of experiencing the world with clarity and peace, enabling your senses to serve as precise guides that enhance the melody of your existence.

10 The Ripples of the Past: Memory – The Maestro's Score

The Transformative Architect

Memory is fundamental to the intricate interplay of cognitive functions, acting as an extensive repository for the thoughts, experiences, and sensory data accumulated throughout one's life. Envision a serene lake, briefly disturbed by the soft splash of a stone; the ensuing ripples embody the intricate nuances and transformations inherent in the essence of memory. Memory serves as a crucial reservoir of our experiences, yet it is not devoid of constraints. Embracing discipline is essential for preserving the accuracy and clarity of this score, enabling you to express the melody of your existence with assurance.

The Nature of Memory's Fluidity

Memory is an ever-evolving tapestry woven from our experiences rather than a mere snapshot in time. Much like ripples on a pond, memories can be shaped and altered by the intricate interplay of emotions, beliefs, and external influences. A recollection of a joyful childhood birthday can evoke a sense of melancholy when revisited in times of sorrow. This fluidity underscores the significance of reflective thought when contemplating past experiences. By recognizing the possibility of distortion, you can cultivate a keen awareness of your memories, navigating through the nuances to reveal the underlying truth.

The Imperfect Archive: Nurturing Self-Discipline

Although the brain serves as a repository for our memories, the organization of this repository is far from flawless. Certain particulars might be misplaced, feelings could tint memories, and the passage of time may diminish the precision of retained knowledge. Here is where the essence of discipline reveals itself. Participating in endeavors that activate your memory, verifying recollections, and recognizing your biases contribute to cultivating a more lucid and precise memory. For example, maintaining a comprehensive journal can act as a reliable source, enabling you to reflect upon and validate previous experiences. This methodical perspective guarantees that the evaluation of your existence stays sharp and unambiguous.

The Importance of Memory: The Cornerstone of What Lies Ahead

Even with its flaws, memory serves as the essential foundation for what will be explored in the "hyper-integration phase" that follows. By weaving together your past experiences—the remarkable triumphs and the significant setbacks—you cultivate insight and guidance for steering through future circumstances. A failed business venture can serve as a profound teacher, imparting invaluable lessons that shape your approach to future entrepreneurial pursuits. Memory serves as a vital link that intertwines the past, present, and future, enabling one to draw insights from experiences and harness that wisdom to create a more profound and satisfying life narrative.

Exploring the Significance of Memory

Envision an artist diligently honing their craft in preparation for a performance. Every rehearsal intricately weaves together the memories of the composition's notes, rhythms, and subtleties. When an error occurs, the artist reflects on it, makes necessary adjustments, and persists in their practice, ultimately leading to a refined and polished performance. Similarly, our recollections, molded through introspection and refinement, elevate our capacity to confidently navigate the symphony of our existence.

Demonstrating the Dynamics of Memory

- **Scenario 1:**

  Embracing Growth Through Errors: Imagine an individual contemplating the lessons learned from an unsuccessful entrepreneurial endeavor. Through thoughtful analysis of previous choices and their consequences, one can extract meaningful lessons that shape future approaches, thereby minimizing the chances of repeating the same mistakes.

- **Scenario 2:**

  Reflective Memory Exploration: Contemplate the profound experience of reconnecting with a long-time companion. You may notice that your recollections vary subtly as you reflect on shared memories. This distinction highlights the dynamic essence of memory and the profound impact that emotions and the passage of time have on our perceptions.

Effective Strategies for Memory Improvement Self-control

a. **Regular Reflection:** Dedicate moments to introspect on previous experiences, examining the insights gained and the emotions experienced. This approach strengthens the reliability of our recollections.

b. **Journaling:** Journaling allows one to chronicle pivotal moments, reflections, and emotional experiences. This document serves as a reliable source for contemplation in the future.

c. **Critical Thinking:** Cultivate the ability to scrutinize the veracity of your recollections, examine the authenticity of memories, and explore various viewpoints.

d. **Mindfulness Practices:** Embrace mindfulness practices to cultivate presence and awareness in your daily life. Practicing mindfulness can significantly diminish the emotional distortions that often accompany our memories.

Final Thoughts

Memory serves as the fluid architect of your existence, intertwining past, present, and future threads. By recognizing the ever-changing essence of memory and fostering a disciplined approach to your reflections, you can enhance and master the art of recollection with greater efficacy. Embrace the journey of thoughtful reflection and intentional remembrance, permitting your experiences to steer you toward a harmonious and purposeful life. Allow your past experiences, whether they be victories or struggles, to compose a more profound and satisfying life narrative.

Let us explore the complex layers of memory with greater depth. As you delve into this chapter, reflect on the fluidity of memory and the critical role of discipline in preserving accuracy. In embracing this approach, you cultivate the ability to traverse the intricate tapestry of existence with assurance, drawing wisdom from previous experiences to orchestrate a balanced and enriching future. Memory transcends mere documentation; it serves as a fluid, transformative melody that shapes your path, enabling you to craft a more profound and harmonious existence.

꿍 꿍 꿍

UNVEILING THE THOUGHT FORGE: PRINCIPLES OF INDUCTIVE REASONING

꿍 꿍 꿍

Venture into the profound depths of consciousness, where each idea serves as a gateway to unraveling the intricacies of being. In this pivotal part of ADAM-GENE, we explore the intriguing relationship between thought and reality, embarking on a journey that invites us to question the essence of our understanding.

Our thoughts serve as the architects of our inner landscape, intricately crafting our experiences and attracting similar energies into our sphere. Explore the profound impact of harnessing your thoughts to attract the life you seek. Inductive reasoning serves as the bedrock for constructing our understanding of reality. Explore the hidden dimensions of this process and its potential to reshape your perspective on knowledge and comprehension.

Explore the practice of nurturing clear and purposeful thoughts. Discover the art of cultivating your inner world, nurturing a sense of clarity and intention that permeates all dimensions of your existence. Faith serves as the driving force that converts ideas into tangible existence. Delve into the significant influence of belief systems on your mind and discover ways to leverage their strength to cultivate a meaningful and enriching life.

Arm yourself with effective strategies and methods to traverse the intricate maze of cognition. Explore techniques that foster a mental landscape characterized by clarity and tranquility, such as mindfulness practices and visualization exercises.

Welcome to the Thought Forge, a space where the intricate dance between consciousness and reality unveils the profound truths that define our being. Get ready to explore a path that will reshape your perception of the mind's limitless capabilities.

Introduction

Envision the human mind as a vast workshop where unrefined thoughts are meticulously crafted into the foundational elements of an individual's reality. Inductive reasoning serves as the skilled artisan, expertly navigating the path toward the precise selection and refinement of thoughts. Individuals can discern patterns and draw meaningful conclusions from their experiences by engaging in inductive reasoning. In due course, he will leverage these insights to shape a life that aligns harmoniously with individual aspirations.

A Look at Thought-to-Reality Correlation

The core principle of Thought-to-Reality Correlation posits that our prevailing thought patterns significantly influence the tangible world around us. Pursuing a precise mechanism continues, yet the overarching concept remains clear: the thoughts we consistently nurture, whether uplifting or detrimental, tend to manifest in our reality. Embracing a mindset filled with optimism and potential attracts opportunities and circumstances that propel you closer to your aspirations, functioning much like a magnet.

On the other hand, negative thinking, filled with fear and uncertainty, manifests as a self-fulfilling prophecy, drawing in more negativity and hindering progress. Gripping the connection between thought and reality lies the power to consciously decide: Will you be the creator of a flourishing city of opportunities or the unaware constructor of a barren landscape of negativity?

The Significance of Inductive Reasoning

Inductive reasoning is the key that will elevate you from mere wishful thinking to the intentional crafting of your reality. When you adopt a systematic perspective on your experiences, you start to identify patterns and formulate rational insights regarding the interplay between your thoughts and the reality you encounter. Moreover, you cultivate the ability to make more informed decisions, nurture positive thought patterns, and consequently mold your reality according to your desires.

1. The Architect Within: Shaping Reality Through Thought

Envision your mind as a masterful creator, where each thought serves as a precise design, constructing the very essence of the reality you inhabit. The notion of "Thought-to-Reality Correlation" implies that our thoughts possess a profound ability to influence the reality we experience. By comprehending and utilizing this force, you position yourself as the designer of your existence.

a. Thoughts as Blueprints

Envision your thoughts as detailed blueprints for what you aspire to manifest. Like blueprints serve as the foundation for constructing edifices, your thoughts establish the essential groundwork for transforming ideas into tangible actions. This idea can be likened to the "CgX sound and unassailable system," illustrating the intricate cognitive mechanisms that shape our thoughts. Consider, for example, an aspiring author who perpetually envisions characters, plots, and settings. These cognitive frameworks ultimately steer them in crafting an engaging narrative. Although mere thoughts won't instantly create your aspirations, they lay the crucial groundwork for transforming them into reality.

b. From Thought to Action; The Power of Manifestation:

This theory suggests that each thought inherently possesses a compelling urge to become a reality. This motivation serves as an intrinsic force, encouraging us to convert our reflections into tangible deeds. Yet, it transcends mere contemplation; it involves directing these reflections through rational and organic pathways to bring them into existence. Envision an innovative tech entrepreneur with aspirations of developing a transformative app. The initial idea slowly transforms into a successful outcome through careful planning and deliberate action. The shift from contemplation to execution necessitates the conversion of concepts into practical strategies and plans, highlighting that realization is a journey steered by purposeful endeavor.

c. Shaping Your World: Taking Charge of Your Thoughts:

This principle highlights the significance of intentional engagement. While it is indeed the case that our thoughts influence our reality, it is crucial to steer our thoughts in the direction of our aspirations consciously. We must reshape our thinking into clear strategies and purposeful actions to transform our aspirations into tangible outcomes. This can be compared to the metaphor of the "impregnable system," emphasizing the significance of comprehending and utilizing our thoughts to realize our aspirations. Students aspiring to achieve academic excellence must intentionally direct their attention toward their studies, developing a well-organized study plan and establishing clear, specific objectives. In this way, individuals channel their cognitive processes to cultivate a fruitful educational experience.

d. The Catalyst for Change: From Thought to Action:

Grasping the influence of our thoughts is merely the beginning; translating that understanding into meaningful change demands proactive engagement. This chapter serves as your personal springboard, guiding you from contemplation to decisive action. The concept of an "unassailable system" serves as a metaphor that highlights a crucial insight: harnessing the strength of your thoughts and directing them purposefully can empower you to take charge of your future. Here are some practical approaches to connect ideas with actions:

- **Igniting the Spark: Establishing Clear Intentions**

  Every transformative path starts with a well-defined purpose. Clarify your goals with unwavering precision. What are your goals and dreams? What type of existence do you wish to manifest? By articulating your objectives clearly, you establish a potent intention that serves as a beacon for your mindset and behaviors. For example, rather than expressing a general desire for success, articulate a clear objective: "I aim to secure a promotion at work within the next year by enhancing my skills and expanding my professional network." This clarity transforms an ambiguous desire into a definitive goal, facilitating the navigation of a purposeful path forward.

- **Constructing the Connection: Developing Strategic Approaches**

  Though thoughts possess considerable influence, they merely act as the starting point for deeper inquiry and subsequent action. Turning your dreams into reality requires a clear and structured plan. Craft a thoughtful action plan that breaks down your goals into manageable, progressive steps. This strategic framework bridges your mental goals and the concrete outcomes you desire, enabling the conversion of intention into practical actions. Consider this: if you aspire to pen a book, deconstruct it into manageable steps such as crafting an outline, composing a chapter each month, and inviting insights from your peers.

- **The Power of Positivity: Cultivating a Growth Mindset**

  Embrace the profound impact of cultivating a positive mindset. Highlight the possibilities that lie ahead, nurturing a deep belief in your ability to achieve your dreams. This unwavering positivity acts as a significant force, attracting the opportunities and circumstances necessary for achieving your goals. Recognizing the importance of fostering a growth mindset is essential. Welcome challenges as essential moments for growth and self-discovery, understanding that setbacks are brief detours on your path to achievement. An athlete who perceives failures as chances for growth is more inclined to persist and enhance their skills than one who regards them as unmanageable barriers.

In summary

By consciously focusing on your thoughts and purposefully directing them, you can steer the course of your life. By grasping the influence of your thoughts and directing that energy toward your ambitions, you essentially take on the role of creator in your own existence, molding a life that resonates with your innermost desires.

Remember!

Thought is a powerful tool, but it needs the partnership of action to truly shape our reality. By harnessing mental resilience, purposeful action, and a flexible outlook, individuals can actively shape their future, transforming dreams into the core components of a fulfilling and successful life. Embrace this journey, allowing your actions to embody the profound intentions you establish, steering you toward the life you aspire to create.

2. The Habit Trap: How Thoughts Take Root in the Subconscious

Imagine the mind as a rich landscape where thoughts take root and blossom into behaviors that shape our existence. This section delves into the fascinating interplay between our conscious thoughts and the subconscious mind, the realm where the roots of our behaviors are formed. This exploration examines the intriguing notion of "Thought Reality Inception and Subconscious Embodiment." This theory reveals how the persistent repetition of thought can create subconscious programming, significantly influencing behavior in deep and meaningful ways.

Envision your conscious mind as a devoted gardener, intentionally planting the seeds of thought into the fertile soil of the subconscious. Each time we reflect on a thought, we are essentially tending to those seeds, enabling them to grow and solidify into the familiar patterns we come to identify as habits. As seeds develop into flourishing plants, these thoughts take root in the subconscious, shaping the groundwork for habitual patterns that subtly steer your behaviors and decision-making, often without conscious realization.

Through the exploration of this process, we uncover the mechanisms behind our habit formation and discover ways to leverage this understanding to foster constructive behaviors and mental frameworks. This consciousness enables us to intentionally craft our existence by cultivating the ideas that drive us toward our aspirations. Embrace this journey into the depths of your mind's garden, where the seeds of thought take root and flourish into the habits that shape your existence.

a. Visual Representations and Case Studies

- **Scenario 1:**

  Cultivating Constructive Routines: Imagine an individual seeking to develop a consistent routine of physical activity. Through intentional contemplation and strategic planning of their exercise regimen, establishing clear objectives, and envisioning the advantages, they cultivate the foundations of this habit within their subconscious mind. Through the power of consistent repetition, these thoughts become ingrained, transforming exercise into an inherent aspect of their daily lives.

- **Scenario 2:**

  Conquering Detrimental Patterns: Envision a person striving to liberate themselves from the confines of detrimental inner dialogue. Through the intentional substitution of negative thoughts with uplifting affirmations and the consistent reinforcement of these new beliefs, individuals can reshape their subconscious minds. With time, cultivating positive self-talk transforms into a natural practice, enhancing one's mindset and overall well-being.

b. Understanding the Power of Repetition

Envision every thought as a wanderer journeying along a winding road. The more frequently this wanderer treads the journey, the more it becomes a well-trodden and intimate experience. Similarly, every time you intentionally interact with a thought, the neural pathways in your brain strengthen. This phenomenon is referred to as Thought Reality Inception, highlighting the profound influence of repetition.

With each instance of a particular thought, you reinforce its neural pathways, leading to a stage where it becomes second nature—deeply ingrained in your subconscious. This illustrates the remarkable power of one-word affirmations and the practice of positive self-talk. By consistently affirming uplifting messages to yourself, you embed constructive patterns into your subconscious, enhancing your behaviors positively.

Take, for instance, an individual seeking to cultivate self-assurance. Consistently engaging in affirmations such as "I am confident" or "I am capable" fosters and strengthens the neural connections linked to confidence. With time, these uplifting thoughts transform into an automatic part of one's mindset, significantly shaping one's actions and self-image.

At its core, repetition serves as a fundamental mechanism for instilling thoughts within the depths of the subconscious mind. This ongoing reinforcement has the power to turn transient thoughts into firmly established habits that influence behavior and mold one's experience of reality.

c. The Two Sides of the Coin: Positive and Negative Habits

Thought Reality Inception. Embedding thoughts into the subconscious through repetition can serve as a double-edged sword, influencing outcomes in both positive and negative ways. Constructive thinking is the foundation for nurturing habits, steering you towards achievement and self-improvement. On the other hand, detrimental thoughts and restrictive beliefs can establish destructive patterns that obstruct advancement and undermine achievement.

Positive Habits

Optimistic reflections serve as the foundation for personal growth and strength. When consistently cultivated, they evolve into robust, advantageous practices. For instance, when you consistently affirm to yourself, "I possess the strength and adaptability," these reflections bolster your confidence in your abilities. As time progresses, this optimistic outlook manifests in proactive actions, embracing challenges with assurance and determination.

o **Example:** Consider an athlete who consistently envisions crossing the finish line in first place. This constructive imagery fosters a sense of self-assurance and concentration, leading to enhanced performance outcomes. Individuals nurture practices that propel them toward achievement by integrating affirmative reflections into their subconscious.

Negative Habits

Conversely, this principle is equally relevant to negative thoughts. Focusing on negativity, fear, and self-doubt can establish profound patterns within the subconscious, resulting in harmful behaviors. For example, perpetually believing "I am not good enough" deepens self-doubt, leading to reluctance to embrace risks or seek opportunities.

o **Example:** Envision a student who continuously affirms their impending failure on an exam. Negative self-talk often cultivates anxiety, fuels procrastination, and undermines preparation, which can culminate in subpar performance. These detrimental thought patterns can solidify into habitual behaviors that undermine one's potential for achievement.

Grasping the Equilibrium

Understanding the dual essence of Thought Reality Inception emphasizes the significance of intentionally guiding your thoughts. By nurturing uplifting thoughts and diminishing the impact of negative ones, you can influence your subconscious programming to align with your ambitions and desires.

d. Actionable Strategies to Cultivate Beneficial Routines

1) **Positive Affirmations:** Embrace the power of affirmations to cultivate and strengthen uplifting thoughts in your daily life. Begin your day by embracing affirmations such as "I am confident and capable" to cultivate a positive mindset.

2) **Visualization:** Envision your aspirations and achievements. Envision yourself realizing your dreams, as this practice reinforces these uplifting possibilities within your subconscious mind.

3) **Mindfulness:** Engage in mindfulness to cultivate awareness of detrimental thought patterns. When you become aware of negative thoughts, intentionally substitute them with positive alternatives.

Gratitude Practice: Embrace the practice of gratitude by taking time to contemplate the positive elements that enrich your life. This redirects your attention from negative thoughts to positive ones, strengthening uplifting habits.

Final Thoughts

As you delve into this idea, recognize that Thought Reality Inception serves as a significant instrument capable of influencing your subconscious in deep and meaningful ways. By intentionally nurturing uplifting thoughts and reducing detrimental ones, you can develop practices that pave the way for a more enriching and prosperous existence. Embrace this duality, allowing your thoughts to shape your reality, constructing a base of empowerment and personal development.

e. Breaking Free from the Trap: Cultivating Awareness

Envision yourself at the threshold of a lush forest, where the trails are frequently entangled with the creeping vines of unproductive thought processes. Awareness is the crucial initial step in liberating oneself from these complex patterns. By cultivating awareness of your mental patterns, you empower yourself to disrupt detrimental thought cycles before they establish themselves.

Mindfulness and Interruption

Mindfulness is like a flashlight in a dark forest, illuminating the hidden pathways of your mind. Mindfulness serves as a beacon in the shadows of your consciousness, revealing the concealed routes within your psyche. By cultivating awareness of your thoughts, you can identify the instances when negativity begins to infiltrate your mind. This heightened awareness enables you to recognize these thoughts at their inception, preventing them from embedding themselves in your subconscious mind. For instance, when you observe a recurring thought such as "I'll never be good enough," you have the power to consciously disrupt this pattern and substitute it with "I am continually evolving and enhancing myself."

Replacing Limiting Beliefs

Upon recognizing these constraining beliefs, you can start to substitute them with uplifting thoughts and affirmations. This journey resembles uprooting unwanted distractions in your mind and nurturing fresh, vibrant thoughts. Affirmations such as "I am capable of achieving my goals" or "I embrace challenges as opportunities to grow" have the potential to transform your subconscious programming gradually.

The Ever-Changing Essence of the Subconscious

It is crucial to understand that the subconscious mind is a dynamic entity. It is ever-changing and adaptable, perpetually shaped by our perceptions and encounters. Through intentional practice and applying Thought Reality Inception principles, one can cultivate a subconscious mindset that resonates with personal aspirations and amplifies the ability to achieve one's highest potential.

Practical Steps to Cultivate Awareness

1) **Mindfulness Meditation:** Mindfulness meditation consistently cultivates a deeper awareness of your cognitive processes. Dedicate a few moments daily to attune yourself to your breath, allowing your thoughts to flow by without any form of judgment.

2) **Thought Journaling:** Journal to observe and reflect on your thoughts. When you observe detrimental patterns, take a moment to document them and intentionally substitute them with uplifting affirmations.

3) **Positive Affirmations:** Embrace the practice of daily affirmations to cultivate and strengthen empowering beliefs within yourself. I possess the confidence and ability to realize my aspirations.

4) **Visualization:** Envision your aspirations and immerse yourself in the experience of realizing your ambitions. This practice of mental imagery facilitates the integration of positive thoughts into your subconscious mind.

5) **Seek Feedback:** Embrace the insights of others. Engage in meaningful conversations with those you trust, whether friends or mentors, to explore your thoughts and beliefs. Insights from others can illuminate and confront negative patterns that may elude your awareness.

In summary

Fostering awareness serves as the initial pathway to liberating oneself from detrimental subconscious habits. Illuminating your thoughts and consciously substituting limiting beliefs with empowering alternatives can turn your subconscious mind into a formidable ally. Keep in mind that your subconscious is a dynamic and evolving aspect of your mind. Through dedicated practice and mindful intention, you can harmonize your actions with your aspirations and realize your true potential. Allow this consciousness to steer you as you explore the corridors of your thoughts, shaping a cognitive environment that nurtures and elevates your pursuit of achievement and satisfaction.

f. Thought Reality Inception and Subconscious Embodiment

Envision the intricate interplay between our awareness and the depths of our subconscious. This notion of "Thought Reality Inception and Subconscious Embodiment" delves into the process by which consistent interaction with a thought can transform it into a habitual pattern, ultimately becoming ingrained as unconscious behavior.

From Thought to Automatic Action: The Power of Repetition

Imagine your mind as a flourishing garden, where each thought is a seed waiting to be nurtured and cultivated. Those that are nurtured with consistent care develop a stronger foundation. Every moment you focus on a thought, it etches a deeper groove in the intricate web of your neural pathways. With consistent practice, this cyclical approach conditions your subconscious to instinctively respond to that thought, bypassing the need for conscious reflection. For example, when you consistently affirm to yourself, "I am capable of handling challenges," you strengthen this conviction until it transforms into an instinctive, empowering reaction during tough times.

The Subconscious Takes the Wheel: Autopilot Engagement

When a thought carves a familiar route in your mind, the subconscious begins to steer your actions, following that ingrained thinking pattern. It employs the most accessible forms of media to manifest its presence in the tangible realm. This medium encompasses any tool or resource available to your subconscious, whether it manifests through your physical being, nudging you towards habitual actions, or through your surroundings, drawing you into scenarios that validate your thoughts. It can extend beyond yourself, subtly shaping how others engage with you without their awareness. Reflect on an individual who perpetually believes they lack the merit for achievement. Their inner thoughts might lead them to shy away from opportunities or emit a sense of self-doubt that others can sense, thus strengthening that belief.

Everything Becomes a Tool: The Subconscious Symphony

This principle underscores the profound impact of the subconscious mind. The world you engage with, including your surroundings and the relationships you cultivate, serves as an unspoken instrument for your deeper cognitive processes. This suggests that the subconscious possesses the capability to direct our actions according to its intentions, frequently beyond our conscious awareness or comprehension. Envision an individual who holds a profound conviction in their inherent creative abilities. This conviction will quietly shape every facet of their existence, from their endeavors to their interactions with others, fostering a self-fulfilling cycle of creativity and innovation.

Practical Steps to Harness Thought Reality

1) **Deliberate Thought Cultivation:** Consistently immerse yourself in uplifting thoughts and affirmations. The more attention you give to these thoughts, the more entrenched their pathways will grow. For instance, to cultivate your resilience, regularly affirm statements such as "I flourish when confronted with challenges."

2) **Environment and Behavior Alignment:** Aligning your surroundings and social circles with your aspirations can significantly enhance your mindset and intentions. To enhance your productivity, consider structuring your environment thoughtfully and surrounding yourself with driven individuals who embody this approach.

3) **Mindful Observation:** Engage in mindful observation to cultivate awareness of the thoughts that spontaneously emerge in various contexts. This consciousness enables you to recognize and shift detrimental thought processes before they become entrenched.

4) **Visualization Techniques:** Regularly envision your desired outcomes. Mental imagery embeds these thoughts within your subconscious, thereby increasing the likelihood of fostering positive behavioral influences.

Breaking Free from Habitual Patterns: Regaining Control

The concept of the subconscious having an impact can appear intimidating, yet there is uplifting news: you possess the power to regain control. Consider these approaches to liberate your mind from unhelpful thought patterns:

1) Illuminate Your Mind's Reflections

Immerse yourself in the art of attentively witnessing your thought patterns. Observe the thoughts that frequently occupy your mind and reflect on any negative patterns that may arise. Mindfulness serves as a guiding light, revealing the hidden corners of your mind and enabling you to recognize and comprehend the thoughts that consistently influence your actions.

2) Challenging Unproductive Thought Processes

It is crucial to thoroughly examine each idea instead of merely accepting them as they are. Explore the validity of limiting or adverse thoughts. Do they exhibit a hint of authenticity? Are they offering you the guidance you require? By examining these thoughts, you can challenge their influence over your inner mind. For example, when you notice a thought like, "I always fail," take a moment to question it by reflecting on your past successes and directing your attention to those accomplishments.

3) Encourage an Environment of Development

Shift negative thought patterns by adopting uplifting affirmations. Feeding your mind with uplifting beliefs can profoundly constructively influence your subconscious. For instance, rather than fixating on "I can't do this," shift your perspective to "I am learning and improving every day." With time, these uplifting affirmations will establish themselves, nurturing a mindset geared towards growth.

4) Embrace the Art of Being Present

Practicing mindfulness techniques like meditation deepens your awareness of your thought processes as they unfold. This increased consciousness enables you to disrupt harmful thought processes and select more uplifting mental frameworks. Envision a straightforward daily practice of meditation, where you center your attention on your breath and witness your thoughts with a sense of detachment and acceptance. This practice fosters a serene and lucid mindset, facilitating the transition from negative thoughts to more uplifting ones.

Remember!

Grasping how thoughts transform into habits and influence our subconscious allows for a deeper awareness of your inner world. Through the application of focused approaches and committed engagement, one can cultivate positive thought processes that contribute to a more fulfilling and meaningful life journey. Embrace this path of introspection and development and take back control over the underlying patterns that shape your existence.

Final Thoughts

As you explore this idea, recognize the deep connection between your conscious thoughts and the subconscious mind.

By harnessing the power of Thought Reality Inception, you can nurture and instill empowering thoughts that influence your actions and mold your reality. Embrace this evolving journey, allowing your thoughts to serve as the bedrock for a life that resonates with your deepest desires, harmoniously guided by the rhythm of your subconscious mind.

3. The Ripple Effect: Thoughts as Catalysis for Change

Unleashing Gravitational Waves of Consciousness. Imagine a peaceful pond where the calm is briefly interrupted by the soft plummet of a pebble into its waters. The initial disruption resonates deeply, affecting every facet of the water's vastness. The mind functions comparably—producing delicate waves, frequently unnoticed, that can catalyze significant changes in the surrounding reality. Though thoughts may not possess a physical presence, their energy wields an extraordinary influence, capable of shaping and transforming our reality.

In this section, we will delve into the deep understanding that thoughts act as powerful agents of change. We will delve into the metaphor of "Gravitational Waves" to demonstrate how our thoughts, much like the delicate ripples formed by a pebble, can spark a chain reaction that extends beyond the limits of our consciousness. When we truly understand the idea and put it into practice, we unlock the ability to channel the power of our thoughts, enabling significant changes in our lives and the world around us.

a. The Butterfly Effect and the Power of Intention

The Butterfly Effect illustrates how minor actions can result in significant, unforeseen consequences—a compelling metaphor for the impact of our thoughts. Much like the delicate flutter of a butterfly's wings can influence distant weather systems, our focused thoughts set off a series of events that resonate outward, ultimately shaping our reality in significant ways.

Intention fuels the strength of our thoughts. By intentionally shaping and guiding your thoughts with a defined intention, you create a ripple effect that draws in experiences and situations aligned with your aspirations. The intensity and positivity of your thoughts amplify their influence, driving you closer to your aspirations.

Practical Application: Using Thought to Shape Reality

Although this idea is intriguing in principle, the essential aspect lies in integrating it into your daily existence. Begin with intentional, incremental shifts in your thought patterns. Rather than fixating on challenges, redirect your attention towards potential solutions. As you engage with this new perspective, you'll begin to observe subtle changes in your environment and connections—these are the manifestations of transformation at play.

Daily Rituals

1) **Meditation:** Engage in daily moments of stillness, allowing yourself to center your thoughts and envision the aspirations you seek to manifest. Meditation purifies your mental space, enabling you to enhance the vibrancy of your thoughts.

2) **Visualization:** Engage in the practice of regularly envisioning your desired outcomes. Envision yourself reaching your aspirations and embracing the profound joy and satisfaction that accompanies such achievements. This mental imagery serves to harmonize your inner self with your aspirations.

3) **Journaling:** Engage in journaling by dedicating a portion of your day to articulate your thoughts, aspirations, and intentions. This practice illuminates your purpose and strengthens an optimistic mindset.

4) **Solution-Focused Thinking:** Emphasizing a solution-oriented mindset: When faced with a challenge, intentionally shift your focus towards possible resolutions. This practice cultivates a mindset that focuses on favorable results instead of dwelling on challenges.

Real-Life Example

Reflect on an individual pursuing a transition in their professional journey. By establishing distinct intentions, such as "I will discover a rewarding career that resonates with my passions," and engaging in practices like visualization, meditation, and journaling, individuals begin to observe opportunities that correspond with their aspirations. These may manifest as job postings, networking events, or serendipitous meetings with individuals in their chosen domain. The currents of contemplation pave the way for realizing professional dreams.

In summary

Integrating these theoretical insights with practical application empowers you to channel the strength of your thoughts in manifesting your desires. By consciously guiding your thoughts and embracing mindful practices, you harmonize your external circumstances with your inner aspirations. Embrace the transformative nature of your intentions and observe how the waves of your thoughts can initiate a profound change in your existence.

b. The Internal Dialogue and the Shaping of Reality

Envision your inner dialogue—the continuous stream of reflections guiding your daily journey—as the maestro orchestrating the symphony of your existence. Your inner conversation shapes the world you experience. When your internal dialogue is steeped in negativity, self-doubt, and fear, it creates a resonance that attracts those experiences into your life. Conversely, a nurturing and uplifting inner dialogue brimming with hope and confidence creates an energy that irresistibly draws in opportunities and success.

By cultivating awareness and transforming your inner dialogue into a constructive force, you take charge of the harmonious orchestration of your internal experience. Envision yourself orchestrating a symphony of potential and intention. These uplifting thoughts emanate outward, shaping your experiences and constructing the essential foundations to manifest your aspirations.

Imagine an individual navigating the complexities of a demanding work assignment. When one's internal narrative is dominated by beliefs such as "I'm not good enough" or "I'll never finish this," it fosters a self-fulfilling cycle of challenge and defeat. By shifting the conversation to "I am capable and resourceful" and "I will complete this successfully," individuals establish a strong intention that directs their actions toward achieving success.

Practical Steps to Cultivate a Positive Inner Dialogue

1) **Mindful Awareness:** Begin by tuning into the conversation happening within yourself. Take moments during your day to reflect and attune yourself to the whispers of your mind. Do they offer encouragement, or do they express skepticism?

2) **Affirmations:** Embrace positive affirmations to transform negative self-talk. For example, when you notice thoughts like "I can't do this," promptly replace them with "I am fully capable and prepared."

3) **Embracing Gratitude:** Nurture a mindset of appreciation. Consistently recognize and value the uplifting elements of your existence. This practice redirects your attention from the negative to the positive.

4) **Visualization:** Envision your achievements. Envision yourself reaching your aspirations and embracing the happiness that accompanies such fulfillment. This cultivates an optimistic perspective.

5) **Embrace an Environment of Upliftment:** Surround yourself with uplifting influences, individuals, literature, or settings. Embracing positivity cultivates a nurturing inner conversation.

Final Thoughts

Keep in mind that your internal dialogue holds the key to shaping your reality. By reshaping your internal dialogue into a positive and empowering influence, you can create a harmonious blend of achievement and satisfaction. Step into the role of the maestro, allowing your thoughts to compose the symphony that leads you to your aspirations.

c. The Gravitational Pull of Thoughts

Consider the concept of gravitational waves—ripples in the fabric of space-time generated by the movement of massive entities. Comparably, our thoughts generate ripple effects that reach beyond ourselves, impacting and molding the surrounding environment. Our thoughts do not simply transform reality; instead, they influence our actions and behaviors, charting the path for our accomplishments.

Thoughts as Catalysts for Action

When we concentrate on a specific goal or concept, our thoughts function like magnetic forces, attracting us to actions that help manifest those aspirations. Imagine a creator contemplating the essence of their forthcoming work of art. The deliberate contemplation behind their creation shapes each brushstroke, choice, and endeavor they undertake. This intentional action resonates with their aspirations, ultimately bringing the imagined artwork into reality.

Practical Examples and Applications

1) **Professional Growth:** Envision an individual striving for advancement in their career. By maintaining a steadfast focus on this objective, their mindset propels them to pursue greater responsibilities, enhance their abilities, and cultivate meaningful connections. Every action driven by these thoughts moves them nearer to realizing the promotion.

2) **Health and Fitness:** A person committed to enhancing their physical well-being may become deeply focused on completing a marathon. This intentional mindset shapes their everyday choices—selecting wholesome foods, following a consistent workout plan, and maintaining dedication to their fitness routine. The force of their reflections propels them toward their envisioned reality.

Harnessing the Power of Thought

To truly leverage the compelling force of your thoughts, reflect on these steps:

1) **Establish Precise Objectives:** Articulate your aspirations with clarity and visualize them regularly. This clarity sharpens your mental focus, amplifying the influence of your thoughts.

2) **Intentional Awareness:** Cultivate awareness to stay aligned with your aspirations. Avoid distractions and maintain your focus on the ideas that resonate with your goals.

3) **Steady Engagement:** Transform your concentrated reflections into steady behaviors. No matter how minor, each deliberate action strengthens the journey toward your aspirations.

Final Thoughts

The compelling influence of our thoughts serves as a significant force that shapes our actions and behaviors. You cultivate influences that mold your reality by directing your thoughts toward your desired outcomes and engaging in consistent action. Recognize that your thoughts serve as powerful agents of transformation, guiding you toward the reality you aspire to create. Allow these introspective actions to bring your dreams and aspirations into the realm of tangible reality.

d. Belief: The Lens Through Which We See the World

Imagine donning a pair of tinted lenses that alter the hue of your entire perception. Our beliefs function as lenses, intricately molding the way we perceive the world around us. Much like how tinted glasses alter our perception, our convictions shape the way we understand the world around us. This chapter explores the profound influence of beliefs, which are reflections of our thoughts, on the trajectory of our lives.

Positive Thoughts and Beliefs

Positive thoughts and beliefs provide a lens that imbues our surroundings with a gentle, hopeful glow. They illuminate possibilities that may escape our notice, turning obstacles into pathways for growth and dilemmas into manageable challenges. This hopeful perspective ignites our drive and enables us to pursue our aspirations purposefully. For example, an individual who has faith in their ability to learn and develop is more inclined to welcome new challenges and perceive setbacks as opportunities for growth.

Negative Thoughts and Beliefs

On the other hand, negative thoughts and beliefs resemble gray-tinted lenses, obscuring the world in a veil of pessimism. When viewed from this perspective, opportunities seem like daunting barriers, while challenges take on an air of inaccessibility. A pessimistic perspective can cultivate self-doubt and paralyze us, hindering our ability to act. Envision an individual who perpetually grapples with the belief, "I am incapable of achieving this." This mindset undermines their self-assurance and deters them from making any attempts.

The Power of Choice: Shifting Your Perspective

Fortunately, you possess the ability to select the perspective from which you perceive reality. By intentionally reshaping your beliefs, you can transform a lens of negativity into a source of potential and opportunity.

Actionable Strategies to Shift Your Perspective

1) **Conscious Presence:** Start by recognizing your existing beliefs. Pay attention to your inner conversation and reflect on whether your thoughts lean towards positivity or negativity.

2) **Confront Limiting Thoughts:** Upon recognizing a negative belief, question its authenticity. Contemplate whether this belief is grounded in reality or simply a constraining viewpoint. Substitute it with a more uplifting option. For instance, transform "I'm not good at this" into "I have the potential to enhance my skills through practice."

3) **Positive Affirmations:** Embrace the power of affirmations to cultivate and strengthen uplifting beliefs. Consistently affirm the beliefs you wish to nurture, such as "I possess the ability to reach my aspirations" or "I view challenges as chances for personal development."

4) **Visualization:** Envision yourself thriving and reaching your aspirations. This mental exercise reinforces constructive beliefs and harmonizes your behaviors with your goals.

5) **Embrace an Environment of Optimism:** Surround yourself with uplifting influences, be they literature, individuals, or your surroundings. These external influences can strengthen your newly adopted, affirmative beliefs.

Final Thoughts

Beliefs serve as profound filters that influence how we interpret the world around us. Embracing a perspective filled with potential and hope can profoundly alter your perception of reality. Embrace the transformative nature of choice and intentionally reshape your beliefs, transforming them into instruments that uplift and empower you on your path to success and fulfillment. Embrace this intentional action as the gateway to a realm of possibilities, transforming your aspirations into tangible outcomes.

e. From Thought to Action: Bridging the Gap

Having contemplated the profound influence of your thoughts, the moment has arrived to translate those reflections into tangible actions. Unexpressed ideas, much like seeds nestled in rich earth, hold immense potential, yet true development requires intentional nurturing. Here are some insights on bridging the divide between contemplation and execution:

Goal Setting: The Catalyst of Aspiration

A catalyst ignites the transition from contemplation to execution, and that catalyst is known as desire. When your aspirations are articulated with clarity and precision, your motivation transforms into a powerful force that propels you toward the goal-setting journey. Clarify your aspirations precisely and design a strategic plan for your endeavors, transforming ideas into concrete actions. Clearly, articulated objectives serve not mere fantasies but powerful catalysts propelling you forward on your path to achievement. For example, rather than expressing a general desire for success, articulate a clear intention: "I aim to secure a promotion at work within the next year by enhancing my skills and expanding my professional network."

Addressing Challenges: From Thought to Strategy

Thoughts are not just passive reflections but potent instruments for traversing challenges. In the face of challenges, the analytical mind transforms into a formidable force for finding solutions. Convert your thoughts into actionable strategies by carefully examining the circumstances, generating potential solutions, and thoughtfully evaluating the practical advantages of each choice. Effective problem-solving demands a blend of analytical reasoning, imaginative inquiry, and a willingness to pivot when the situation demands it. When confronted with a multifaceted project, it is beneficial to deconstruct it into smaller, more manageable tasks, consider various methodologies, and select the most practical option.

Decision-Making: The Compass of Your Journey

Each movement you make is rooted in a choice. Choices originate from our cognitive frameworks, convictions, and principles. The relationship between our thoughts and the choices we make is profound; cultivating a growth mindset fosters a constructive inner conversation, enhancing your ability to make decisions that align with your aspirations and sense of purpose. Your thoughts serve as the guiding force in your life's journey, steering each decision toward achievement and fulfillment. Clarity and focus in thought pave the way for choices that resonate with your innermost desires. Every choice represents a crucial moment, a shift that has the potential to redefine your path. Make thoughtful choices, allowing your intellect to lead you toward a life that truly aligns with your inner essence.

The Strength of Action: Putting Thought into Practice

Thought serves as a formidable catalyst; however, shaping your reality requires an essential companion: action. This chapter seeks to elevate your thoughts into meaningful action. Understanding the immense power of thought and dedication to action empowers you to shape your future. Ideas, no matter how brilliant, exist only in the realm of thought until they are transformed into tangible actions. Embrace the journey, manifest your intentions, and observe the profound changes unfold around you.

Channel your thoughts, define your objectives, plan your steps, make resolute decisions, and initiate your journey. Your existence is poised to be molded by the strength of your mindset and the authenticity of your deeds.

f. The Ripple Extends: Beyond the Individual

The profound impact of our thinking reaches well beyond the self. Our thoughts are intricately connected in a magnificent fabric known as humanity. This chapter delves into the profound influence of our thoughts on the collective consciousness, generating a ripple effect that nurtures collaboration, inspires positive change, and cultivates an optimistic vision for the future of our world.

Envision yourself beside a tranquil pond, gently casting a pebble into its serene waters. The initial disruption sends waves across the entire expanse of the water, influencing every aspect of its surface. Similarly, our thoughts—imbued with optimism and intention—generate waves that reach far beyond our consciousness. By sharing our thoughts with others, we create an influence that goes beyond our personal lives.

The Influence of Collective Optimism: Amplifying the Ripple

When we share positive and nurturing thoughts, we plant seeds of possibility in fertile ground. These seeds have the potential to spark dialogues, foster partnerships, or inspire collective efforts toward improvement. Envision a collective where individuals elevate one another, fostering a culture of positivity and a unified aspiration for a brighter tomorrow. The harmonious interplay of this shared energy has the potential to be transformative, cultivating a sense of unity and purpose that transcends individual limitations.

The Collective Consciousness: An Harmonious Blend of Unified Ideas

The idea of a collective consciousness implies that our thoughts are intricately connected within a broader tapestry of collective energy. By intentionally cultivating uplifting thoughts and expressing them through our words and deeds, we play a vital role in enhancing the collective harmony of consciousness. The harmony of a symphony surpasses that of a solitary instrument, much like how the collective force of positive thoughts can profoundly transform and inspire meaningful change in the world.

Utilizing Shared Positivity in Everyday Life

1) **Community Projects:** Participate in initiatives that foster meaningful transformation within the community. Working together enhances uplifting energy, cultivating a shared sense of belonging and intention.

2) **Support Networks:** Engage in and cultivate support networks where individuals inspire one another through uplifting thoughts and encouragement. This shared optimism fortifies personal determination and fosters communal health.

3) **Public Speaking and Advocacy:** Utilize avenues like public speaking and social media to disseminate uplifting messages. Your ideas have the power to motivate those around you, initiating a chain reaction that fosters significant transformation.

The Power of Collective Energy

Consider the historical movements propelled by shared beliefs and collective efforts, like the civil rights movement or the push for environmental awareness. The dynamics of these movements were driven by a common vision and uplifting thoughts among numerous individuals, highlighting the significant influence of collective energy.

In summary

You are not an isolated whisper in the boundless realm of being. Your mindset, behaviors, and uplifting energy are vital in shaping humanity's shared journey. Embracing optimism, fostering collaboration, and dedicating oneself to positive transformation positions you as a conductor within the grand orchestra of humanity, guiding the creation of a harmonious symphony of hope and advancement for everyone. Embrace your place in this vast tapestry, allowing your thoughts to resonate and create waves that touch and transform the world around you.

4. The Power Within: Shaping Your Thoughts with Willpower

Our minds are fluid entities, constantly evolving and adjusting to new experiences. This concept invites us to consider that our thoughts are not fixed and immutable. The idea of "Thought Manipulation" is presented, indicating that with intention and focused effort, we have the ability to consciously shape, steer, and govern our thoughts according to our wishes.

a. The Mind: A Work in Progress

Envision your thoughts as malleable clay rather than rigid statues carved in stone for eternity. They exist in a state of perpetual change, shaped by their experiences, emotions, and learning processes. It is empowering to recognize that we can intentionally influence our circumstances. Much like a sculptor shapes clay into a work of art, we have the power to refine our thoughts to resonate with our deepest aspirations and core values.

For instance, an individual who has consistently believed, "I'm not good at public speaking," can start to transform this perception. Through the regular practice of speeches, actively pursuing constructive feedback, and envisioning successful presentations, individuals begin to shift this restrictive belief into one that fosters their development, such as "I am evolving into a more confident public speaker."

Understand that our minds are adaptable, and with the appropriate resources and dedication, we can steer our thoughts toward constructive transformation. This continuous journey of transforming our mindset enables us to liberate ourselves from constraining habits and foster new, empowering beliefs.

b. Willpower: The Key to Transformation

Envision willpower as the precise tool wielded by an adept artisan, shaping the raw material of our lives into something extraordinary. Much like an artist chisels away at stone to reveal a stunning creation, we, too, can refine our thoughts into empowering and constructive patterns through intentional effort and disciplined habits.

Willpower serves as the essential catalyst, empowering us to counteract negative thoughts and intentionally steer our minds toward our aspirations. For example, if you frequently battle procrastination, harnessing your willpower to implement time-management strategies and cultivate disciplined work habits can shift this inclination into a productivity pattern.

Imagine an individual dedicated to the rigorous journey of preparing for a marathon. Each morning, they rise with determination, navigating through discomfort and weariness fueled by an intrinsic desire for growth and achievement. Similarly, consistent and purposeful effort can transform our thought patterns from barriers into pathways leading us toward our aspirations.

Harnessing willpower transcends a singular endeavor; it embodies an ongoing commitment to deliberate and concentrated effort. By nurturing practices that foster our psychological and emotional development, we tap into our inner strength to reshape our thinking and, in turn, our existence.

c. The Art of Thought Transmutation

Imagine "thought transmutation" as a profound transformation, akin to the alchemical journey of turning base metals into gold, yet occurring within the intricate landscape of the mind. This notion revolves around the understanding that our thinking patterns can be transformed through intentional and sustained endeavor. Transmutation is not a passive process; it requires active involvement and cultivating habits that nurture the new thought patterns we seek to establish.

Deliberate Effort in Transmutation

To transform your thoughts, it is essential to participate in intentional practices that strengthen emerging patterns. For example, to shift from a pattern of self-doubt to one of self-confidence, it is essential to intentionally substitute self-critical thoughts with affirmations that reinforce your sense of self-worth. Whenever you notice a thought of self-doubt, respond with affirmations such as, "I possess the ability and deserve to achieve success." With consistent intention, this process will transform your inner world, akin to the alchemical change of base metal into gold.

Habit Formation

Successful transmutation fundamentally hinges on cultivating habits. Create habits and strategies that regularly support the thought processes you wish to cultivate. Consider establishing a daily practice of reflecting on your accomplishments and the positive attributes you possess. This practice enhances the neural connections linked to self-assurance, facilitating the automatic emergence of these thoughts.

o **Practical Example**

Envision an individual seeking to transition from a perspective of scarcity to one of abundance. One could start by engaging in a daily practice of gratitude, reflecting on the aspects of life they appreciate and envisioning the abundance that surrounds them. By consistently directing their attention towards gratitude and abundance, individuals gradually transform their mindset, drawing in more positive experiences and opportunities.

In summary

The practice of transforming thoughts involves intentionally crafting your mindset through focused effort and the establishment of consistent habits. By immersing yourself in practices that align with your desired thought patterns, you initiate a transformation in your mental state, resulting in significant shifts in your behavior and overall life experiences. Embrace this journey with patience and determination, and observe how your thoughts transform, crafting a more empowering and enriching reality.

d. Building Scaffolding for New Thoughts

Transforming your mindset resembles the intricate work of building a structure; it requires a robust base to support what you aim to create. The concept of "scaffolding for new thoughts" entails embracing practical habits that serve as foundational supports as you nurture positive and empowering mental frameworks. These practices offer a framework and direction as you cultivate a new mindset. As your new perspectives solidify, you can slowly dismantle the support structures, resulting in a robust and empowering mental framework.

1) Positive Affirmations: The Power of Self-Talk

Embracing positive affirmations serves as a profound method to cultivate and strengthen the mindset we aspire to achieve. It is crucial to eradicate detrimental inner dialogue and substitute it with affirmations that empower and bolster your aspirations. Consider transforming the disempowering thought "I am unable to do this" into a more empowering perspective by saying, "I am capable, and I am learning." By consistently practicing these affirmations, you are actively reshaping your neural pathways, creating an environment conducive to a more positive and self-assured mindset.

Effective Approaches to Implement Positive Affirmations

i. **Recognize Detrimental Self-Talk:** Be mindful of your inner conversation and recognize any detrimental thoughts that arise.

ii. **Create Positive Affirmations:** Create affirming statements that challenge and transform these detrimental thoughts. For instance, when you find yourself thinking, "I'm not good enough," shift that narrative to "I am worthy and capable."

iii.   **Engage in Consistent Practice:** Regularly embrace these affirmations, particularly during times of uncertainty or when encountering obstacles. These uplifting thoughts will gradually embed themselves in your subconscious with consistent practice.

iv.   **Envision Achievement:** Integrate positive affirmations with the power of visualization. As you engage in your affirmations, envision yourself reaching your aspirations and embracing the essence of success.

Final Thoughts

Constructing a framework for fresh ideas requires cultivating and strengthening affirmative thought processes through intentional practices such as positive affirmations. These practices act as provisional frameworks, guiding you toward cultivating a resilient and empowering mindset. Over time and with persistent effort, these emerging thought patterns will seamlessly integrate into your mental framework, enabling you to realize your aspirations and embrace a life of fulfillment. Continue to affirm, visualize, and trust your abilities, and observe the transformation of your inner world.

2) **Visualization: Painting a Picture of Success**

Visualization stands as a remarkably potent instrument within your reach. By vividly envisioning your desired outcomes, you effectively condition your subconscious for achievement while simultaneously inspiring yourself to take action.

Creating a Clear Picture

Start by gently closing your eyes and vividly imagining the outcome you wish to achieve. Observe it with the utmost attention to detail. Envision yourself achieving your aspirations, whether standing triumphantly on a podium, earning that well-deserved promotion, or crossing the finish line of a marathon. Immerse yourself completely: notice the texture of the podium underfoot, listen to the crowd's applause, savor the sweetness of triumph, and embrace the profound sense of achievement and fulfillment.

Regular Visualization Practice

By engaging in consistent visualization, you strengthen these uplifting images within your consciousness, rendering them more tangible and achievable. This practice communicates profound messages to your inner mind, harmonizing your thoughts and actions with your aspirations. For example, a competitor may imagine reaching the finish line, experiencing the thrill of triumph and the power coursing through their body. This striking visualization elevates their drive and improves their execution by establishing a cognitive framework for achievement.

Actionable Strategies for Powerful Visualization

i. **Allocate Time:** Allocate a few moments daily to engage in your visualization practice. This can seamlessly integrate into your morning practices or serve as a calming pre-sleep ritual.

ii. **Seek a Serene Environment:** Choose a serene and cozy environment that allows for uninterrupted reflection. Gently close your eyes and take a series of deep breaths to ground your awareness.

iii. **Involve every sense:** Enhance your visualization by immersing yourself in a rich sensory experience.

Envision the vivid imagery, auditory experiences, aromas, flavors, and emotions that accompany the realization of your aspirations.

iv. **Affirmative Feelings:** Embrace the opportunity to feel the uplifting emotions associated with your achievements genuinely. Feel the joy, pride, and satisfaction as though you have already reached your goal.

v. **Consistency:** Regularly engage in visualization. As you do, you enhance the neural connections linked to your aspirations, facilitating a deeper alignment of your subconscious with these objectives.

In summary

Through the art of visualization, you can vividly illustrate your path to success, tapping into your mind's immense potential to construct a mental framework for realizing your aspirations. This approach conditions your inner mind for achievement and inspires you to engage in the essential steps. Embrace the power of visualization on your journey and observe how your aspirations start to take shape, one vivid image at a time.

3) Gratitude Practice: Cultivating an Attitude of Appreciation

Engaging in gratitude practice serves as a transformative mechanism, redirecting your perspective from a sense of lack to one rich in abundance and appreciation. Daily reflection on your gratitude fosters a mindset that encourages your mind to seek out the positive aspects in every situation.

Daily Reflection

Take a moment each day to reflect on the things you appreciate in your life. Engaging in practices such as journaling, meditation, or quiet reflection can facilitate this process. Identify the elements, individuals, and moments in your life that you hold in high regard, regardless of their perceived insignificance. This practice gradually cultivates a mindset that acknowledges and values the positive aspects of your existence.

Rewiring the Brain

Transforming the Mind Engaging in gratitude practice reshapes your brain by establishing neural connections linked to fulfillment and positivity. It cultivates your capacity to recognize and value your existence's positive aspects, fostering abundant uplifting experiences. For example, consistently recognizing the contributions of your friends and family can lead to deeper and more enriching connections in your relationships.

o **Illustration**

Imagine an individual who starts their morning by noting three aspects of their life for which they appreciate. These experiences may vary from a bright morning to a thoughtful act from a coworker to a personal milestone. This straightforward practice slowly transforms their perspective, enhancing their awareness of positivity and alleviating stress. Over time, individuals might observe a significant enhancement in their emotional state and perspective on existence.

Actionable Approaches to Cultivating Gratitude

i. **Gratitude Journal:** Maintain a journal that records several things you appreciate daily. Engaging in this practice in the morning can set a positive tone for your day, and doing so in the evening allows for a thoughtful reflection on the blessings experienced throughout the day.

ii. **Gratitude Meditation:** Engage in a brief meditation practice, allowing yourself to center on the aspects of life for which you feel gratitude. Envision them distinctly and embrace the uplifting feelings that accompany them.

iii. **Express Gratitude:** Cultivating a practice of expressing gratitude towards others can profoundly impact your relationships and overall well-being. Expressing gratitude through a note, a spoken word or a simple act enhances positive energy flow in our interactions.

iv. **Gratitude Reminders:** Incorporate reminders or cues into your daily routine to pause and reflect on something you appreciate. This might manifest as a simple reminder on your workspace, a gentle nudge from your phone, or a contemplative pause amidst your day.

Final Thoughts

Embracing a mindset of appreciation can profoundly reshape your inner world. Consistently engaging in the practice of gratitude allows you to redirect your attention towards abundance and appreciation, fundamentally reshaping your mindset for a more positive outlook. This practice enriches your well-being and fosters a wave of positivity in your interactions and experiences. Adopt gratitude as a regular practice and observe how it cultivates greater joy, fulfillment, and deeper connections in your life.

4) **Mindfulness Meditation: Becoming the Observer of Your Thoughts**

Mindfulness meditation empowers you to witness your thoughts and emotions with a sense of detachment and acceptance. This practice cultivates a heightened awareness of your inner dialogue, empowering you to take action when unproductive thought patterns emerge. Mindfulness empowers you to witness your thoughts rather than be confined by them. Through consistent effort, you will cultivate the ability to distance yourself from negativity, creating room for the selection of more positive and enriching thoughts.

Actionable Approaches to Mindfulness Meditation

i. **Set a Regular Practice Time:** Set aside a designated daily time to engage in mindfulness meditation. This practice can be embraced in the morning to cultivate a positive mindset for the day ahead or in the evening to facilitate relaxation and reflection.

ii. **Find a Quiet Space:** Select a serene and cozy environment that allows for undisturbed reflection. Assume a comfortable posture, whether seated or reclined, allowing your body to unwind.

iii. **Center Your Awareness on Your Breath:** Gently close your eyes and bring your awareness to your breath. Notice the gentle rhythm of the air as it moves in and out through your nostrils. This grounds your consciousness in the here and now.

iv. **Notice Your Thoughts:** During meditation, it is natural for thoughts to emerge. Rather than becoming entangled in your thoughts, recognize them and allow them to drift away, much like clouds moving across the sky. Redirect your attention to the rhythm of your breath.

v. **Non-Judgmental Awareness:** Foster an attitude of open-minded observation. Witness your thoughts and emotions without categorizing them as "positive" or "negative." This approach fosters a deep and empathetic awareness of your inner thoughts and feelings.

o **Illustration**

Reflect on an individual navigating the pressures of their professional environment. By engaging in mindfulness meditation, individuals cultivate the ability to witness their thoughts regarding work without becoming trapped by them. They observe the anxiety yet opt for a measured response, allowing time for reflection. This awareness establishes a space between the stressor and the individual's response, enabling the choice of a more constructive reaction, like taking a deep breath or finding a moment of solitude to restore balance.

In summary

Mindfulness meditation is a transformative practice that allows you to witness your thoughts with a sense of detachment and acceptance. By stepping back and observing your thoughts, you empower yourself to intervene and select more positive ones, leading to a profound transformation of your mental landscape. Embrace this practice, allowing it to lead you toward a more mindful, present, and positive existence. Through consistent effort and patience, you will cultivate a greater resilience to negativity and enhance your ability to nurture a peaceful inner conversation.

e. A Journey, Not a Destination

Keep in mind that transforming your thought patterns is an ongoing process rather than a conclusive endpoint. Throughout your journey, you will face challenges. Rather than allowing discouragement to take hold, embrace these moments as valuable chances for personal development. Every setback serves as a hidden lesson, a crucial stepping-stone on your journey toward mental resilience.

Consider these challenges as a workout for your mind, with each hurdle enhancing your cognitive resilience. In the face of adversity, it becomes essential to reaffirm your commitment to your aspirations, strengthening your resolve for transformative growth. Each time you navigate a challenge, you cultivate mental grit and resilience, empowering you to confront future obstacles with enhanced assurance.

Consider a scenario where you strive to enhance your productivity, yet you notice a tendency to revert to familiar procrastination patterns. Instead of perceiving this as a setback, consider it an opportunity to reevaluate and enhance your approaches. It might be beneficial to reevaluate your approach to time management or explore fresh strategies to enhance your motivation. By reflecting on these experiences, you cultivate an increasingly resilient and flexible mindset.

Pragmatic Approaches to Welcoming the Path Ahead

1) **Engage in consistent self-reflection:** Pause and contemplate your journey thus far. Recognize your achievements and pinpoint growth opportunities. This

contemplation fosters an awareness of your path and strengthens your dedication to personal development.

2) **Embrace the significance of minor achievements:** Honor your accomplishments, regardless of their size. Every achievement serves as a significant marker along your path, fueling your drive and strengthening constructive mental frameworks.

3) **Embrace Challenges:** In moments of adversity, take the time to reflect on the factors that contributed to the outcome and the underlying reasons behind it. Embrace this understanding to implement essential changes and return with renewed strength.

4) **Embrace Adaptability:** Embrace the possibility of evolving your approaches. When faced with challenges, embrace the opportunity to explore alternative strategies. Adaptability is essential for traversing the highs and lows of your path.

5) **Reaffirm Your Aspirations:** Consistently reflect on your aspirations and their significance in your life. This renewed dedication sustains your drive and hones your concentration.

Final Thoughts

Embrace the transformative journey of reshaping your thought patterns, recognizing that it is a continuous process rich with growth opportunities. Through unwavering dedication and a strong mental framework, you will cultivate the inner fortitude necessary to navigate obstacles and persist in your journey toward achieving your aspirations. Embrace the lessons each step of your journey offers, and let your commitment to self-improvement lead you to an empowered and deeply fulfilling life.

f. Influence, Not Control

It's important to recognize that while we may not have total control over our thoughts, we do possess the ability to shape and guide them. Our thoughts emerge from a complex interplay of various influences, such as our past experiences, emotional states, and the stimuli we encounter in our environment. We can effectively steer and mold our thoughts toward a more positive trajectory through dedicated practice, heightened awareness, and the strategic use of particular techniques.

Developing Awareness

Awareness is the initial stride in shaping your thoughts. By cultivating awareness of your inner conversation and identifying moments when detrimental or unhelpful thoughts emerge, you can start to take action. This consciousness enables you to identify unproductive thoughts before they establish themselves and guide them toward more uplifting alternatives.

Effective Strategies for Influencing Thoughts

1) **Mindfulness Meditation:** Consistent mindfulness meditation cultivates an awareness of cognitive patterns. This approach encourages you to witness your thoughts impartially, fostering an environment where you can select more uplifting and beneficial ones.

2) **Positive Affirmations:** Embracing positive affirmations can transform your mindset, allowing you to gradually shift away from limiting beliefs and cultivate a more empowering inner dialogue. Statements such as "I am capable" and "I embrace challenges" can cultivate a more resilient mindset.

3) **Visualization:** Envisioning your goals and desired outcomes harmonizes your thoughts with your aspirations. By vividly envisioning success, you condition your inner self to align with and progress toward these aspirations.

4) **Gratitude Practice:** Engaging in gratitude practice transforms your perspective from one of scarcity to one of abundance, fostering a more positive view of life. This approach cultivates a mindset that actively seeks and values the positive aspects in all circumstances.

5) **Cognitive Restructuring:** This approach focuses on recognizing and questioning detrimental thought patterns. You shape your mental environment by examining the authenticity of negative thoughts and substituting them with more realistic and uplifting alternatives.

Final Thoughts

Although complete mastery over our thoughts may elude us, we possess the capacity to shape them through intentional mindfulness and conscious endeavor. We steer our thoughts toward a more uplifting and empowering path by cultivating awareness and employing mindfulness meditation, positive affirmations, visualization, gratitude exercises, and cognitive restructuring. Adopt these practices, and observe how you nurture a mental landscape that fosters your development and overall wellness.

g. **The Power of Choice**

Ultimately, "Thought Manipulation" reveals that our thinking processes are subject to our influence. Through the cultivation of determination and supportive routines, we can steer our thoughts toward creating a more fulfilling existence. We possess the ability to shape our mental narratives, turning ephemeral ideas into the foundational elements of the reality we aspire to manifest.

Embracing the Power of Will and the Formation of Habits

Embracing the essence of choice involves a deliberate engagement in shaping your thoughts. It's about harnessing your inner strength to guide your thoughts toward optimism, achievement, and personal development. Creating nurturing habits sets the stage for a robust and adaptable mental structure. Incorporating mindfulness practices, positive affirmations, and visualization into your daily life enables you to take charge of your thoughts and harmonize them with your aspirations.

Embracing the Role of Your Own Mind's Architect

Envision yourself as the creator of a narrative, where every thought serves as a word, sentence, or chapter that shapes the unfolding tale of your existence. You create a story that resonates with your deepest desires and ambitions by selecting the thoughts you wish to embrace and cultivate. Much like a masterful author hones their prose, you have the power to shape your thoughts, ensuring they enhance the story of your life.

Actionable Strategies to Harness the Power of Choice

1) **Conscious Decision-Making:** Periodically evaluate your thoughts and intentionally choose which ones to embrace and which to let go of. This approach fosters a deep connection with your aspirations and principles.

2) **Intentional Thought Selection:** When encountering a negative or unhelpful thought, consciously substitute it with a more uplifting and constructive alternative. For

instance, substitute "I can't do this" with "I am capable and open to growth."

3) **Routine Reinforcement:** Consistent engagement in practices that nurture and strengthen positive thought patterns is essential. Daily affirmations, gratitude journaling, and mindfulness meditation are profound methods for effectively harnessing and directing thoughts.

4) **Reflect and Adjust:** Allocate time to examine your cognitive patterns and their influence on your existence. When you identify aspects that require enhancement, recalibrate your strategy and reaffirm your dedication to your objectives.

In summary

Embracing the power of choice allows you to navigate your mental landscape with intention and awareness. Through the strength of your will and the cultivation of nurturing habits, you have the power to steer your thoughts toward manifesting a reality that embodies your most profound desires and aspirations. Take charge of your mental narrative, allowing your thoughts to serve as the foundation for a meaningful and prosperous existence.

5. The Mind-Body Connection: Thoughts as Messengers of Health

Neuronal Messengers: The Influence of Thought on the Body! This idea delves into the fascinating connection between mental functions and overall health. The idea of "Thought as Neuronal Messenger" suggests that our thoughts act as signals, influencing the functioning of our bodies on a cellular level.

a. **The Harmony of Thought and Being: A Tapestry of Interconnectedness**

The journey of being human unfolds like a magnificent symphony, a profound interplay between our thoughts and physical existence. This chapter delves into the profound connection between our mental processes and physical state, highlighting how our thoughts, particularly the subconscious ones, act as a guiding force in the intricate orchestration of our existence.

The human body resembles a sophisticated orchestra comprising trillions of cells, each functioning as a distinct instrument in the grand symphony that contributes to the organism's overall health. In this section, we explore a captivating idea: all our thoughts, especially those hidden within the depths of our subconscious, serve as the conductor, shaping the performance of this internal orchestra.

The Healing Power of Positivity: Cellular Repair and Growth

Positive thinking can produce miracle healing and growth within the body. Some experts think a positive mindset can activate cellular repair mechanisms and significantly augment the body's natural healing and regeneration processes. Also, focused thought, impregnated with a belief in growth and maturation, can potentially feed the body and support particular life phases, such as those occurring during childhood and puberty.

Optimizing Performance: Thought's Influence on Organs

The impact of cognition reaches far beyond mere cellular repair and growth processes. The interplay of our cognitive processes may significantly influence the operational dynamics of our bodily organs, akin to a conductor meticulously refining the performance of an intricate internal orchestra. For example, cultivating positive thoughts and emotions can enhance cardiovascular health and optimize respiratory function. Similarly, maintaining a calm and focused mindset can improve digestive processes, whereas persistent stress may adversely affect the digestive system.

The Body's Defense System: The Power of Positive Thinking

Positive thinking transcends mere emotional well-being; it possesses the potential to profoundly influence one's physical health. Evidence indicates that maintaining a positive perspective could enhance the body's ability to fend off illness by fortifying the immune system. Positive thoughts can mitigate stress and enhance well-being, fostering conditions less prone to illness.

Remember!

The mind and body are two sides of the same coin. As you nurture a positive mindset with empowering thoughts, you become a conductor of your internal symphony, conducting your body on the cellular level to find the way to optimal health and well-being.

b. The Power of Focused Intention: Harmonizing Your Well-Being

The human body is a magnificent instrument, and our thoughts hold the power to be its most skilled conductor. This section looks at a concept called "Focused Attention," a concept that seeks to prove that our will can be used to enhance the connection between mind and body and to improve health and well-being. Although the scientific mechanism is still obscure, the potential benefits are undeniable. In the following section, we shall review practical ways of tapping into the power of focused intention.

Visualization: Rehearsing for Health

Visualization is an essential tool in designing your reality and determining your physical health. Take a few minutes daily to mentally paint a colorful picture of yourself in a healthy and vibrant state. Visualize your body performing at the highest level, energized with stamina. This mental rehearsal serves your subconscious mind with a blueprint for making positive physiological changes in the body and aligns your internal orchestra for peak health performance.

Positive Affirmations: Self-Fulfilling Prophecies for Wellness

The power of positive affirmations is not only in the conditioning of the mind, but they also affect the realm of the body. Positive statements about one's health and well-being regularly deeply impact the subconscious mind. Consistently affirming your belief in your body's power to heal and thrive provides the foundation for a self-fulfilling prophecy and lets the body act on the positivity you mean for it.

Stress Management: Quieting the Conductor of Chaos

Chronic stress can be considered a disruptive conductor of one's mind-body symphony. If allowed to take hold, it sends the internal orchestra into a mess and may cause a cascade of ill effects on health. You will learn and practice relaxation techniques, such as deep breathing or meditation, that will give you ways to quiet the conductor of chaos. The daily integration of this practice brings calmness and wellness into the body; thus, the body is able to function at optimal levels.

Remember!

It is essential to keep this in mind! The capacity to shape your health is not solely dependent on external influences; it is equally rooted in the remarkable strength of your concentrated intention. Through the strategic application of visualization, positive affirmations, and effective stress management techniques, one can take command of one's health, orchestrating a harmonious balance of well-being within the body.

c. Beyond Duality: A Symphony of Wholeness

The essence of being human transcends the limitations often associated with personal identity. This section explores the intricate relationship between the mind and body, presenting them as a unified entity that profoundly enriches the essence of existence. This viewpoint transcends the conventional understanding of these elements as separate entities, recognizing them as two facets of a cohesive whole.

Our thoughts and emotions transcend simple ideas; they possess significant influence, directly affecting our physical health. The complex relationship of our existence is shaped not by isolated parts but through a seamless interaction between the flow of our thoughts and the tempo of our physical reality. The interplay between these elements significantly influences our physiological processes, including biochemical reactions, immune system activity, and vulnerability to various health concerns.

The Harmony of Mind and Body

Envision the mind and body as components of a grand symphony, each playing a vital role in creating a harmonious masterpiece. When thoughts and emotions harmonize positively, they compose a symphony that elevates overall well-being. For example, embracing a positive mindset can trigger the release of endorphins, the body's inherent pain relievers, enhancing mood and alleviating stress. On the other hand, persistent stress and adverse emotions can disturb this balance, resulting in chemical imbalances and health complications like hypertension or compromised immunity.

Concrete Example

Consider an individual navigating the complexities of persistent stress in their professional environment. The experience of stress may manifest in various physical symptoms, including headaches, digestive disturbances, and a compromised immune system. Individuals can find a sense of equilibrium and harmony by engaging in practices like mindfulness, physical activity, and positive affirmations. Engaging in these practices aids in regulating stress hormones such as cortisol, ultimately fostering a greater sense of well-being.

Final Thoughts

The mind and body exist as interconnected components of a singular, cohesive system. Exploring and cultivating this relationship can elevate our holistic health and well-being. Embrace practices that foster a deep connection between your mind and body, and witness the transformative effects of this holistic approach to well-being. Allow your mind and body to harmonize, crafting a masterpiece of unity beyond personal identity's confines.

d. A Call to Exploration: Unveiling the Mysteries of the Mind-Body Connection

The emerging scientific study suggesting that our thoughts can directly influence cellular processes is equally thrilling. This concept is undoubtedly captivating; however, it's important to acknowledge that our comprehension of the intricate mechanisms at play is still developing. This encourages us to consider the transformative potential of a positive mindset within a wider context of holistic health rather than perceiving it as an isolated remedy.

The Interplay of Cognition and Biological Mechanisms

Recent findings indicate that uplifting thoughts and feelings could impact cellular well-being. Research indicates that stress may influence telomeres, the protective structures at the ends of chromosomes, which could affect aging and health outcomes. On the other hand, engaging in practices such as mindfulness and positive thinking appears to correlate with increased telomere length, suggesting a nuanced relationship between our mental state and cellular well-being.

An Expansive Perspective on Well-Being

Exploring the interplay between the mind and body encourages us to embrace a comprehensive view of well-being. Although the impact of positive thinking is significant, it is essential to combine it with additional health practices to achieve optimal results. Integrating an optimistic outlook with healthy lifestyle choices, strong social connections, and attentive mental health care fosters a holistic strategy that enhances our overall well-being.

In summary

Exploring the intricate relationship between the mind and body is a continuous path of revelation. The evolving science surrounding the interplay between thoughts and cellular processes presents a captivating realm of exploration. Adopt this comprehensive perspective on well-being, merging optimistic thought with various wellness techniques, and observe how you cultivate a more harmonious, vibrant, and satisfying existence. This path encourages a sense of wonder and receptivity, urging you to delve into how your mindset and behaviors influence your overall wellness.

e. A Holistic Harmony: Cultivating Well-being Through Integration

It is essential to understand that while positive thinking holds value, it is not a cure-all and should not substitute for medical care or a balanced way of living. What we strive for is a comprehensive sense of well-being. By integrating healthy living, effective stress management techniques, and positive thinking, we create a profound sense of well-being that resonates deeply within our being.

The Harmony of Comprehensive Wellness

Embracing a mindset of positivity is essential, yet it must be integrated into a holistic and balanced perspective on well-being. Much like a symphony that thrives on the interplay of diverse instruments to produce harmonious melodies, our overall well-being blossoms when we integrate positive thinking with other beneficial practices. Envision your mind and body as a finely tuned orchestra, where every element of your lifestyle plays a vital role in creating a harmonious symphony.

Wellness and Vitality

Embrace a harmonious blend of nutritious eating, consistent physical activity, and restorative sleep in your daily life. The essential components serve as the vital framework your body requires to operate at its best. A nourishing diet abundant in fruits, vegetables, lean proteins, and whole grains energizes both body and mind, while consistent physical activity alleviates stress and enhances mood.

Managing Stress

Embrace dynamic approaches to releasing built-up tension, including practices like yoga, meditation, deep breathing techniques, or engaging in activities that foster joy and tranquility. These practices foster equilibrium between the mind and body, cultivating tranquility and fortitude. Daily meditation can potentially lower cortisol levels, enhancing overall well-being and fostering mental clarity.

Embracing an optimistic mindset

Foster a constructive mindset through regular gratitude practice, affirming positive beliefs, and employing visualization strategies. Embracing a positive mindset fosters emotional strength and nurtures mental well-being, yet its true power emerges when combined with additional healthy practices. Starting and concluding your day with a gratitude journal can transform your perspective, highlighting the positive elements of your life and nurturing a more hopeful mindset.

In summary

A comprehensive perspective on well-being encompasses the fusion of optimistic thought, nutritious lifestyle choices, and adept stress management techniques. By adopting this balanced perspective, you cultivate a harmonious resonance of well-being that profoundly echoes throughout your entire self. Acknowledge that every facet of your lifestyle plays a role in your overall well-being, and allow this holistic perspective to lead you toward a more enriching and dynamic existence.

f. The Power of the Neuronal Messengers: Taking Charge of Your Symphony

Imagine standing confidently before a grand orchestra, baton in hand, ready to guide each instrument into a harmonious blend of melodies. Embracing the intricate balance of mind and body, coupled with a deep understanding of how our thoughts function as "neuronal messengers," enables us to consciously and harmoniously manage our well-being. We assume the role of our conductors in the personal symphony of life, steering it towards vitality and well-being with the purposeful intention of a maestro.

Understanding Neuronal Messengers

Neuronal messengers act as essential conduits for the chemical and electrical signals that facilitate communication within our nervous system. The interplay of our thoughts and emotions is fundamental in releasing neurotransmitters, hormones, and other chemical messengers, which profoundly influence our physical health. Welcoming uplifting thoughts can trigger the release of neurotransmitters linked to joy, like serotonin and dopamine, promoting overall mental and physical well-being. Conversely, ongoing stress and negative thinking can disrupt this balance, leading to various health issues.

Perfecting the Craft of Your Composition

Understanding the connection between our thoughts and neuronal messengers empowers us to intentionally guide our mental and physical health. Here is a guide to establish your impact:

1) **Mindful Intention:** Approach each day with intentionality, guiding your mindset towards optimism and growth. Setting clear and positive intentions in the morning can significantly impact how you approach your day, influencing your actions and reactions. Start your day with a strong affirmation like, "Today, I intentionally choose positivity and embrace each moment with a heart brimming with gratitude."

2) **Stress Management:** To navigate stress with greater ease, consider incorporating practices like deep breathing, meditation, and physical exercise into your routine. Engaging in these practices can facilitate the regulation of stress hormone release, such as cortisol. Taking a few moments for deep breathing exercises during stressful times can profoundly calm your mind and body.

3) **Healthy Lifestyle Choices:** Adopt a comprehensive perspective on wellness: Foster a harmonious diet, maintain regular physical movement, and emphasize restorative rest to amplify the effectiveness of your brain's communicators. Nourishing foods, regular physical activity, and restorative sleep are essential for harmonizing the mind and body.

4) **Positive Social Interactions:** Fostering meaningful connections is vital, as well as nurturing relationships and engaging deeply in fulfilling social interactions. Participating in uplifting social exchanges stimulates the production of oxytocin, a hormone that nurtures affection and bonds, enhancing our overall wellness.

o **Illustration**

Contemplate a person's journey navigating the complexities of recovery from a health obstacle. Individuals can profoundly enhance their recovery by consciously nurturing uplifting thoughts, engaging in mindfulness techniques, emphasizing a wholesome lifestyle, and building nurturing connections. Their positive perspective and actions influence their neural interactions, promoting healing and holistic well-being.

To Conclude

Embracing this intertwined harmony of mind and body and deepening our understanding of how our thoughts function as "neuronal messengers," we are in an appropriate position to manage our health actively and much more in balance. We become our own conductors in our personal orchestra of life, guiding it toward vitality and well-being with the baton of focused intention.

Absolutely, the body is not just a vessel but an intrinsic part of your whole self. By fostering a positive mindset, you pave the way for a harmonious connection between mind and body, creating a symphony of health that resonates through every aspect of life. Yet, it's crucial to remember that while a positive mindset can work wonders, it shines brightest when complemented by proper medical care, a healthy lifestyle, and a holistic approach to well-being. Think of it as a beautiful harmony where every note counts—mind, body, and soul, all playing their parts to create a life of balance and fulfillment.

6. Designing Your Destiny: The Engine of Thought

Begin an exploration where your reflections act as the catalyst steering your fate. This inquiry reveals the deep understanding that our minds, with their relentless flow of thoughts, desires, and motivations, possess the ability to mold our reality. As previously mentioned, thoughts serve as the driving force that propels us to action, whether consciously aware of it or not. Through a deep exploration of the "Nine Primary Motives," we reveal the underlying forces that drive our thoughts and actions. This section encourages you to unravel the fundamental aspirations that drive your progress, providing insights to harmonize your decisions with your intrinsic values.

Envision your thoughts as the driving force behind a vehicle, steering the course, pace, and ultimate goal of your life's expedition. Whether consciously selected or influenced by deep-seated beliefs, your journey is fundamentally guided by the nature of your thoughts. By consciously choosing your thoughts and aligning your motivations with your aspirations, you navigate your life's journey, guiding yourself toward fulfillment and achievement. Embrace the power of choice as you journey through the vast seas of knowledge, shaping your future with deliberate intention and clarity.

a. The Powerhouse Within: Thoughts as the Engine of Action

Our minds are relentless in their activity, perpetually crafting thoughts, aspirations, and perspectives. At the heart of ADAM-GENE lies the notion of the mind as "the Engine of Thought." These reflections drive us toward action, whether we are aware of it or not.

Your thoughts serve as the compass guiding your journey; they shape the direction you take, influence the speed of your advancement, and define where you ultimately arrive. The way you think significantly impacts your path, whether it is a deliberate choice or molded by ingrained beliefs. Your thought patterns shape the choices you make and the steps you take in life. Each action we engage in, whether it stems from deliberate contemplation or occurs instinctively, is fueled by the essence of our thoughts.

Envision a learner striving for excellence in their studies. Their reflections on their ambitions and desires propel their behaviors—engaging in thorough study, reaching out for support when necessary, and maintaining concentration throughout their learning experiences. On the other hand, an individual harboring a negative mindset may experience their actions swayed by self-doubt and procrastination, resulting in stagnation.

Recognizing that thoughts drive actions allows you to guide your mental focus intentionally. By cultivating constructive, purpose-driven thoughts, you chart a path toward achievement and satisfaction. Harness the strength of your consciousness as the force that shapes your future, directing it with clarity and intention.

b. The Fuel of Motivation: Understanding the Why Behind Our Choices

Not every thought holds the same value. Some spark a momentary impulse, while others stoke an intense passion for engagement. This notion presents the "Nine Primary Motives" as the driving force that catalyzes thought into action. The spectrum of these motives reflects the complexity of human desires, spanning from fundamental needs like safety and enjoyment to elevated ambitions such as acknowledgment and the quest for understanding.

Grasping these hidden drives empowers us to unravel the reasons behind specific choices. By examining our motivations, we uncover the underlying forces that propel us, allowing us to make decisions that resonate more deeply with our fundamental principles.

The Nine Core Motivations: Unraveling the Essence of Action

Grasping these fundamental desires is vital for profoundly comprehending the motivations that drive our progress. The core motivations act as essential elements of human drive, profoundly influencing our decisions and actions meaningfully:

1) Safety

Security is the cornerstone of human motivation, embodying a core impulse for safety, stability, and comfort. This notion encompasses our fundamental requirements for nourishment, shelter, security, and the aspiration for emotional and financial equilibrium. For instance, people may prioritize saving money or pursuing stable employment to cultivate a sense of security for their future.

2) Pleasure

The pursuit of enjoyment, happiness, and fulfillment serves as the fundamental impetus for the pleasure principle. This inner drive compels us to seek out experiences that bring joy, excitement, and a deep sense of fulfillment. Engaging in a cherished pastime or organizing a getaway exemplifies actions motivated by this yearning.

3) Connection

Connection is essential to our human experience, reflecting our nature as social creatures. The drive for connection highlights our fundamental desire for love, belonging, and significant social engagement. This inner drive inspires us to foster significant connections with others, ultimately nurturing a deep sense of community and belonging. Contemplate the energy we invest in nurturing friendships and cultivating familial connections.

4) Power

The power motive embodies a fundamental urge for influence, control, and accomplishment in social interactions. It's not just about dominating others; it highlights the significance of having agency and actively shaping the world around us. For instance, seeking leadership positions or aiming for career achievements are endeavors driven by this underlying motive.

5) Growth

The pursuit of growth is marked by a deep-seated curiosity and an intense yearning to learn, evolve, and expand our capabilities. This drive urges us to face our boundaries, embrace fresh experiences, and seek continuous personal growth. Engaging in educational pursuits or embracing demanding projects reflects this intrinsic motivation.

6) Contribution

Contributing reflects a profound aspiration to create a positive influence on the world and foster significant transformation. This aspiration inspires individuals to support others, participate in endeavors that go beyond self-interest, and forge a significant legacy. Engaging in community service or participating in charitable endeavors exemplifies actions motivated by this purpose.

7) Recognition

The quest for validation, respect, and social status serves as the fundamental impetus for the desire for recognition. This should not be seen as mere self-importance; instead, it speaks to the fundamental human need to feel valued for our efforts and to have our accomplishments acknowledged. The pursuit of recognition, commendations, or admiration for one's endeavors reveals a deeper yearning.

8) **Justice**

The journey towards justice is inherently tied to the search for fairness, equality, and ethical principles. This aspiration compels us to advocate for our beliefs and foster a more just and equitable society. Championing social justice initiatives or participating in activism stems from this foundational belief.

9) **Ideals**

The quest for individual values, beliefs, and principles clearly defines the driving force behind our ideals. This unwavering commitment to fundamental principles profoundly shapes our priorities and guides our actions. For example, aligning one's life with ethical principles or following spiritual convictions exemplifies this drive.

Exploring the Unique Blend of Your Motivations

These nine motives seldom function independently. Our actions frequently emerge from a nuanced interaction of diverse motivations collaborating harmoniously. Contemplate the circumstances that invigorate you and the decisions that cultivate your happiness to uncover your primary blend of motivation. By grasping this integration, you can make intentional decisions rooted in your fundamental beliefs, guiding yourself toward a more enriching existence.

Actionable Strategies to Discover Your Unique Motivational Blend

1) **Reflect on Peak Experiences:** Reflect on those moments of profound fulfillment and vitality. Recall the instances when you experienced your highest sense of achievement and energy. Examine the underlying motivations present in these instances.

2) **Reflect on Your Decisions:** Consider the choices that have led you to feelings of joy and fulfillment. Explore the underlying motives that shaped these decisions.

3) **Design a Motivational Map:** Illustrate or articulate your core motivations and their interconnections.

4) **Harmonize with Fundamental Principles:** Ensure your decisions resonate with your essential beliefs and primary motivations.

By acknowledging and harmonizing with these nine fundamental motives, you cultivate a profound understanding of your inner drives, empowering you to make more purposeful and satisfying choices. Embrace this self-awareness, allowing your motivations to steer you toward a journey that aligns with your authentic self and deepest aspirations.

c. Shaping Your Destiny: Taking the Wheel of Your Life

Our behaviors stem from our thoughts and are driven by our motivations, ultimately influencing the tapestry of our life experiences and the situations we encounter. This does not imply that we possess complete mastery over every facet of our existence, as external circumstances frequently arise that lie beyond our influence. By consciously directing our thoughts and aligning them with suitable motivations, we possess significant influence over the trajectory of our lives.

Reflect on the narrative of Sarah, a woman who found herself confined in a role that failed to resonate with her true passions. Amidst her frustration, she resolutely shifted her focus to her aspirations. Rather than fixating on her discontent, she directed her energy toward her ambitions. Sarah established purposeful intentions, picturing herself in a position aligned with her core values and innate abilities. This transformation in perspective inspired her to pursue advanced studies and connect with others in her chosen area of interest. In under two years, she embraced a rewarding and thriving career that brought her joy.

Envision yourself, like Sarah, grasping the reins of your existence, fueled by a potent force within you. This engine empowers you to steer your journey in any direction you desire, gracefully maneuvering through the complexities and nuances that arise along the path. By honing your mental clarity and establishing purposeful intentions, you enhance your ability to navigate the unfolding path of your life.

Actionable Strategies to Craft Your Future

1) **Establish Clear Intentions:** Articulate your goals with precision and intention. Visualize your aspirations and design a strategic path to achieve them.

2) **Embrace Positivity:** Shift your mindset from the shadows of negativity to the light of hopeful aspirations. Foster a perspective that highlights possibilities and personal development.

3) **Harmonize Your Actions with Inner Motivations:** Your actions must stem from motivations that truly reflect your fundamental values and aspirations. This alignment fosters a compelling drive for transformation.

4) **Continual Learning and Networking:** Embrace the journey of lifelong learning and cultivate meaningful relationships within your area of passion, much like Sarah does. These steps create pathways to fresh possibilities and achievement.

Final Thoughts

Crafting your future requires a deliberate focus on your thoughts and a commitment to aligning them with profound motivations. By mastering your mental processes, you guide your existence toward a sense of purpose and achievement. Embrace this transformative journey, allowing your authentic intentions to illuminate a path that aligns profoundly with your essence. Keep in mind that although you may not have power over every situation that arises, you always possess the ability to steer your path forward.

d. The Power of Choice: The Captain at the Helm

Though thoughts hold considerable sway, they do not serve as an inflexible command that governs our every behavior. The notion of "The Power of Choice" highlights our remarkable ability to consciously choose the thoughts we entertain and the aspirations we nurture in our existence. This enables us to steer our thinking towards desired results and harmonize our actions with our ultimate objectives.

Envision yourself as the leader of a ship, navigating the expansive seas of knowledge and understanding. While external influences such as currents and winds may impact your path, you hold the power to decide the direction and set sail toward your desired horizon.

The Influence of Intentional Thought Selection

To be the captain is to consciously select the thoughts you wish to engage with. In challenging situations, one has the opportunity to direct one's thoughts toward resilience and problem-solving rather than allowing defeatist attitudes to take hold. This intentional choice enables you to approach obstacles with an optimistic and forward-thinking attitude.

Harmonizing Motivations with Objectives

Recognizing and enhancing the motivations aligning with your fundamental values allows you to harmonize your thoughts and actions with your overarching goals. For example, if your main drive is to attain career advancement, you may focus on ideas that foster ongoing education and resilience. This harmony guarantees that your behaviors steadily guide you toward your envisioned results.

Actionable Strategies to Embrace the Potential of Decision-Making

1) **Mindful Awareness:** Nurture an understanding of your mental processes. Consistently engage in introspection regarding the prevailing thoughts in your mind, assessing how they influence your actions and aspirations.

2) **Intentional Thought Replacement:** When unhelpful or detrimental thoughts emerge, consciously substitute them with uplifting and constructive alternatives. For example, transform "I can't do this" into "I am capable of figuring this out."

3) **Goal Alignment:** Harmonize your thoughts and actions with your overarching aspirations. Consistently evaluate your aspirations and refine your mindset to align with them.

4) **Visualize Success:** Picture yourself as a captain navigating the waters toward achievement. This mental imagery strengthens your dedication to making intentional and empowering decisions.

o **Illustration**

Imagine an individual striving to enhance their well-being. By directing attention towards thoughts that highlight well-being and self-nurturing, individuals find themselves increasingly inspired to pursue healthier options. Consider incorporating a balanced diet, committing to regular physical activity, and exploring various stress management strategies. Their intentional choices in thought and alignment with health-focused motivations steer them toward the pursuit of enhanced well-being.

Final Thoughts

Seize the opportunity to shape your path and navigate the course of your existence. By consciously choosing your thoughts and harmonizing them with your motivations, you guide your mental processes toward the outcomes you wish to achieve. As the leader of your journey, you steer through the expansive seas of thought, shaping your path and setting sail toward the destination you envision. By harnessing your intention and carefully choosing your thoughts, you pave the way toward a life filled with fulfillment and achievement.

Designing Your Destiny: The Engine of Thought

Begin a voyage in which your reflections act as the catalyst shaping your future. This inquiry uncovers the deep understanding that our minds, with their relentless flow of thoughts, desires, and motivations, possess the ability to mold our reality. As previously mentioned, our thoughts serve as the vibrant energy driving us toward action, whether consciously aware of it or not. Through a deep exploration of the "Nine Primary Motives," we reveal the underlying forces that drive our thoughts and actions. This section encourages you to unravel the fundamental aspirations that truly drive you, providing you with insights to harmonize your decisions with your intrinsic values.

Envision your thoughts as the driving force behind a vehicle, steering the course, pace, and ultimate destination of your life's path. Whether consciously selected or influenced by deep-seated beliefs, your journey is ultimately directed by the nature of your thoughts. By consciously choosing your thoughts and aligning your motivations with your aspirations, you can navigate your life's journey, guiding yourself toward fulfillment and achievement. Embrace the power of choice as you journey through the vast seas of intellectual discovery, shaping your future with deliberate intention and clarity.

7. Thought's Symphony: The Conscious and Subconscious in Harmony

This chapter deals with an exciting concept known as "Thought's Multidimensionality": the detailed concept that human thought is not a one-dimensional process but rather a layered collaboration between our minds' conscious and subconscious components. The dynamic interplay unravels the secret of how we can use our brains' powers to the fullest.

a.   The Duality of Thought: A Tale of Two Minds

Our minds operate on two primary levels, each playing a crucial role in the grand orchestra of thought.

The Conscious Mind: The Conductor in the Spotlight. The conscious mind is that more logical, analyzing aspect of our being with which we are most familiar. It is that part of our mind that reaches out into the world via the senses, informing us about our experiences by referring to previously internalized knowledge structures. Think of the conscious mind as the conductor in an orchestra, holding the baton of logic and reason, guiding the symphony of thought into order and purpose. For the most part, we can control just what our conscious thoughts are focusing on through our conscious direction. Thus, we can look at situations, make decisions, and plan for the future.

The Subconscious Mind: The Vast Reservoir of Potential. On the other hand, the subconscious mind is an underground process operating beneath our awareness. This huge container contains a great number of memories, emotions, implicit knowledge, cumulative wisdom, and experience of a lifetime. The "infinite intelligence" you referred to earlier would be understood to mean the gigantic arena of the subconscious as a processor of information, constructor of creative solutions, and influencer upon all of our behaviors in the most powerful ways. While the modus operandi of the subconscious mind remains veiled in a lot of mystery, its influence upon everything from what we think to what we do is simply undeniable.

b. Collaborative Thinking: A Beautiful Duet

Thought isn't a singular process located in one specific brain region; it's a beautiful duet between the conscious and subconscious minds.

The Conscious Mind Functions as a Discerning Filter. The conscious mind functions as a discerning filter, meticulously choosing which thoughts, impulses, and information from the depths of the subconscious emerge into our conscious awareness. Envision the conscious mind functioning as a selective filter, permitting only the most pertinent or beneficial information from the subconscious to permeate our conscious awareness. Our conscious mind serves as a powerful tool for analyzing, refining, and directing the flow of subconscious thoughts. We can transform these thoughts into actionable ideas that effectively guide our behaviors by harnessing this capability.

The Subconscious Mind: A Profound Source of Inspiration. The subconscious mind is a continuous source of information, inspiration, and creative potential. It can harbor limiting beliefs and emotional patterns that subtly shape our thoughts and behaviors. Engaging with the subconscious's extensive capabilities allows us to unlock enhanced creativity, refine our intuition, and improve our problem-solving skills.

c. Beyond the Five Departments: Exploring the Faculties of the Mind

In certain psychological frameworks, the concept of "five departments" may emerge, yet the core notion remains that the conscious mind utilizes various faculties to engage with and interpret information. The interplay of faculties such as logic, reason, memory, emotional intelligence, and spatial reasoning allows for a distinctive and personal approach to thought.

1) Reasoning

Reasoning is the capacity that enables us to comprehend our surroundings through organized and progressive thought processes. It involves drawing conclusions based on established premises. In situations that require problem-solving, such as mathematics or chess, applying logic enables us to dissect the circumstances, evaluate different strategies, and foresee potential results through rational reasoning. Envision navigating a multifaceted mathematical challenge; reason steers you through every phase, guaranteeing that your resolution is rational and precise.

2) Rationality

Reason intertwines with logic, yet it also encompasses abstract and critical thinking capacities. The process entails integrating diverse information from various sources to arrive at cohesive conclusions. In a debate, the power of reason enables the construction of arguments, the evaluation of evidence, and the anticipation of counterarguments. Imagine an individual constructing a narrative; logic enables them to connect elements, principles, and historical context into a compelling discourse.

3) Recall

Memory serves as the vault of our past experiences, knowledge, and acquired skills. It holds significant importance in the processes of decision-making and learning. For instance, acquiring a new language involves the intricate interplay of memory, which aids in retaining vocabulary, grammar rules, and usage patterns. Envision an artist immersed in their craft, where the essence of the music flows effortlessly from memory, capturing every nuance and emotion, resulting in a performance that resonates deeply.

4) Understanding Emotions

Emotional intelligence (EI) refers to the capacity to comprehend and regulate both your own emotions and the emotions of others. It encompasses understanding others, managing oneself, and navigating social interactions. Emotional intelligence is crucial in navigating conflicts, establishing rapport, and nurturing collaboration in personal and professional relationships. For example, a manager with a strong emotional awareness can identify an employee's feelings of frustration, respond with understanding, and inspire the team meaningfully.

5) Understanding Space

Spatial reasoning encompasses the capacity to envision and alter objects within a spatial context. It is crucial for endeavors that engage with physical environments and the organization of items. An architect uses spatial reasoning to craft buildings, meticulously ensuring that every element aligns harmoniously. Envision a surgeon engaged in a sophisticated procedure; their adept spatial reasoning directs meticulous movements and navigation through the intricacies of the human body.

Practical Application: Interaction of Abilities

Envision the intricate process of orchestrating a significant occasion like a wedding. Rational thinking enables you to manage your finances and establish a schedule. Let your intellect lead you in selecting a theme that embodies the couple's narrative. Reflecting on previous weddings can provide valuable insights and practical advice for future celebrations. The ability to navigate emotions plays a crucial role in alleviating the stress experienced by the couple, while an understanding of spatial dynamics aids in the thoughtful arrangement of the venue's layout. Every aspect plays a distinct role, weaving together to form a harmonious and effective result.

In summary

The faculties of the conscious mind—logic, reason, memory, emotional intelligence, and spatial reasoning—interact harmoniously, allowing us to think and act in distinctly personal manners. We can elevate our mental functions by comprehending and utilizing these abilities, leading to more insightful and impactful choices. Embrace the dynamic relationship between these faculties, allowing them to steer you toward a life enriched and purposeful.

d. The Power of Awareness: Bridging the Gap for More Holistic Thinking

Grasping the complexity of our thoughts allows us to embrace a more comprehensive perspective on self-awareness and mental health. Practices like meditation and mindfulness serve as pathways connecting the conscious and subconscious realms, offering a profound understanding of the unseen forces that shape our thoughts and actions. Utilizing the conscious mind as a guiding force, we can compose a harmonious blend of thoughts that paves the way for a more enriching existence in our pursuits and creations.

The Significance of Meditation and Mindfulness

Meditation and mindfulness practices act as profound instruments to connect the realms of conscious and subconscious thought. In the practice of meditation, one nurtures a heightened state of awareness, enabling the observation of thoughts in a non-judgmental manner. This approach uncovers the fundamental patterns and forces that mold your thoughts and actions. Consider an individual grappling with anxiety; they may employ mindfulness techniques to recognize persistent thoughts that provoke their anxiety, thereby gaining a deeper understanding of how to navigate these thoughts with greater efficacy.

Utilizing Mindfulness Meditation in Everyday Life

Reflect on the benefits of incorporating daily mindfulness meditation into your routine. Dedicate 10-15 minutes daily to finding stillness, concentrating on breathing, and reflecting on your thoughts. As thoughts emerge, recognize them without criticism and softly redirect your attention to your breath. As you engage in this practice, you gradually cultivate a deeper awareness of the subtle forces at play within your mind, empowering you to make intentional decisions that resonate with your aspirations and principles.

o   **Illustration: Enhancing Creativity**

Envision a creator grappling with a profound sense of stagnation in their artistic expression. Through the practice of mindfulness meditation, individuals can silence the incessant noise of their thoughts and access profound depths of creativity. This approach enables individuals to reveal concealed wells of creativity and attain a clearer understanding of their artistic aspirations, leading to a more seamless and enriching creative journey.

Utilizing the Awareness of the Mind

The conscious mind is a discerning guide, allowing us to intentionally prioritize and navigate our thoughts. Through mindfulness and cultivating self-awareness, we can sharpen our cognitive patterns and engage in decision-making that promotes our overall well-being. This method enables us to traverse the complexities of existence with enhanced insight and intention.

Final Thoughts

Embracing the transformative potential of awareness through mindfulness and meditation connects the realms of conscious and subconscious thought, nurturing a comprehensive approach to self-awareness and mental wellness. By exploring and integrating the complexities of thought, we can cultivate a rich tapestry of purposeful, satisfying, and balanced thinking that enhances our experiences and pursuits. Allow mindfulness to illuminate your inner landscape, uncovering the intricacies of your thoughts and enabling you to embrace decisions that align with your authentic essence.

e. The Power of Understanding: A Key to Unlocking Your Potential

Throughout this journey of discovery, we have explored the world of thought and unraveled how it creates our reality. Truly magical, though, is knowing that thought has several dimensions. This knowing is empowering in deep ways:

Unveiling the Subconscious: A Wellspring of Potential

The subconscious mind is a treasure trove of creativity, intuition, and problem-solving skills. Imagine consciously prompting this wellspring for solutions. By employing techniques like visualization or journaling, we can spark a dialogue with the subconscious, allowing it to surface innovative ideas and creative solutions to our challenges.

Mastering the Conscious Mind: Taking the Wheel of Your Thoughts

Though not the only player, this conscious mind is a conductor in this thought traffic. In so doing, training will enable it to become a more active filter and director. In this way, it's possible to determine ways of thinking and acting that align with what we want. The first step is often discovering ineffective patterns in our subconscious repertoire that tend to defeat and limit us from being at our best. By conscious effort and cognitive reframing, we can choose to replace these patterns with more empowering thoughts and create a deeper purpose.

Building Bridges: Forging a Unified Mind.

Meditation and mindfulness are some bridging techniques used to bridge the conscious and subconscious mind. As we nurture this connection, our thinking becomes more integrated and effective. With this, one could imagine a symphony where the conscious mind acts as the orchestra, drawing upon the deep, deep well of creativity residing in the subconscious to create a true masterpiece. These practices will thus give us an idea of the undiscovered motivational factors in our thoughts and behaviors, allowing us to make informed choices grounded on our objectives and values.

A Holistic Approach to Unlocking Your Potential

Understanding multidimensional thought is more than a concept; it is a valued tool for releasing one's potential. As we begin to realize the interaction between conscious and subconscious thought, a more holistic approach to self-awareness and mental health begins to develop. This integrated approach will enable you to think more clearly, act purposefully, and build a life of creativity, fulfillment, and success.

Remember!

Your mind functions as a complex orchestra, harmoniously led by two influential conductors: the conscious and subconscious minds. By comprehending their functions and promoting synergy among them, one can orchestrate a harmonious exchange of ideas that facilitates clear thinking, purposeful action, and realizing one's full potential.

8. The Flexible Mind: Shaping Your Reality Through Thought Amenability

Our thoughts are not concrete entities but fluid and tend to be shaped by the habits formed within ourselves. Referred to herein as "thought amenability," this concept gives meaning to the outstanding trait of both our conscious and subconscious minds: their tendency to change and adapt according to patterns formed within us. Understanding how habits affect our thoughts unleashes the power to pattern thinking and, consequently, reality.

a. Habit: The Architect of Thought

We are constantly learning something new and reorganizing our minds. The tendencies we create involve not only conscious habits that we choose but unconscious routines, too. Now, let's see exactly how this works:

- **Conscious Habits: Carving Pathways in the Mind.** Every conscious repetition that we do from time to time of some specific thought or behavior carves its way into the neural pathways. Think of it this way: if you are trying to cut through a dense forest, the more you travel that path, the easier it is to get through. The more we consciously and consistently practice some kind of thinking pattern, the more that is going to be our automatic way of seeing things. And this can work for good or ill. We can willfully decide to empower ourselves with the right thoughts, enforce repetition, and open avenues to a brighter, more resilient mindset.

- **Subconscious Habits: The Hidden Influencers.** Our subconscious mind isn't ignorant of patterns, either. The very emotional reactions can get habitual; beliefs are usually subconscious and become habits in information processing. These subconscious habits may affect conscious thinking unbeknownst to us. For example, if someone has subconscious beliefs that they are bad at math, they may unconsciously avoid challenges that involve some form of mathematics. This could serve to reinforce the harmful thought pattern in one's brain. As we become conscious of our unconscious habits, we can begin to break down and remake limited beliefs into more resourceful ways of thinking.

136

b. The Ever-Shifting Landscape of Thought: A Dynamic Web of Connections

It is not a static process but rather dynamic- dance through the millions of interconnections in our brains. Every single thought we create is a derivative of this complex wiring system. The interlinkages are constantly being strengthened or weakened by the different experiences and life habits one develops. Imagine the brain's connections as a complex web. The more one travels a particular path through that web, the stronger that path becomes. By becoming more mindful of our thoughts and developing more positive habits, we can actually strengthen those neural pathways that support the empowering thoughts and weaken the ones that lead to negativity and self-doubt

c. Modification and Alteration: Shaping Your Neural Landscape

The principle of thought amenability says such linkages are not permanent. We have enormous potential to change and reshape our line of thinking through deliberate effort and practice with full awareness. By being consciously selective with thoughts and actions that match our objectives, we can break the tight grip of habits serving no good purposes and simultaneously build up new, more enabling patterns of thought.

Imagine for a moment that you are going for a walk in the woods. The trails are very indistinct and overgrown at first. After many people travel along them over and over again, the pathway becomes distinct. Similarly, by making conscious choices of empowering thoughts and reinforcing them with action, we create new pathways within our neural landscape and loosen the hold of negativity and self-doubt.

d. Choice: The Key to Redefining Your Mind

While habits have a powerful influence, they do not dominate our destinies. We have the power of decision, and herein comes probably the most effective way of reshaping our thought patterns. Conscious interference gives us that strength that may deliver us from the clutches of negative habits and enable us to embrace positive habits.

The influence of choice in shaping our thought patterns. Imagine yourself positioned at a pivotal intersection. The established route often guides us toward recognizable yet possibly constraining cognitive frameworks. An underexplored avenue invites exploration, offering potential avenues for development and advancement. Through the deliberate selection of empowering thoughts and the proactive measures we take to strengthen them, we have the capacity to reshape our mental landscape.

Here are various methods to purposefully interact with your cognitive processes:

1) **Mindfulness Practices:** Engaging in mindfulness practices, such as meditation, allows individuals to cultivate awareness of their automatic thoughts, thereby fostering an environment conducive to conscious decision-making.

2) **Cognitive Reframing:** Cognitive reframing involves recognizing negative thought patterns and transforming them into more positive and empowering perspectives.

3) **Positive Self-Talk:** Positive self-talk involves actively challenging detrimental self-beliefs. Individuals can cultivate a more supportive internal dialogue by substituting these with affirmations that foster self-compassion and bolster confidence.

e. Harnessing Amenability for Growth

Understanding thought amenability empowers us in several ways:

1) **Recognizing Limiting Habits:** Cultivate an awareness of the habits that influence your thoughts in unproductive manners. Engaging in journaling or meditation serves as an effective methodology for fostering self-reflection. By identifying these patterns, one can start dismantling them and pave the way for innovative, empowering modes of thought.

2) **Fostering Constructive Habits:** Cultivate new routines and practices that align with your intended cognitive frameworks. Engaging in practices such as positive affirmations, visualization exercises, or immersing oneself in nature can be highly beneficial. These practices will reinforce the neural pathways linked to positive thinking, thereby enhancing your mental resilience.

3) **Embracing Continuous Learning:** Adopt a growth mindset towards education, acknowledging that your cognitive processes are perpetually in flux. Embrace the opportunity to venture beyond familiar boundaries and engage in novel experiences that can foster innovative cognitive frameworks. Engaging in lifelong learning and broadening your intellectual horizons allows for introducing novel information and experiences, thereby intricately influencing the architecture of your cognitive landscape.

Conclusion

By leveraging the principle of thought amenability, we can effectively navigate and shape our mental landscape. By cultivating positive thinking habits, individuals can unlock their full potential and actively shape the trajectory of their lives. Our thoughts do not govern us; rather, they serve as instruments through which we can shape the reality we aspire to achieve.

Your thoughts do not define your fate; rather, they serve as instruments through which you can shape your reality. Through a comprehensive understanding of thought amenability and the strategic application of habitual practices, one can effectively position oneself as the architect of one's cognitive landscape, thereby influencing one's thoughts and, in turn, manifesting the life one aspires to achieve.

9. The Illusory Certainty: Unveiling the Subjectivity of Our Truths

Let's delve into this interesting concept of "perceived reality" and how it clings strongly to the thoughts generated in our minds. We will introduce the term "self-perceived unassailable truth," proposing that our thoughts are indeed very personal and can even be flawed, but they are absolutely true to our perception. Once the perceived truths are grasped and understood for what they are, we open our minds toward a newfound openness to the world.

a. The CgX System's Veil of Certainty: A Glimpse into the Mind's Processing

Introducing the "CgX System" embodies the internal mechanism through which we process information and formulate thoughts, providing a deep understanding of our perception of truth. This system engages with our understanding of truth profoundly:

Thoughts as Unquestionable Truths

When a thought is put into action, it transforms into an "unquestionable fact" within our consciousness. This notion of truth arises from the CgX System's focus on integrating thoughts already manifested in action. We frequently perceive these manifested thoughts as indisputable truths solely due to their influence on our actions. Consider this: when you have consistently achieved success through a specific approach, it can become a deeply ingrained belief, often perceived as an absolute truth, despite emerging evidence that may challenge that perspective.

The Blinding Power of Bias

However, this principle recognizes that these thoughts may not be accurate. They may be infused with individual biases, perspectives, prejudices, and various emotional conditions. In moments of heightened emotion, rationality often takes a backseat, allowing our subjective perceptions to steer our thinking. Consider a scenario where you experience an intense fear of speaking in front of others. Any adverse encounter associated with public speaking could potentially strengthen this conviction, regardless of whether the experience was singular or misconstrued. This limitation hinders your ability to perceive the larger context and transcend your apprehensions.

o **Example: Exploring the Dynamics of Social Media Echo Chambers**

Reflect on the influence of social media algorithms that foster echo chambers. These platforms frequently validate our pre-existing convictions by presenting material that resonates with our inclinations. This solidifies our beliefs as "absolute certainties" while excluding opposing perspectives. With time, this fosters a skewed understanding of reality, leading us to believe that our convictions are widely embraced, regardless of their actual acceptance.

Practical Steps to Unveil Subjectivity

1) **Question Your Thoughts:** Consistently scrutinize your convictions and ideas. Contemplate whether these beliefs stem from objective realities or subjective interpretations. Consider, for instance, the thought, "I'm terrible at presentations." Take a moment to examine the evidence that underpins this belief.

2) **Seek Diverse Perspectives:** Open yourself to various opinions and viewpoints. This expands your perspective and aids in mitigating biases. Participate in dialogues with individuals with contrasting viewpoints and truly absorb their rationale.

3) **Emotional Awareness:** Acknowledge the moments when your feelings shape your thinking. Pause for a moment and let your analytical mind evaluate the circumstances. When experiencing anxiety regarding a decision, take a moment to reflect and assess the facts prior to taking action.

4) **Reflect on Past Experiences:** Examine past experiences with a discerning eye. Recognize moments when preconceived notions may have shaped your views and explore different perspectives. Contemplating instances where your initial beliefs were later challenged can yield profound understanding.

In conclusion

The CgX System uncovers the layers of certainty, illustrating how our thoughts can morph into perceived truths shaped by biases and emotions. We can reveal the personal nature of our realities by exploring our thoughts, pursuing varied viewpoints, being aware of emotional impacts, and thoughtfully examining our past. This method enables us to traverse the intricacies of our perceptions, allowing for more thoughtful and equitable choices. Embrace this path of introspection, allowing it to illuminate your perception of existence.

b. The Deceptive Power of the Senses: The Five Untrustworthy Witnesses

Another potential factor that can skew our understanding of truth arises from our sensory experiences—sight, sound, taste, smell, and touch. The senses, crucial for our interaction with the environment, can often be swayed by the power of our emotions. Intense feelings such as fear, love, or anxiety can intertwine with our sensory experiences, resulting in distorted interpretations of the physical reality around us.

Illustrating Sensory Distortions

Imagine a situation in which the sound of a car backfiring reaches your ears. When experiencing a sense of unease or instability, it's possible to perceive a sound as something more alarming, like a gunshot. This illustrates the profound impact emotions can have on our perception of sensory information. In times of deep affection or exhilaration, one may find that everyday occurrences take on an extraordinary glow, merging the boundaries between what is real and what is felt.

Example: Anxiety and Perceptual Alteration

Envision a solitary stroll under the night sky, where apprehension lingers in the air. A subtle rustling emerges from the bushes, inviting curiosity and contemplation. In a tranquil mindset, you may perceive it as a benign creature. Yet, when fear takes hold, it can distort your perception, transforming situations into perceived threats and resulting in increased anxiety and irrational actions. Your perceptions, shaped by fear, create a skewed interpretation of reality.

The Balancing Act of Reason

Reason acts as an essential equilibrium to these perceptual distortions. This process enables us to understand the information we receive through our senses, sifting through biases and emotional factors. By engaging our rational faculties, we can assess sensory data with greater precision, leading to more informed choices.

Practical Steps to Balance Sensory Input with Reason

1) **Pause and Reflect:** When faced with intense emotions, take a moment to pause and reflect before responding to what you perceive. This helps avoid hasty, prejudiced reactions.

2) **Question Your Perceptions:** Scrutinize your first sensory impressions. Consider whether your feelings could be shaping the way you see things. For instance, when you experience anxiety following a sudden loud sound, take a moment to explore different interpretations of that reaction.

3) **Engage in Mindfulness Practices:** Mindfulness techniques allow you to remain anchored in the present, diminishing the influence of intense emotions on your sensory experiences. Consistent engagement can refine your capacity to interpret sensory stimuli with precision.

4) **Seek External Validation:** In moments of uncertainty, looking for affirmation from those around you can be beneficial. Different viewpoints can offer a clearer understanding, aiding in separating truth from emotional bias.

Final Thoughts

The misleading nature of our senses underscores the necessity of harmonizing sensory experiences with rational thought. By acknowledging the impact of emotions on our perceptions and activating our rational thinking, we can more adeptly maneuver through the intricacies of sensory information. Embrace this equilibrium, allowing your rationality to steer you toward a more lucid and precise comprehension of existence.

c. Rethinking "Unassailable Truth": A Call for Nuanced Understanding

The concept of "unassailable truth" challenges the belief that our individual truths are immune to scrutiny. It indicates that our cognition and perception are profoundly shaped by individual frameworks—our unique biases, experiences, and feelings. This acknowledgment does not diminish our personal experiences; instead, it encourages us to embrace a more reflective and sophisticated perspective on the world around us.

Illustrating Subjectivity in Perception

Imagine two individuals observing the same occurrence, like a debate. Some may concentrate on the rational reasoning offered, whereas others could be influenced by the speaker's charm and emotional resonance. Each person departs with a unique interpretation of the occurrence, influenced by their biases and life experiences. This illustration underscores the profound impact of personal filters on our understanding of reality.

Embracing Complexity and Introspection

Embracing a deeper and more nuanced perspective of existence compels us to examine our convictions and remain receptive to the possibility that our truths might not be definitive. It invites us to recognize that a complex interplay of factors, such as cultural background, personal history, and emotional state influences our perceptions.

Example: Exploring the Dynamics of Interpersonal Relationships

In personal relationships, acknowledging the subjective nature of our truths can cultivate empathy and deepen understanding. A disagreement with a friend may arise from varying interpretations of a shared experience. Recognizing that unique biases and experiences influence individual viewpoints allows us to engage with the situation more empathetically and openly, fostering pathways to more constructive solutions.

Practical Steps for Nuanced Understanding

Reflect on Personal Biases: Consistently examine your personal biases and their impact on your perceptions. Recognize that personal experiences and perspectives influence your understanding.

Seek Diverse Perspectives: Connect with individuals from various backgrounds and outlooks. This will expand your perspective and prompt you to reconsider your beliefs.

Practice Empathy: Endeavor to grasp the viewpoints of others, even when they diverge from your own. Understanding others nurtures profound relationships and shared regard.

Question Assumptions: Challenge your foundational beliefs by consistently examining the assumptions that support them. Embrace diverse perspectives and remain receptive to evolving your beliefs.

Final Thoughts

Reevaluating the notion of "unassailable truth" encourages us to acknowledge our perceptions' intricate and subjective nature. Embracing a nuanced perspective allows us to delve into our thoughts and feelings, cultivating a sense of empathy and forging more profound connections with those around us. Allow this consciousness to steer you toward a deeper and more reflective understanding of the world, where individual truths harmonize with respect for varied viewpoints.

d. Cultivating a More Objective View: Embracing Multiple Perspectives

Embracing the subjectivity of our so-called 'unassailable truths' invites us to embark on a journey toward a deeper and more authentic understanding of ourselves and the world around us. Fostering a sense of objectivity towards reality encompasses a variety of essential practices:

1) Examining Bias

Awareness of your biases is crucial for grasping how they may influence your thought patterns. Consider the practice of journaling or employing personality assessments to deepen your self-reflection in this area. For instance, engaging in regular journaling about your thoughts and choices can aid in recognizing persistent biases that shape your perceptions.

Illustration: Bias in Decision-Making

Envision a tendency within yourself to steer clear of confrontation. Reflecting on instances where you opted to sidestep conflict can illuminate how this tendency fosters lingering challenges. Recognizing this bias empowers you to cultivate approaches that confront conflicts head-on, resulting in more favorable resolutions.

2) Exploring Varies Viewpoints

Explore viewpoints that differ from your own. Engage with literature and academic works that stimulate deep reflection, and immerse yourself in conversations with people from various walks of life. This approach expands your perspective and questions your beliefs.

Example: Understanding Diverse Perspectives

Engaging with literature from diverse cultural perspectives or participating in discussions led by experts who challenge your beliefs can be profoundly enriching. Conversations with individuals who possess contrasting viewpoints cultivate a richer comprehension and respect for a variety of perspectives.

3) Reasoning as a Form of Counterbalance

Refine your capacity for critical thought and engage in a rational examination of evidence before accepting any notion as absolute truth. Consider inquiries such as, "Might this circumstance be perceived through a different lens?" or "What proof supports this specific idea?"

Example: Critical Analysis in Everyday Life

Imagine encountering an article asserting that a particular diet is the epitome of health. Rather than taking it at face value, engage in a thorough examination of the evidence provided. Explore further research, evaluate diverse perspectives, and reflect on possible biases present in the materials. This comprehensive examination enables you to cultivate a more nuanced perspective.

Final Thoughts

By embracing the diverse essence of truth and fostering a more objective outlook on life, we connect our limited self to a wider understanding. This path of self-exploration enhances our lives by fostering analytical thought, clear expression, and the cultivation of profound connections rooted in shared comprehension. Allow this method to lead you to a deeper and more impartial comprehension of reality, cultivating an attitude that appreciates varied viewpoints and reflective examination.

༄༅༄༅

CRYPTIC INSIGHTS: THE ENIGMA OF THOUGHT INDUCTION

༄༅༄༅

Within the intricate labyrinth of the human psyche exists a realm cloaked in enigma and profound potential—the sphere of thought induction. Here, within the shadowy corridors of the Thought Forge, the principles of purified thought inception linger, poised for revelation. These principles are essential guides for traversing the intricate maze of human thought, where desire sparks action, and the echo of belief molds our reality.

Step into the depths of the Thought Forge, where the intricate dance of logic, creativity, and morality intertwines to forge the most captivating creations of the psyche. Discover the hidden truths of channeling emotional power, and explore how focused intellects convert conviction into the rich soil for achievement. In this exploration, we will delve into the elusive power of conviction, its function as the catalyst for extraordinary events, and its enigmatic sway that transcends the boundaries of observable reality.

Get ready to explore the deep and unsettling nature of human belief—an unsettling gift that allows us to construct the very fabric of our existence. With every move, we unveil the instruments of perception, hone our cognitive abilities, and carve out routes to unwavering reality. The Thought Forge transcends the ordinary; it beckons you to delve into a profound journey of self-discovery, mental expansion, and life-altering decisions.

Welcome to the Thought Forge, a realm where shadows twist into clarity, and the strength of conviction emerges as the very foundation of our reality. Let us embark on this journey together, delving into the complex interplay of thought and belief while tending to the remnants of the Creator as we construct our realities.

Unveiling the Thought Forge: Principles of Purified Thought Inception

This concept invites us to engage in the fundamental process of "thought inception," allowing us to examine the nuances of fostering clear and actionable thinking. Let us begin our exploration by delving into the significance of prioritizing information, which serves as the cornerstone for effective decision-making and attaining our objectives.

1. Navigating Through the Noise: Discerning Fact from Fiction

The path to clear and precise thinking starts with recognizing the difference between solid evidence and mere conjecture or rumor. It's about distinguishing between noise and signal—sifting through to identify what truly matters. Distinguishing between what is factual and what is simply an indication of personal opinion represents the initial phase of understanding.

Envision yourself as a seeker of treasures, sifting through the flowing waters in pursuit of glimmering rewards. As you navigate through the murky depths, you cleanse the chaos, uncovering the invaluable treasures hidden beneath. In our pursuit of clarity in thought, it is essential to navigate through an overwhelming sea of information, discerning meaningful truths from the noise of conjecture and rumor.

o **Example: Exploring the Landscape of Media**

Reflect on the constant stream of news and information we encounter each day. We are inundated with a constant stream of content from social media, news outlets, and our daily interactions. To distinguish reality from illusion, one must engage in thoughtful analysis. Imagine encountering a distressing news headline while scrolling through your social media feed. Before responding, you verify with trustworthy news outlets, seek out evidence, and assess the reliability of the information presented. This approach guarantees that your responses are grounded in reality rather than driven by exaggerated narratives.

Practical Steps to Discern Facts from Fiction

a) **Source Evaluation:** Analyze the reliability of the information source. Reliable sources are often recognized for their commitment to precision, openness, and responsibility.

b) **Cross-Verification:** Ensure the accuracy of information by consulting various trustworthy sources. This process of cross-referencing serves to validate the precision and coherence of the information presented.

c) **Bias Awareness:** Acknowledge the possible biases inherent in the information provided. Reflect on the viewpoint and possible intentions of the origin.

d) **Pose Thought-Provoking Inquiries:** When assessing information, consider asking yourself insightful questions like: Is there substantiation for this assertion? Is the information grounded in verified data or derived from anecdotal experiences?

Final Thoughts

Distinguishing truth from falsehood amidst the chaos is essential for cultivating lucid and practical thought. We establish a strong basis for sound decision-making by emphasizing trustworthy information and eliminating conjecture. Engage in the art of critical thinking, assess your sources, and practice cross-verification to ensure that your beliefs and actions are rooted in reliable and credible information. Allow this structured method of engaging with information to serve as the foundation for your path to a more enlightened and intentional existence.

2. Fact Values: Prioritizing Information for Peak Performance

In our pursuit of clarity and practical reasoning, it is crucial to recognize that not every fact holds equal significance. Emphasizing the importance of information prioritization is essential for navigating decision-making processes and realizing our aspirations. This section explores the importance of distinguishing pertinent information from extraneous, steering us toward optimal achievement.

Envision your mind as a meticulously crafted instrument, with each fragment of knowledge serving as a note that adds to a cohesive melody. To achieve optimal performance, it is essential to discern which notes to emphasize and the timing of your actions, grounding your decisions in the most relevant insights. This requires the ability to differentiate between essential truths and trivial distractions, to see through the illusions of preconceived notions, and to reshape your mindset to prioritize what is genuinely important.

Embracing these principles allows you to elevate your cognitive processes into a sophisticated "Thought Forge," where unrefined information is shaped into potent instruments for achievement. Let's delve into the process of filtering out distractions, emphasizing the importance of facts, and nurturing a mindset that fosters thoughtful and intentional decision-making.

a. **Significance Assumes Prominence:** After establishing a solid foundation of facts, organizing these facts according to their pertinence to our objectives becomes essential. This process entails categorizing facts into two clearly defined groups: those that are significant and those that are not.

    i. **Important Facts: The Cornerstones of Progress:** These are the cornerstones that can propel you towards your goals. An important fact is any piece of information that can be used to help you achieve your desired outcome. For example, if your goal is to run a marathon, important facts would include information on training plans, proper nutrition, and injury prevention strategies.

    ii. **Relatively Unimportant Facts: Background Noise vs. Actionable Intelligence:** These other facts constitute background noise rather than actionable intelligence. They might be interesting but don't directly help you achieve your goals. Using the example of a marathon, information on the history of marathons or what celebrities wear for running shoes would more than likely fall into this category.

b. **The Mirage of Assumptions: Navigating Inferences:** This man surmises that people live their lives based on assumption and inference without ever grounding themselves in any hard-core reality of fact. An undiscerning attitude as to what is important and what is not is likely to result in poor decisions leading to failure. This implies that decisions for the average person depend upon "inferences" based on undependable sources of information. They rarely discipline themselves to insist that facts form the basis of their thinking. Furthermore, most individuals never learn to distinguish between what is insignificant and what is important, one of the prime reasons for the many failures in the world.

c.   **Redefining Thinking: Prioritization is Key.** Here is a useful rephrasing of our thinking: Genuine thinking is selection, which means that thinking is not simply a question of garnering information but making priorities. It is a sorting process in which we put "first things first" in a ranking order of importance and action. Effective thinking involves critically looking at information to determine what is important for achieving our goals. It shows fact prioritization is important while filtering out the unimportant, which refines our thoughts and will make informed decisions to move us forward. In other words, the "Thought Forge" symbolizes the human mind where base information is refined and polished. By living up to these principles above of purified thought inception, raw thoughts can be transformed into strong tools for success.

3. The Thought Forge: Where Desire Ignites Action

Here, we will delve into the concept of the "Spark of Desire," which serves as the essential catalyst for the initiation of thought processes. We explore the intricate relationship between desire and motivation, examining how a well-defined purpose drives us to engage in intentional thought and action, culminating in personal success.

a. Desire serves as the catalyst, embodying the seed of possibility

The concept of desire, anchored in a specific motive, serves as the foundation for all intentional thoughts and actions linked to personal accomplishment. It serves as the catalyst that fuels our internal drive, inspiring us to establish objectives and pursue them with determination. Contemplate the profound aspiration to acquire proficiency in a new language. When combined with a distinct motivation, the aspiration to connect with a different culture serves as a powerful catalyst for engaging in research on language learning techniques, enrolling in educational courses, or committing to daily practice.

b. Imagination Driven by Aspiration: Shaping Your Reality

A profound yearning stimulates the creative faculties, encouraging them to formulate routes toward fulfilling that yearning. Envision a dynamic scenario where you articulate the new language with fluency and confidence. The concept of "reality adjustment driven by a potent desire-fueled imagination" serves as a catalyst for motivation, enabling individuals to envision the favorable outcomes of their endeavors vividly.

c. Subconscious Activation: The Habitual Blueprint

Exploring Subconscious Activation: Understanding the Habitual Blueprint. When a desire is persistently cultivated through contemplation, it becomes ingrained in the subconscious, facilitating its manifestation through the most effective avenues. Envision the subconscious mind as a rich and fertile terrain, a space where the seeds of your aspirations take root and flourish. Your subconscious mind, through established routines, assimilates your aspirations and actively explores avenues to manifest them into reality. For example, the motivation to acquire a new language may lead you to instinctively pursue avenues for practice, such as participating in conversation groups or engaging with music in the language you intend to learn.

d. The Spark That Ignites Action

"Thought Forge" represents the intersection of desire and concentrated cognition. Through the strategic utilization of desire, coupled with imaginative faculties, we engage our subconscious to facilitate the necessary actions to realize our objectives. This dynamic synergy catalyzes action and advances us along the trajectory of personal success.

4. The Wellsprings of Thought: Fueling the Multidimensional Mind

The following discussion will delve into the "Wellsprings of Thought," examining the diverse origins that invigorate and influence our cognitive processes. Grasping these foundational elements is essential for the emergence of "multidimensional intelligence," as they serve as the fundamental components from which our cognitive processes are constructed.

a. Environmental Input: The Raw Data of Experience

The five senses serve as crucial conduits for raw data from the external environment, facilitating the interaction between the mind and its surroundings. Although environmental input may be subject to biases in perception, it is essential in fostering critical thinking and intellectual engagement. Observing an act of kindness can evoke reflections on the concepts of compassion and social justice.

b. **Memory's Echoes: Shaping Our Present with the Past**

Memory functions as a repository of past thoughts and experiences, serving as an internal library from which we draw to inform our current thinking. The phenomenon of "reconstructed thoughts," akin to the ripples of memory, plays a significant role in shaping our interpretations of the world and directing our decision-making processes. A positive recollection of acquiring a new skill can significantly enhance your confidence as you embark on the journey of learning something novel.

c. **Subconscious Intuition: A Gateway to Unseen Potential**

The subconscious mind, frequently described as a wellspring of creativity, possesses a significant capacity to inspire intellectual engagement. It is widely posited that it serves as a conduit for the influence of what some refer to as "infinite intelligence" on our cognitive processes. The phenomenon of "hyper-integration through morphic intelligence" emerges as a form of intuitive power, enabling us to reach solutions or insights that appear to materialize effortlessly. Reflect on the phenomenon of a sudden flash of inspiration during problem-solving; this may indicate the subconscious mind providing valuable insights.

d. Emotional Catalysts: The Wellspring of Desires

Emotions serve as the fundamental source of desires, effortlessly igniting cognitive engagement. These elements serve as the emotional subconscious activators that influence our aspirations and construct our human identity. The inherent emotional capacities within us serve as the foundation for all human cognition, driving us to take action. For instance, the emotion of fear can evoke thoughts centered around self-preservation, whereas joy may serve as a catalyst for creative expression.

e. Mastery of Willpower: Beyond the Limit Controller

The Will's Command! Emotions serve as a potent motivational force, yet they can also function as a double-edged sword, potentially circumventing the faculties of reason. They will, which may lead to erroneous judgments. This is precisely where the faculty of will becomes relevant. The will serves as the paramount authority of the mind; however, it remains underutilized by the majority of individuals. To effectively manage one's thought processes, it is essential to recognize cognitive boundaries and exercise a disciplined will that governs all avenues of thought. "Beyond the Limit Controller" represents the intricate process of regulating and mastering willpower by harnessing various cognitive resources.

It is important to recognize that, in many instances, our thoughts primarily influence our emotions rather than the reverse. In theory, the development of enhanced willpower control allows individuals to harness and direct their mental faculties toward constructive outcomes effectively.

Remember!

Regulating Intuition, Sensory Perception, and Memory: The Disruptive Triad. The content explored "The Unruly Trio": intuition, the five senses, and memory. The facilities that stimulate thought most frequently are regarded as the least influenced by willpower. Such pursuits necessitate a steadfast commitment to discipline in order to safeguard the mind from being swayed by its capricious inclinations. For example, intuition may guide us into a labyrinth of assumptions; unreliable sensory input can skew our perception of reality, and imperfect memories can obscure our judgment.

By cultivating self-discipline, we can enhance our ability to navigate and refine the impact of these unpredictable sources of cognitive stimulation. It is essential to develop the ability to differentiate between intuitive insights and emotional influences, to assess sensory data rigorously, and to recognize the distinction between reliable memories and deceptive recollections.

In conclusion, The Symphony of Thought: A Multidimensional Source

The "Wellsprings of Thought" offers an intensely rich and complex landscape. Understanding the many sources of inspiration and information upon which our thinking draws permits cultivating a more disciplined and multidimensional mind. In light of self-awareness and directed effort, we can powerfully tap into our emotions, intuition, senses, and memory to foster creative thought, sound judgment, and purposeful action.

It is not a thought created in a vacuum but a symphony played within the "Thought Forge." The input of the environment, the echoes of memory, and subconscious intuition are the rich tapestry of our thinking. Understanding these wellsprings makes it possible to foster a multidimensional intelligence drawing upon the full spectrum of available resources to fuel creative problem-solving, inspired action, and realization of our highest potential.

5. Harnessing the Power Within: Information Resonance and Cohesion

Embarking on a journey to grasp the essence of Information Resonance and the art of Cohesion: a deep exploration into aligning with the subconscious realm. This idea reaches its peak with the intriguing concept of "information resonance and cohesion mastery." This suggests individuals can align their inner thoughts with their desired goals through dedicated and intentional practice.

This idea proposes that by understanding the principles of information resonance and cohesion, we can tap into the vast potential of infinite intelligence for meaningful insights. At its core, harmonizing our thoughts and aspirations with the subconscious opens the door to an immense well of wisdom and possibility.

Aligning with the Infinite

Envision the subconscious mind as an expansive ocean teeming with information. By silencing the external noise of our conscious thoughts and honing our focus, we can create a harmonious connection with this profound level of awareness. The attainment of this cohesion realized through rigorous self-discipline and consistent practice, enables us to tap into the profound "power of infinite intelligence" for insightful guidance.

Practical Applications

The notion of "infinite intelligence" invites diverse interpretations; however, its fundamental message holds significant value. By cultivating a harmonious relationship between our conscious and subconscious minds, we can unlock our full potential, thereby enhancing our capacity for creative problem-solving, intuitive decision-making, and inspired action.

a) **Meditation:** Meditation practices quiet the conscious mind, thereby facilitating a deeper connection with the subconscious. This process opens up avenues for introspection and self-discovery.

b) **Self-hypnosis:** Self-hypnosis techniques are powerful tools for programming the subconscious mind, allowing individuals to integrate positive suggestions and achieve their desired goals.

c) **Visualization:** Visualizing exercises can enhance the alignment between your conscious aspirations and the subconscious mind.

The Power of Belief: A Crucial Ingredient

Recognizing that scientific evidence has yet to substantiate the notion of "infinite intelligence" existing within the subconscious mind is crucial. Nonetheless, one must not overlook the significant influence of belief. A robust conviction in one's capacity to tap into the subconscious is a significant motivation catalyst and can effectively promote transformative outcomes.

In conclusion, repealing the principle of information resonance and cohesion mastery gives us a fascinating insight into what the human mind may be mature for. While this great concept promotes the touchstone of unlocking new levels of creativity, solution-seeking, and growth, one must realize that lining up our conscious thoughts with the vast potential of the subconscious is a process, not an instant one.

Bringing this about will depend on disciplined practice and sustained efforts. Overcoming the forces of resistance from within, which are sometimes deeply ingrained, can slow one's journey toward mastery of information resonance and cohesion. One must, therefore, be patient and resilient, knowing this comes in successive stages rather than by any singular breakthrough.

But, beyond all question, mastery of this philosophy will give one direct control over the great mental storehouse of infinite intelligence for guidance; it does not promise instant or easy success. There are certain difficulties and reverses in all this work, which are to be taken as opportunities for growth and not as defeats.

Ultimately, only the person who becomes able to control the subconscious mind and direct it toward a definite end through self-discipline and regular practice has the greatest access to infinite intelligence. This alignment can provide valuable guidance in pursuing one's aims and purposes, but it requires ongoing effort, patience, and a realistic understanding of the gradual nature of personal growth.

6. The Thought Forge: The Artisan's Touch

The Mind's Craftsmen. This concept explores the "Principle of Knowing Thought Modifiers," presenting the three "Mind's Craftsmen": reason, imagination, and conscience. Although these faculties do not generate thoughts independently, they are essential in molding and enhancing the fundamental elements derived from the "Wellsprings of Thought."

Reason, Imagination, and Conscience: The Architects of Thought

Reason, imagination, and conscience serve not as the creators of our thoughts but as the skilled artisans who meticulously shape and refine them. Imagine a sculptor meticulously shaping a raw block of stone into an exquisite work of art. Comparably, these "thought modifiers" engage with the foundational elements of our cognition, shaping them into coherent and significant concepts.

a) Reason: The Judge of Experience

The faculty of reason functions as an evaluative mechanism, juxtaposing novel ideas against prior experiences to cultivate informed judgments and opinions. The evaluation of evidence put forth by our cognitive processes occurs within the context of our recollections and established knowledge framework. For example, one might rigorously assess a novel business concept by drawing comparisons with analogous enterprises from history.

b) Imagination: The Sculptor of Possibilities

The faculty of imagination serves as a catalyst, transforming abstract thoughts into concrete ideas, actionable plans, and strategic frameworks aimed at realizing specific objectives. The sculptor embodies the process of converting an abstract concept into a tangible strategy for execution. Reflect on the ways in which creativity can transform a novel business concept into a comprehensive marketing strategy or an intricate product development plan.

c) Conscience: The Moral Compass

The conscience serves as a guiding force for moral reasoning, facilitating the alignment of one's thoughts with established ethical principles. It serves as our intrinsic guide, directing our cognitive processes toward intentional actions that resonate with our core values. Consider the scenario where one's conscience rigorously evaluates a business plan, ensuring it is in harmony with ethical standards and promotes equitable treatment of employees and customers.

The Art of Thoughtful Action

By comprehending and implementing these principles, we can foster a disciplined mindset adept at producing and honing thoughts that culminate in intentional action. The collaborative efforts of the "Mind's Craftsmen" serve to refine the abundant flow of information sourced from the "Wellsprings of Thought." This process yields clear, constructive, and ethically grounded reasoning, ultimately driving us toward successfully realizing our objectives.

Remember!

Increasing consultation enhances the efficacy of these "Mind's Craftsmen." By continuously integrating reason, imagination, and conscience into our cognitive processes, we can enhance our thought patterns and enable ourselves to undertake impactful and ethical actions within the wider context of the world.

Key Takeaway: The "Wellsprings of Thought" serve as the foundational resources, whereas the "Mind's Craftsmen" transform these resources into practical applications. By comprehensively understanding reason, imagination, and conscience and effectively leveraging their synergistic potential, we can enhance our cognitive processes and align ourselves toward realizing our objectives.

In conclusion

The Symphony of the Mind: A Unifying Force. Our exploration of the Wellsprings of Thought" has revealed a multifaceted landscape. We have examined the role of environmental input, memory s echoes, subconscious intuition, emotions, willpower, and even the unruly trio of intuition, senses, and memory. By understanding these influences and practicing self-discipline, we can orchestrate a symphony within the Thought Forge" of our minds. This harmonious alignment of our conscious and subconscious will empower us to think critically, feel deeply, and act purposefully on the path to achieving our goals.

Unveiling the Thought Forge: Harnessing the Power of Belief

This segment explores the concept of the "Power of Belief," an influential yet elusive phenomenon whose essence and origins continue to intrigue scholars and thinkers alike. The discourse posits that, notwithstanding its elusive essence, belief represents the "most remarkable power accessible to humanity."

1. The Intangible Force: A Mystery to Behold

Belief embodies an intriguing and powerful essence, its origins and characteristics shrouded in deep mystery. Though it remains an enigmatic force, belief stands as the unparalleled strength accessible to humankind. This concept is regarded as the singular force that can be exercised with complete assurance in the tangible aspects of existence, underscoring its profound impact on our behaviors and results.

Demonstrating the Power of Belief

Envision an individual who possesses an unwavering conviction in their potential to thrive, even in the face of significant obstacles. This conviction drives their determination, shaping their choices and behaviors as they strive to realize their aspirations. For instance, Thomas Edison maintained an unwavering conviction in his capacity to create the electric light bulb. In the face of countless setbacks, his steadfast conviction propelled him to persist in his experiments until he ultimately succeeded. Despite being abstract, this demonstrates how belief can significantly influence our actions and successes.

The Influence of Belief on Outcomes

The essence of belief lies in its profound ability to mold our reality, guiding our thoughts and actions in significant ways. Embracing the potential for success empowers us to actively pursue our objectives, maintain our determination amidst challenges, and recognize opportunities that resonate with our dreams. On the other hand, the absence of belief may obstruct advancement, resulting in uncertainty and a failure to act.

Example: The Placebo Phenomenon

The placebo effect in medicine compellingly illustrates the profound influence of belief. Patients who believe they receive effective treatment often experience real improvements in their health, even if the treatment is inactive. This occurrence illustrates how belief can initiate physiological transformations, highlighting its significant influence on overall well-being.

Harnessing the Power of Belief

To tap into the transformative potential of belief, reflect on these practices:

a) **Affirmations:** Consistently reinforce empowering beliefs regarding your identity and capabilities. Statements like "I am capable and resilient" reinforce a mindset of confidence and determination.

b) **Visualization:** Imagine your aspirations and the milestones you've reached. Imagine yourself achieving your goals and embracing the profound joy and fulfillment that accompanies such success. This mental imagery enhances your conviction in your capabilities.

c) **Surround Yourself with Positivity:** Connect with uplifting influences, such as literature, guidance from mentors, or nurturing communities. This setting strengthens your convictions and sustains your drive.

d) **Reflect on Past Successes:** Remember moments when your conviction resulted in favorable results. Contemplating previous successes enhances your self-assurance and strengthens the conviction that your beliefs can mold your future.

Conclusion

The essence of belief, while elusive, holds significant sway over our behaviors and the results we achieve. By comprehending and utilizing this mysterious energy, we can synchronize our thoughts and actions with our objectives, shaping a reality that embodies our profound desires. Embrace the transformative nature of belief, allowing it to steer you toward a life rich with purpose and fulfillment.

2. The Key: Channeling Emotional Energy with Self-Discipline

Belief wields significant influence, yet its authentic strength is realized through the practice of self-discipline. Harnessing emotional and mental energy through concentrated intention turns belief into tangible action. Self-discipline channels these energies into a singular, potent focus, like directing sunlight through a magnifying glass to spark a fire.

Demonstrating the Strength of Personal Discipline

Envision the challenge of igniting a flame from disorganized fragments of kindling. While there may be some signs of disturbance, it's improbable that it will escalate into something more significant. Envision the act of channeling a concentrated ray of sunlight through a lens, honing in on a precise location. The focused energy sparks the tinder, igniting a flame. This metaphor demonstrates how self-discipline can unify our emotional and mental energies, igniting the flame of belief that manifests our desires into reality.

Example: Completing a Marathon

Reflect on the possibility of establishing a goal to complete a marathon. Self-discipline involves directing your emotions and energy purposefully to reach your desired outcome. This encompasses formulating a training regimen, nurturing motivation during challenging moments, and sustaining concentration on the event day. By harmonizing your emotional energy and minimizing distractions, you enable your subconscious mind to express your dedication to finishing the marathon.

Effective Approaches for Harnessing Emotional Energy

a) **Establish Distinct Objectives:** Articulate precise, achievable aims that resonate with your values. For instance, if your conviction centers on enhancing your fitness, establish a target to cover a specific distance each week.

b) **Develop a Strategy:** Formulate a comprehensive strategy for implementation. Detail the necessary steps to realize your objective, including a structured training plan for completing a marathon.

c) **Embrace Mindfulness:** Immerse yourself in mindfulness practices to still the mind and channel your energy effectively. Meditation and deep breathing practices foster a sense of balance and alignment with your aspirations.

d) **Embrace Consistency:** The foundation of self-discipline lies in unwavering consistency. Remain committed to your intentions, even when faced with difficulties. For instance, commit to your training regimen, even when your drive diminishes.

e) **Envision your success:** Consistently picture yourself reaching your aspirations. Envision the profound feelings and experiences accompanying achievement, solidifying your conviction and dedication.

Final thoughts

Self-discipline serves as the essential mechanism for directing emotional energy and converting belief into tangible action. By directing your mental and emotional energies with purpose, you spark the flame of conviction, manifesting your aspirations into reality. Embrace the strength of self-discipline, allowing it to steer you toward your aspirations with steadfast resolve. Engaging in a marathon or any other goal requires a steadfast belief, complemented by consistent effort, to achieve extraordinary results.

3. The Success Mandate: Acts of Believing

The Doctrine of Leadership

Exceptional leaders are, at their core, individuals who possess a deep-seated belief in their vision. They hold a steadfast conviction in their potential, aspirations, and capacity to motivate those around them. This belief serves as the foundation for their achievements. The "Creed of the Leaders" notion suggests that the foundation of success lies in essential beliefs crucial for attaining greatness. Those who nurture and leverage these convictions are more inclined to gain backing and achieve remarkable outcomes.

o **Demonstrating the Influence of Conviction in Leadership**

Reflect on a transformative figure such as Martin Luther King Jr. His steadfast conviction in fairness and righteousness drove him to spearhead the civil rights movement. His conviction in his vision and capacity to motivate others galvanized millions, resulting in profound societal transformation. This illustration highlights the capacity of belief to elevate simple concepts into significant movements.

Belief as the Soil for Success

Belief cultivates the rich ground from which achievement flourishes. A robust belief framework, cultivated through self-discipline, empowers us to unlock our true potential and transform our aspirations into concrete accomplishments. Much like a gardener tending to seeds in fertile ground, our beliefs cultivate our aspirations, enabling them to thrive.

o **Example:** Achievement in Business Ventures

Consider an individual embarking on the journey of launching a new venture. A deep conviction in their offering, aspirations, and capacity to navigate obstacles propels them onward. This conviction drives their determination, creativity, and capacity to engage investors and customers. Through their conviction in the endeavor, they cultivate an environment where success can flourish and develop.

Actionable Strategies for Nurturing Conviction

a) **Develop a Clear Vision:** Articulate a distinct and inspiring vision for your aspirations. This vision acts as a beacon, illuminating the path for your choices and behaviors.

b) **Nurture Self-Belief:** Foster a deep conviction in your capabilities. Consistently reflect on your inherent abilities and previous achievements to cultivate a sense of self-assurance.

c) **Inspire Others:** Articulate your vision and motivate others to follow your path. Influential leaders convey their convictions with fervor, inspiring others and igniting a sense of enthusiasm.

d) **Practice Self-Discipline:** Transform your convictions into consistent, purposeful actions. Keep your attention directed toward your aspirations, engage in steady diligence, and embrace obstacles with a spirit of adaptability.

e) **Continuous Learning:** Embrace the journey of continuous learning by adopting a mindset that thrives on growth and actively pursuing opportunities for enhancement and development. Your conviction in your ability to evolve is the driving force behind continuous growth and achievement.

Final Thoughts

Faith serves as the foundation for effective leadership and achievement. By cultivating a solid belief framework and applying self-discipline, individuals in leadership positions can attain remarkable success and motivate those around them to follow suit. Embrace the transformative nature of belief, cultivate your vision, and allow it to steer you toward a life rich in purpose, fulfillment, and remarkable achievements. It is essential to recognize that belief serves as the catalyst that turns aspirations into tangible outcomes, laying the foundation for lasting achievement.

4. Diverse Belief Systems: Seeds of Success

Seeds of the New CgX$_{new}$ System

This idea delves into different belief frameworks that can serve as catalysts for creating innovative CgXnew systems, establishing a groundwork for achievement. These frameworks interact with the subconscious and create pathways toward realizing our aspirations.

a)   **Belief in a boundless intellect (The Divine)**

The belief in Infinite Intelligence, commonly known as God, reflects a deep trust in a transcendent force or divine direction. This framework provides individuals with resilience, solace, and a deep sense of meaning. For example, individuals who believe in a higher power might discover comfort and inspiration in difficult moments, steering their choices with a profound sense of purpose.

o   **Example: Individual Drive**

Reflect on a person confronted with a challenging life choice. Their conviction in a boundless intellect instills a sense of assurance, suggesting they are under the guidance of a transcendent force, which brings clarity and confidence to their decisions. This belief serves as a driving force for inspiration and guidance as individuals traverse the intricacies of existence.

b) Belief in One's Abilities: Self-Confidence

Conviction in one's capabilities and potential for success is essential for overcoming self-doubt and reaching one's goals. Believing in ourselves empowers us to step outside our comfort zones and face obstacles with a positive mindset and unwavering strength.

o **Example: Navigating Challenges**

Envision an individual embarking on the journey of establishing a novel enterprise. Their self-belief catalyzes resilience, enabling them to navigate early challenges while sustaining an optimistic perspective. This unwavering self-assurance propels individuals to explore new ideas, adjust to challenges, and ultimately thrive in their endeavors.

c) Confidence in Collaborators: Reliance and Cooperation

The conviction in partnerships highlights the significance of trust and cooperation, drawing upon the skills and backing of chosen allies. Fostering a space filled with uplifting and encouraging people amplifies our efforts and plays a crucial role in achieving success.

o **Example: Cultivating a Flourishing Collective**

Envision a project manager guiding a multifaceted team. A shared conviction in the group's capabilities nurtures an environment rich in trust and cooperation. This conviction inspires individuals within the team to invest their utmost effort, culminating in a fruitful project result.

d) Belief in Righteousness: Perseverance

The belief that justice will ultimately triumph through unwavering commitment emphasizes the importance of upholding values and striving for what is right, especially in difficult times. Consistency and moral integrity are ultimately acknowledged and valued.

o **Example: Moral Guidance in Leadership**

Consider a leader who steadfastly maintains ethical values within their organization, even in the face of challenges. Their steadfast dedication to what is right serves as a beacon for others, fortifying the organization's moral foundation and paving the way for enduring achievement.

e) **Belief in Science: Evidence-Based Approach**

The dependence on established laws and empirical evidence, which form the foundation of scientific inquiry, highlights the significance of analytical reasoning and logical thought processes. This framework emphasizes the importance of basing choices on reliable data and credible sources of information.

o **Example: Choices in Medical Care**

Reflect on a healthcare practitioner navigating the complexities of treatment choices. Their commitment to empirical understanding fosters reliance on contemporary research and clinical evidence, ensuring optimal care for individuals seeking assistance. This method, grounded in evidence, improves patient results and cultivates trust.

f) **Belief in the Mind's Potential**

The belief in the mind's ability to connect with limitless intelligence is a powerful force. We unlock profound strength and possibilities by intentionally guiding our thoughts and ambitions.

o   **Example: Creative Problem-Solving**

Envision an individual unlocking the depths of their imaginative capabilities. Their conviction in the mind's potential enables them to delve into creative concepts and resolutions, leading to pioneering endeavors that motivate and impact those around them.

In summary

Recognizing that choosing a belief system profoundly reflects personal inclination is vital. Moreover, nurturing a perspective that actively drives you toward your aspirations and desires is paramount. Furthermore, adopting a belief framework that aligns with your fundamental principles and cultivating it through unwavering self-discipline empowers you to tap into the profound potential of belief, enabling you to realize your ambitions. Embrace the belief that resonates deeply within you, permitting it to act as the foundation for a life abundant in significance and accomplishment.

Unveiling the Thought Forge: The Enigma of Belief System within CgX (ADM-GENE Theory)

Cognitexis   Unveiled! Cognitexis   encapsulates   a fundamental concept that reflects the intrinsic essence of cognitive existence. This segment illuminates a crucial element of the intricate ADAM-GENE hypothesis, delving into the profound mystery of Cognitexis. The forthcoming book will explore Cognitexis, a concept embodying the fundamental state of cognitive existence. This intriguing notion will be examined in greater detail in the upcoming part three of the series: The Cognitexis Enigma.

To explore the intricacies of Cognitexis, one must immerse oneself in the rich tapestry of interdisciplinary research that characterizes cognitive science. This field integrates knowledge from various domains, such as psychology, neuroscience, linguistics, philosophy, and artificial intelligence, to enhance our understanding of the fundamental nature of the mind. Moreover, modern theories and frameworks shed light on cognitive processes, including perception, reasoning, memory, attention, language, and problem-solving, reaching far beyond the limits of this text.

Although the ADM-GENE theory is not detailed in this context, we can glean significant insights into CgX's unique perspectives. Through exploring Cognitexis, we cultivate a deep awareness of the fundamental processes that influence our mental landscape and propel our quest for knowledge. This journey encourages us to delve into the intricacies of cognitive science, revealing the mysterious essence of belief systems and their significant influence on our existence.

The Hallmark of Humanity: The Capacity to Believe

The Capacity to Believe: A Core Human Trait

Belief is a distinguishing trait of mankind, differentiating us from other beings. It is our inherent capacity to adhere to particular ideas and convictions with unwavering resolve. This capacity profoundly affects our viewpoint, shapes our actions, and eventually defines our identity. Let us examine how science, philosophy, and religion enhance our comprehension of this extraordinary characteristic.

Cognitive Science and Belief

Cognitive science investigates the processes behind our ability to believe. Studies demonstrate that belief development is intricately connected to the neurological circuits of the brain. The prefrontal cortex, which governs higher-order cognition and decision-making, is integral to forming and preserving beliefs. Neurotransmitters such as dopamine bolster beliefs by rewarding congruent behaviors, establishing a feedback loop that fortifies our opinions.

o **Example: Placebo Effect**

The placebo effect illustrates the influence of belief on physical well-being. Patients administered a placebo, under the impression it is an actual treatment, frequently exhibit authentic enhancements. This event underscores the brain's capacity to affect physiological functioning through belief, demonstrating the significant effect of our mental state on physical health.

Philosophy: The Nature of Belief

Philosophers have always contemplated the essence and importance of belief. René Descartes, a distinguished philosopher, underscored the significance of skepticism and conviction in his renowned maxim, "Cogito, ergo sum" ("I think, therefore I am"). This assertion emphasizes that confidence in one's existence is fundamental to all other knowledge. In "The Will to Believe," American philosopher William James contended that belief is fundamental for action. James posits that ideas direct our behaviors and construct our world, even without empirical substantiation.

o **Example: Existential Philosophy**

Existential thinkers such as Jean-Paul Sartre and Søren Kierkegaard examined the significance of belief in forming meaning and purpose. They asserted that individuals must develop their ideas to traverse an intrinsically meaningless world. This viewpoint highlights the active influence of belief in forming identity and directing life decisions.

Religion: Faith and Belief

Religion is intricately connected to the notion of believing. Faith, a fundamental element of several religious systems, entails steadfast conviction in a superior entity or divine purpose. Religious convictions furnish individuals with a feeling of purpose, ethical direction, and communal belonging. In Christianity, belief in God and the teachings of Jesus Christ are the foundation of a believer's existence, shaping their behaviors, ethics, and perspective on life.

o **Example: Spiritual Resilience**

Research indicates that persons with robust religious convictions frequently have enhanced resilience when confronted with hardship. Faith in a supreme being offers solace and optimism, allowing individuals to navigate difficulties and derive significance from adversity. This spiritual resilience highlights the transformational influence of belief in altering an individual's perception of reality.

Final Assessment

The ability to believe is a defining characteristic of humans, intricately embedded in our cognitive functions, philosophical explorations, and religious practices. This inherent capacity to maintain beliefs profoundly affects our viewpoint, motivates our actions, and eventually defines our identity. Comprehending the scientific, philosophical, and theological aspects of belief enhances our grasp of this extraordinary human characteristic and its significant influence on our existence.

The Engine of Miracles: Belief and the Unexplained

Miraculous Power: The Catalyst for Extraordinary Outcomes

The notion of miraculous power asserts that belief has always acted as the impetus for miracles—events that defy scientific explanation. The effect of belief is a compelling phenomenon that may yield extraordinary results, frequently surpassing the limits of current scientific understanding. This concept corresponds with the idea of the placebo effect, where a firm belief in a therapy can produce positive results, irrespective of the treatment's actual ineffectiveness.

Science: The Placebo Phenomenon

The placebo effect is a thoroughly proven scientific phenomenon in which individuals perceive genuine health gains following a therapy devoid of therapeutic efficacy. This impact highlights the influence of belief on physiological results. When patients perceive their treatment as helpful, their bodies respond favorably, initiating genuine biochemical alterations that facilitate recovery. This demonstrates how belief may materialize in concrete, quantifiable forms, even without direct physical involvement.

o **Example: Placebo in Pain Management**

Examine a clinical experiment in which chronic pain patients get a placebo rather than an active analgesic. Although the placebo contains no active components, several patients experience considerable pain alleviation just due to their belief in receiving an efficacious treatment. This conviction triggers the brain's analgesic pathways, illustrating the significant influence of mental thought on physical well-being.

Philosophy: Belief and Metaphysical Realities

Philosophers have extensively examined the essence of belief and its capacity to influence reality. The metaphysical argument asserts that belief may affect the universe in ways that are beyond empirical proof. William James contended that belief significantly influences our experiences and reality. He proposed that when we fully embrace a belief, we establish circumstances that increase the likelihood of its realization, a notion referred to as "the will to believe."

o   **Example: Self-Fulfilling Prophecy**

A self-fulfilling prophecy transpires when an individual's belief or anticipation affects their behavior, ultimately leading to the realization of that belief. A student who anticipates excelling in a topic is inclined to exert greater effort in their studies and thus achieve superior performance, thereby validating their conviction. This demonstrates how belief may construct its reality via the influence of anticipation and behavior.

Religion: Faith and Miracles

In religious contexts, belief is frequently associated with miracles, which are manifestations of divine intervention. Numerous religious traditions narrate accounts of miraculous healings, transformations, and supernatural events resulting from steadfast faith. Although not necessarily explicable by scientific methods, these miracles offer believers a deep feeling of optimism and validation of their faith.

o   **Example: Miraculous Healing in Religion**

Examine the narratives of miraculous healings throughout several religious traditions. In Christianity, the miraculous healings performed by Jesus, including restoring sight to the blind and resurrecting the dead, are fundamental to the belief system. These narratives motivate adherents to trust in the potential for divine intervention and the transformational efficacy of belief.

Final Assessment

Belief is a catalyst for miracles, capable of yielding astonishing results that surpass scientific comprehension. Belief significantly impacts our lives, as evidenced by the placebo effect in medicine, the philosophical notion of self-fulfilling prophesies, and religious miracles. Harness the potency of conviction, acknowledging its capacity to influence reality and catalyze extraordinary transformations. Allow belief to serve as the impetus that propels you toward accomplishing the seeming unattainable as you use its extraordinary potential in your pursuit.

The Mystery Within: Beyond Scientific Grasp

Elusive and Intangible: The Enigma of Belief

The CgX paradigm posits belief as a phenomenon that surpasses the limits of scientific understanding, highlighting its elusive and intangible characteristics. It continues to be enigmatic even to the most discerning minds, defying attempts at logical analysis. The constraints of our current scientific comprehension may impede our capacity to properly appreciate the intricacies and impact of believing. This indicates that belief functions on a different plane, apart from the strictly physical domain analyzed by scientific investigation.

Science: The Constraints of Empirical Research

Although science proficiently elucidates occurrences in the physical realm, belief is a complex notion that is difficult to define and assess. Neuroimaging studies have identified the brain areas implicated in belief formation, including the prefrontal cortex and limbic system. However, these findings just represent a preliminary understanding. The subjective and personal characteristics of belief render it challenging to examine using conventional scientific methodologies.

Philosophy: Beyond Empiricism

Philosophical studies have historically contended with the elusive essence of belief. Pivotal philosopher Immanuel Kant asserted that certain dimensions of human experience, such as belief, transcend factual observation. Kant's notion of the "noumenal world" denotes the reality that exists autonomously from our sensory impressions, implying that belief pertains to this transcendent domain.

o   **Example: The Role of Faith in Philosophy**

Philosophers such as Søren Kierkegaard examined the notion of faith, highlighting the necessity of transcending logic that believing frequently demands. Kierkegaard contended that authentic faith necessitates the acceptance of uncertainty and the unknown, an endeavor that surpasses scientific proof and rational thought. This viewpoint emphasizes that belief is fundamentally based on personal conviction rather than empirical evidence.

Religion: The Spiritual Dimension

In religious contexts, believing is sometimes considered a spiritual phenomenon surpassing the mortal realm. Belief in a higher power or divine design is seen as a fundamental element of several religious systems. These convictions give humans significance, purpose, and a sense of affiliation to a transcendent entity existing beyond empirical quantification.

o   **Example: Mystical Experiences**

Religious mystics describe deep encounters with spiritual connection or enlightenment that elude scientific understanding. These experiences, however profoundly influential and transformational for the person, pose significant challenges for scientific investigation due to their subjective character. They emphasize that belief includes aspects of human experience that transcend empirical examination.

Conclusion

Belief is a significant and enigmatic force that functions outside the limits of scientific understanding. The ethereal quality and resistance to rational scrutiny underscore its unique position in human experience. Recognizing the constraints of scientific investigation and examining religion's philosophical and spiritual aspects enhances our understanding of its intricacy and impact. Embrace the enigma inside, acknowledging that belief operates on a distinct level that enhances our comprehension of the world and ourselves.

A Force of Its Own: Operating Outside Logic

Investigating the Realm Beyond Logic

Belief can operate independently of rational thinking, following a distinct framework that sometimes surpasses conventional cognitive processes. The power of conviction may frequently eclipse logic and reason, profoundly affecting our perceptions and behaviors in unexpected manners. This event highlights belief systems' profound and entrenched nature, functioning beyond the limits of logical reason.

o **Example: The Power of Ideological Convictions**

Consider an individual with a strong belief in a certain philosophy. This conviction may cause individuals to dismiss evidence that opposes their perspective, resulting in behaviors that may seem unreasonable to external observers. A person fervently devoted to a political ideology may disregard real evidence that contradicts their convictions, concentrating only on sources that reinforce their viewpoint. This may lead to a distorted perception of reality, influenced by belief rather than rationality.

Science: Cognitive Biases and Belief

Cognitive biases frequently influence the predominance of believing over rationality. Confirmation bias is the inclination to pursue and prioritize information that validates our preexisting ideas while disregarding or rejecting opposing evidence. This bias fortifies belief systems, rendering them impervious to alteration despite the presence of rational reasons. Psychological studies have demonstrated the profound impact of biases on human cognition, underscoring the significant role of belief in shaping our mental processes.

Philosophy: Faith and Rationality

Philosophers have historically examined the connection between belief and rationality. An 18th-century philosopher, David Hume, contended that human behavior is predominantly influenced by passions and beliefs rather than rationality. He asserted that reason frequently serves as the "slave of the passions," implying that our convictions and emotions influence our actions more than rational consideration. This viewpoint emphasizes the independence of belief from logical reasoning.

Religion: Belief Beyond Reason

In religious situations, faith is frequently esteemed as a virtue that surpasses rationality. Adherents may possess certain truths grounded in spiritual belief rather than empirical proof. The belief that miracles or divine intervention exists beyond scientific examination and is grounded in faith and spiritual experience. This underscores how belief may influence conduct and perception in manners that reasoning alone cannot elucidate.

o   **Example: Faith in Healing**

Examine the phenomenon of faith healing, when individuals believe in divine or supernatural intervention to remedy diseases. Notwithstanding the absence of scientific validation, a conviction in healing abilities might result in authentic sensations of alleviation and recuperation. This demonstrates that belief functions autonomously from rational thinking, yielding tangible outcomes grounded in trust.

Practical Steps to Harmonize Belief and Reason

1) **Identify Cognitive Biases:** Acknowledge biases such as confirmation bias that validate existing ideas. Consistently interrogate your assumptions and pursue varied perspectives to contest your viewpoints.

2) **Employ Critical Thinking:** Utilize critical thinking to assess evidence impartially. Evaluate many perspectives and critically examine the integrity of material before drawing judgments.

3) **Reflect on Beliefs:** Consistently examine your beliefs and their sources. Recognize the influence of emotions and experiences in forming your beliefs.

4) **Cultivate Open-Mindedness:** Adopt open-mindedness to harmonize belief with rationality. Be open to modifying your opinions based on fresh data and logical reasoning.

Conclusion

Belief functions as an independent force, frequently beyond the limits of logic and reason. Although it may significantly influence behavior and perception, it is crucial to equilibrate belief with critical thinking and open-mindedness. By acknowledging belief's independence and influence on our cognitive functions, we may traverse the intricacies of faith and reason, cultivating a more sophisticated and profound comprehension of our beliefs and their significance in our lives. Adopt the distinctive belief system, allowing it to direct you with insight and clarity.

The Great Leveler: Belief for All

The Great Equalizer: Belief's Inherent Accessibility

The belief system of CgX highlights a significant trait of belief—its intrinsic accessibility. People from diverse backgrounds, regardless of their socioeconomic status, can harness the transformational power of conviction. This intangible type of power is universally accessible, promoting a sense of equality in its potential impact. In contrast to money or privilege, belief functions as a democratizing agent, empowering individuals to construct their own realities actively.

Science: The Universal Capacity for Believe

Research demonstrates that the ability to believe is an inherent characteristic of humanity, intricately woven into our cognitive functions. Psychological research indicates that belief formation transcends socioeconomic conditions and is a fundamental component of human cognition. Neuroplasticity, the brain's capacity to restructure by creating new neural connections, enables individuals from all backgrounds to cultivate and reinforce their beliefs, illustrating the egalitarian essence of belief.

o   **Example Educational Aspirations**

   Contemplate a student from an economically disadvantaged background who possesses confidence in their academic abilities. Despite financial difficulties, their conviction propels them to thrive academically, seek scholarships, and finally realize their educational aspirations. This situation demonstrates how conviction may surpass financial boundaries, enabling individuals to influence their future.

Philosophy: The Egalitarian Nature of Belief

Philosophers have historically acknowledged the egalitarian influence of belief. John Locke, a prominent philosopher, contended that all persons have the ability for logical thought and belief development, regardless of their social standing. This viewpoint underscores the inherent equality of beliefs, positing that personal convictions may direct individuals toward fulfilling and worthwhile lives, irrespective of their external conditions.

o   **Example: Grassroots Movements**

Grassroots movements frequently illustrate the egalitarian essence of conviction. Individuals united by a shared conviction in social justice or environmental sustainability may organize and instigate substantial change, even in the absence of conventional power or privilege. The shared conviction in a cause enables them to contest the status quo and influence society's standards.

Religion: Belief as a Universal Gift

Numerous religious systems perceive belief as a universal gift available to everyone. In Christianity, faith is regarded as a heavenly gift accessible to all believers, irrespective of their upbringing. This inclusive methodology underscores the global accessibility of faith and its capacity to offer spiritual fortitude and meaning.

o   **Example: Community Support**

In religious societies, faith frequently cultivates a sense of cohesion and assistance among members. Individuals from varied backgrounds gather by their common religion to assist one another in navigating life's obstacles. This shared conviction highlights the unifying power of faith, offering comfort and resilience to all individuals.

Final Assessment

Belief serves as a profound equalizer, naturally available to all persons, irrespective of their social status or upbringing. This democratizing impulse enables individuals to actively influence their circumstances, surpassing the constraints of affluence or position. Harness the transforming capacity of belief, acknowledging its ability to promote equality and catalyze good change in your life and the lives of others. Allow conviction to serve as the cornerstone for constructing a future characterized by intention, grit, and collective humanity.

Belief as the Fuel: Powering Thoughts and Plans

The World Belongs to Believers

The belief extends past mere recognition of its influence, delving into the examination of methods to harness its potential meaningfully. This highlights the importance of integrating belief systems into our cognitive frameworks and strategic planning to realize our objectives. The assertion that "the world belongs to believers" highlights the notion that individuals who steadfastly maintain their convictions are more inclined to realize their goals.

Structure Your Cognitive Potential

Integrate your strategies with a strong foundation of positive belief. A clearly articulated vision, supported by conviction, creates a strategic framework for attaining success. Cognitive research corroborates this strategy by demonstrating that explicit objectives and affirmative attitudes stimulate the brain's reward system, hence enhancing motivation and perseverance. Neuroplasticity enables our brains to adapt and fortify neural connections linked to goal-oriented cognition, improving our capacity to attain desired results.

o **Example: Strategic Planning in Business**

Consider a firm that aspires to become a market leader in sustainable products. The corporation integrates this vision with a firm conviction in its plans, establishes precise objectives, allocates resources to research and development, and aligns its operations with sustainable principles. This belief propels the organization towards success, generating a beneficial effect on both the environment and the market.

Believe In, Not Against

Prioritize developing a mentality focused on your ambitions instead of dwelling on anxieties or constraints. This change in emphasis markedly improves your pursuit of your objectives. Positive affirmations and a future-oriented perspective are crucial for personal growth and development. Research in positive psychology indicates that emphasizing strengths and favorable outcomes enhances resilience, creativity, and well-being.

o **Example: Overcoming Personal Challenges**

Envision a person recuperating from a significant adversity, such as unemployment. By redirecting their attention from the apprehension of failure to confidence in their abilities and potential, they embrace positive affirmations such as "I am competent and resilient." This mentality allows people to pursue new chances, network efficiently, and ultimately obtain a gratifying new role.

Agency Through Belief

The core of conviction acts as the impetus that stimulates action, propelling your ideas and intentions into actualization. Belief without action is akin to fire without fuel; it holds great potential but requires appropriate guidance to realize its strength. Philosophers like William James have highlighted that belief drives action, while action reinforces belief, establishing a circle of success.

o **Example: Transforming Vision into Reality**

Contemplate a community leader with a mission to enhance local schooling. Their conviction in the possibility of transformation drives them to mobilize volunteers, get financing, and execute educational initiatives. This proactive strategy, driven by conviction, results in measurable enhancements in the community's educational achievements.

Practical Steps to Harness the Power of Belief

1) **Establish Clear Objectives:** Articulate your aims distinctly, ensuring they are grounded in your convictions. Clarity offers a strategic framework for your endeavors.

2) **Cultivate Positive Affirmations:** Consistently utilize affirmations corresponding to your goals. Affirmative self-dialogue strengthens your conviction in your capabilities.

3) **Visualize Success:** Use visualization methods to visualize achieving your objectives. Mental rehearsal enhances your conviction and drive.

4) **Engage in Consistent Action:** Deconstruct your objectives into concrete actions and dedicate yourself to their execution. Steadfast endeavor, fueled by conviction, advances you towards achievement.

5) **Reflect and Adapt:** Consistently assess your advancement, acknowledge achievements, and modify your approaches as necessary. This iterative approach, driven by conviction, maintains your focus.

Final Assessment

Belief is the catalyst that propels ideas and intentions into actualization. You may use the transformational power of belief by organizing your cognitive abilities with positive conviction, fostering an optimistic mentality, and engaging in persistent action. Adopt this methodology and allow conviction to direct you in forging a future characterized by intention, success, and satisfaction. The world truly belongs to those who believe, and by harnessing the power of belief, one may transform ambitions into reality.

Contagious and Double-Edged[5]

The Ripple Effect of Belief: A Contagious Phenomenon

Belief is an infectious phenomenon propagating from person to person. Positive beliefs have the extraordinary capacity to motivate and elevate others, while negative or skeptical ideas can have opposing effects. This phenomenon is accurately characterized as a "double-edged sword."

Comprehending the Ripple Effect

1) **The Dynamics of Conviction**

   Belief systems can permeate various cognitive domains and influence the environment that surrounds them. The convictions we hold deeply shape our thoughts, actions, and interactions with the world around us. Cognitive science illuminates the interplay between neural networks associated with belief and their influence on behavior. For example, when people believe in their ability to succeed, their minds activate pathways that enhance focus, drive, and perseverance, leading to more effective actions.

   o **Example: Influence in Education**

      Contemplate an educator who has faith in their pupils' capabilities. This conviction influences their relationships,

---

[5] Remember, meanwhile, that belief is contagious; that belief in one thing tends to open the way for belief in many things, while unbelief works in the same manner.

inspiring and motivating pupils to reach their full potential. The educator's affirmative belief system fosters an environment where pupils feel supported and assured, enhancing academic achievement.

2) The Influence of Positive Belief

Fostering an atmosphere abundant in affirmative thoughts might trigger a ripple effect, augmenting general positivity. Associating with persons who inspire and uplift you may profoundly impact your thinking. Research in positive psychology underscores the advantages of an optimistic atmosphere, such as improved well-being, superior stress management, and strengthened social ties.

o Example: Team Dynamics in the Workplace

In a professional environment, a team leader who is confident in their team's qualities and capabilities cultivates a culture of trust and collaboration. This optimistic conviction penetrates the team, elevating morale, enhancing creativity, and augmenting production. Team members see their worth and are more inclined to put in the utmost effort.

3) Philosophy: The Impact of Collective Belief

Philosophers have always acknowledged the influence of communal belief on society. In "The Republic," Plato examined the concept of collective ideas influencing society's moral and ethical structure. He contended that a society's shared conviction in justice and morality directs its laws, traditions, and overall disposition. This philosophical viewpoint underscores the influence of collective ideas in molding societal norms and actions.

o **Example: Social Movements**

Social movements often exemplify the profound impact of collective belief. Movements like the civil rights movement emerged from a shared belief in the fundamental principles of equality and justice. This common belief inspired individuals to take action, leading to significant changes in the social and political landscape.

4) **Religion: Belief and Community**

Religious societies frequently exhibit the ripple effect of faith. Common beliefs and ideals foster a robust sense of community and assistance among members. Adherents derive fortitude and motivation from their group, augmenting their spiritual and emotional wellness.

o **Example: Religious Gatherings**

Examine the effects of religious assemblies, including church services and meditation retreats. These gatherings unite individuals, strengthening their common ideas and cultivating a sense of solidarity. The shared conviction in a higher power or spiritual tenets offers solace and inspiration, favorably impacting persons' lives.

In Conclusion: Cultivating a Belief System for Success

The belief system inside the CgX framework offers an intriguing perspective on the essence of belief. It highlights its accessibility, ability to motivate action, and contagious nature. By fostering a strong belief system and interacting with positive influences, you may harness the power of the intangible to transform your ideas, tactics, and, eventually, the essence of your reality.

Practical Steps for Cultivating Positive Beliefs

1) **Surround Yourself with Positivity:** Associate with persons who inspire and motivate you. Their upbeat perspective may elevate your mentality and promote a good atmosphere.

2) **Practice Gratitude:** Consistently recognize and value the favorable elements of your existence. Gratitude strengthens affirmative convictions and enhances well-being.

3) **Disseminate Optimism:** Convey affirmative convictions through your engagements. Inspire and elevate others, generating a ripple effect beyond your individual influence.

4) **Reflect on Positive Outcomes:** Dedicate time to consider previous achievements and beneficial experiences. This exercise strengthens your confidence in your capabilities and potential.

Final Assessment

Belief is a contagious and dual-faceted phenomenon that may significantly influence our reality. By comprehending the ripple impact of believing and fostering good convictions, we may motivate and elevate others, therefore establishing a supportive and hopeful atmosphere. Embrace the transformational potential of belief, allowing it to direct you toward a future characterized by purpose, success, and collective optimism.

Freedom Through Belief: A Disciplined Mind

Unveiling the Sanctuary of the Mind

Genuine freedom through conviction is attained when the mind is disciplined. A mind shaped by self-discipline and anchored in a robust belief system becomes a refuge, fearless and devoid of inner turmoil. Consequently, belief functions as a psychological barrier that repels negativity and self-doubt, simultaneously cultivating mental resilience.

Neuroscience: The Role of Neuroplasticity

Neuroplasticity, the brain's capacity to restructure by creating new neural connections, is essential for cultivating a disciplined mind. By exercising self-discipline and reinforcing affirmative attitudes, we fortify these brain connections, rendering them more resilient and automatic. This change converts our thoughts into bastions of tranquility and fortitude, making us more adept at confronting life's adversities.

Self-Discipline: The Fortifying Force

Self-discipline offers a protective mental sanctuary. It clarifies cognition, organizes emotional turmoil, and enhances mental capabilities. Envision a disordered room; self-discipline constitutes the process of organizing it, fostering clarity and concentration in your mind. A trained mind enables us to tackle our concerns and traverse uncertainty with a composed resolve.

o **Example: Mindfulness and Self-Discipline**

Mindfulness activities, including meditation, cultivate self-discipline by conditioning the mind to concentrate and stay present. Consistent meditation facilitates the elimination of mental clutter, enhancing cognitive clarity and emotional balance. This methodical technique strengthens the mind, allowing us to confront obstacles with composure and concentration.

Belief as a Source of Strength

An unwavering belief system functions as a source of strength and resilience. It provides meaning, direction, and unwavering faith as a psychological anchor during life's tumultuous challenges. Similar to a tower enduring a storm, a robust belief system serves as the foundation that supports us throughout challenging times, offering solace and the capacity to inspire ourselves through hardship.

o   **Example: Faith and Resilience**

Examine persons possessing profound spiritual convictions, particularly those who are resilient from their religion in challenging circumstances. This spiritual system imparts a feeling of purpose and perseverance, utilizing their faith as a source of solace and strength.

Freedom from Fear and Strife

The amalgamation of self-discipline with a robust belief system fosters a condition of liberation from fear and conflict. This does not imply eradicating all negative emotions since fear may serve as a normal and advantageous reaction. Disciplined minds, fortified by strong convictions, manage fear adeptly, averting its potential to undermine our actions and thoughts. We assume the role of witnesses to our fears and choose our responses instead of being dictated by them.

o   **Example: Cognitive Behavioral Therapy**

Cognitive Behavioral Therapy (CBT) illustrates this idea by instructing clients to identify and restructure problematic beliefs. Through rigorous practice and a conviction in their capacity for transformation, individuals acquire the skills to regulate anxiety and dread, exerting control over their reactions and diminishing the influence of adverse emotions.

The Ever-Evolving Sanctuary

Acknowledging that this "sanctuary of the mind" is an ongoing endeavor, persisting even through eternity, is essential. Like self-discipline necessitates continual exercise, belief systems may require refining via development and new experiences. The pursuit of liberation from fear and conflict is an enduring endeavor. Through diligent effort and commitment to personal growth, we may cultivate a realm of psychological safety inside ourselves.

o **Example: Lifelong Learning**

Reflect on the concept of lifelong learning, wherein individuals continuously seek out new knowledge and skills. This commitment to personal growth and self-discipline enhances psychological resilience and adaptability. By refining our belief systems and embracing new experiences, we cultivate a robust sanctuary within our minds, equipped to face the challenges that life presents.

Final Assessment

Liberty via conviction is attained with a trained intellect. By amalgamating self-discipline and robust belief systems, we establish a mental refuge devoid of internal discord and durable against hardship. This road is perpetual, necessitating constant refining and commitment to self-enhancement. Harness the potency of conviction and self-regulation to establish a mental refuge, promoting psychological security, resilience, and autonomy throughout your existence.

Efficiency in an Organized Mind

This section explores the notion of a structured mind and its importance in cultivating belief as a powerful psychological influence. A well-structured mind reveals an enhanced ability to harness belief's influence in the quest to attain one's goals.

Ingredients of Belief: Crafting Your Cognitive Terrain

Belief is an intricate construct, not simply a random occurrence. Our comprehension is profoundly influenced by the information we interact with and the approaches we utilize to make sense of it. Our cognitive processes resemble thriving gardens of the mind.

The information we engage with acts as the foundational elements that shape the beliefs we embrace. Just as a gardener carefully selects seeds to cultivate a vibrant garden, we must practice discernment in the information we allow to take root in our minds.

Science: Cognitive Filtering

The process of cognitive filtering is a fascinating exploration of how we perceive and interpret the world around us. The realm of cognitive science underscores the critical role that selective attention and filtering play in forming our beliefs. The capacity of the mind to hone in on pertinent information while filtering out distractions is essential for effective cognitive functioning. This focused awareness guarantees that only the most relevant information shapes our convictions and choices.

o   **Example: Media Consumption**

Reflect on how engaging with various forms of media shapes our understanding and beliefs. One can foster a nuanced and informed perspective on the world by intentionally choosing reliable news outlets and consciously avoiding sensationalist narratives. This intentional involvement cultivates a mental landscape abundant in precise and beneficial insights.

Discipline and Direction: Channeling Belief for Success

Self-discipline is crucial in shaping and directing our belief systems toward specific outcomes. It allows us to discern the elements that support or hinder our aspirations—what to embrace and what to let go. Imagine an exceptional creator wielding an expansive array of hues. To create a true masterpiece, one must cultivate the self-discipline necessary to select the most fitting shades and hues. In a similar vein, grounding our consciousness with uplifting and empowering beliefs cultivates a mental momentum that propels us toward achievement.

o **Example: Strategic Focus**

Envision an individual dedicated to pursuing excellence, rigorously preparing for the pinnacle of athletic achievement. Their commitment to a disciplined approach in choosing and following a stringent training routine, nutritional plan, and mental preparation harnesses their conviction in reaching optimal performance. This intentional mindset, rooted in affirmative convictions, drives them forward on their journey to success.

The Starting Point: Taking Inventory of Your Mental Inputs

To cultivate a well-ordered mind, it is essential to reflect on the nourishment you provide to your thoughts. This encompasses all aspects of your environment, including the media you engage with, the individuals you choose to associate with, and even the conversations you have within yourself. Are you often enveloped in an atmosphere of negativity? Do the skeptical attitudes of those around you deplete your vitality? Through a thoughtful examination of both external influences and your inner dialogue, you have the opportunity to cultivate a mental landscape that nurtures empowering and affirming belief systems.

o **Example: Personal Reflection**

Imagine an individual grappling with a pervasive sense of negativity in their professional environment. Through introspection regarding their mental influences, individuals recognize detrimental coworkers and unproductive media engagement as significant sources of stress. Opting to reduce exposure to detrimental influences while immersing oneself in encouraging and enriching content fosters a more nurturing cognitive landscape.

The Organized Mind: A Psychological Powerhouse

A well-structured mind enables you to tap into the full capacity of your belief systems. Careful selection and refinement of your beliefs create a robust foundation for your mental landscape, empowering your cognitive processes. This inner fortitude guides you through the complexities of existence and propels you toward the aspirations you seek.

o **Philosophy: Mind as an Organized System**

The mind can be understood as a meticulously structured system, with each component playing a vital role in the overall functioning and coherence of our thoughts and behaviors.

Thinkers like Aristotle highlighted the significance of structuring one's thoughts and beliefs as a path to living virtuously. Aristotle's notion of "eudaimonia" embodies the pursuit of flourishing through the harmonious alignment of one's beliefs and actions with one's authentic potential. An intentional framework for thought and action cultivates a life rich in fulfillment and meaning.

In summary

Efficiency within a well-structured mind entails creating a mental landscape that is nourished by intentional and affirmative beliefs, steered by self-regulation, and perpetually enhanced through thoughtful reflection. This structured methodology elevates the mind into a formidable force, propelling you toward achievement and personal satisfaction. Embrace these facets of intentional belief to mold your reality and realize your aspirations with precision and intention.

Belief in Action: The Spark that Ignites Change

This segment highlights the deep connection between our beliefs and our actions. The assertion implies that conviction is fortified by tangible efforts directed toward attaining a specific goal.

From Thought to Action: Putting Belief into Motion

Simply possessing a belief does not suffice. Translating this concept into tangible actions is essential to unlock its full potential. Reflect on belief as a powerful catalyst. Without action, this initial spark lies dormant, unable to ignite the transformative blaze of change and progress. When our actions align with our fundamental beliefs, they spark our passions and drive us toward a more fulfilling existence.

o **Example: Starting a Business**

Envision an individual driven by an unwavering conviction in their groundbreaking vision. Merely believing in its potential does not suffice to transform it into reality. It is essential to engage in deliberate actions—crafting a comprehensive business plan, pursuing financial support, and initiating the launch of their product. Every action driven by conviction propels them toward achievement, turning their aspirations into tangible outcomes.

The Importance of Action: Validating Belief Through Deeds

A belief system diminishes in credibility when aligned actions do not support it. When beliefs do not manifest in tangible actions, they risk becoming nothing more than hollow philosophies or expressions of hopeful longing. Just as cognitive abilities wane without consistent practice, our beliefs may become stagnant if we do not actively incorporate them into our daily existence. This concept echoes the saying, "Faith without action is lifeless." The expressions of our behaviors stand as tangible evidence of our beliefs, reinforcing their strength and our commitment to them.

o   **Example: Environmental Activism**

Reflect on an individual deeply committed to conservation principles and their vital role in our world. When individuals express their concerns without accompanying them with action, the validity of their beliefs diminishes significantly. Through their engagement in clean-up initiatives, promotion of policy reforms, and efforts to enlighten others, they embody their convictions, showcasing a profound dedication to safeguarding the environment.

The Mind Forged Through Action

The evolution and fortification of the mind rely on purposeful involvement. Actively pursuing our goals challenges our boundaries and broadens our comfort zones, urging us to gain new insights and adjust with purpose. Engaging with our environment enriches our mental faculties, especially concerning our belief systems. By consistently aligning our actions with our beliefs, we strengthen and elevate them, transforming them into powerful forces that profoundly shape our experiences.

o   **Example: Exploring the Process of Acquiring a New Ability**

Envision an individual embarking on the journey of mastering a musical instrument. Their conviction in their capacity to master the instrument finds affirmation solely through dedicated practice and active involvement. As individuals engage with new compositions and refine their skills, their confidence in their musical potential deepens, thereby enriching their cognitive and motor capabilities.

The Belief-Action Cycle: A Catalyst for Growth

The dynamic relationship between what we believe and how we act acts as a powerful force for individual growth. Strong beliefs ignite involvement and encourage proactive actions. The behaviors we engage in serve to affirm and strengthen our convictions. Our confidence and conviction rise profoundly as we attain successes rooted in our belief-driven actions. This positive cycle propels us forward in a continuous quest for self-improvement and achievement.

o **Example: Achievement in Academia**

Imagine a student who is deeply committed to thriving in their academic pursuits. This conviction drives individuals to dedicate themselves to their studies, seek assistance when necessary, and confront difficult topics head-on. Their confidence in their abilities deepens as they attain academic milestones, further fueling their dedication to scholarly achievement.

In summary

The conviction to act catalyzes transformation. Translating belief into concrete actions affirms our convictions and drives us forward on our journey toward our aspirations. The intricate relationship between our convictions and behaviors cultivates individual development and strengthens our belief frameworks, establishing a profound cycle of success and satisfaction. Embrace the harmonious interplay of conviction and effort, allowing it to propel you toward fulfilling your dreams and creating a significant legacy.

The Ascendancy of Self: Belief as a Tool for Self-Mastery

The Art of Shaping Your Own Fate

Achieving mastery over oneself through organized endeavors indicates that a well-defined belief framework, when paired with intentional actions and a spirit of humility, empowers individuals to reach self-mastery. This idea suggests that belief transcends mere passive acceptance; it serves as a dynamic instrument for directing and molding one's future.

The Mastery of Self: Navigating the Journey to Inner Triumph

Belief acts as an essential compass, steering individuals along their path to personal mastery. By organizing our cognitive processes, intentionally expressing our beliefs through deliberate actions, and fostering humility, we can develop the psychological resilience necessary to master our thoughts, emotions, and behaviors. This resonates with the idea of taking charge of our inner being, steering it intentionally towards the aspirations we hold dear.

o   **Science: Cognitive Behavioral Therapy (CBT)**

Cognitive Behavioral Therapy (CBT) represents a profound exploration into the intricacies of the human mind, offering insights into the interplay between thoughts, emotions, and behaviors. It serves as a transformative tool for individuals seeking to navigate the complexities of their mental landscapes.

Cognitive Behavioral Therapy focuses on structuring thought patterns to facilitate attaining specific behavioral goals. Individuals can steer their behaviors toward achieving self-mastery by recognizing and confronting detrimental thought patterns and substituting them with constructive, organized beliefs. This method highlights belief's significant role in influencing behavior and cultivating psychological strength.

Structured Pursuit: The Strength of Intentional Engagement

A carefully organized mindset, fueled by strong beliefs and purposeful actions, stands out as a powerful tool for attaining self-mastery. Imagine an artist, deeply attuned to their inner vision, meticulously shaping their masterpiece. A structured mindset envisions the desired result, while a deep-seated confidence in one's abilities drives the person to meticulously chisel away at the stone. In a parallel manner, by organizing our thoughts and channeling our beliefs into concrete actions, we position ourselves as the designers of our own path toward personal growth.

o   **Example: The Artisan**

Envision the profound moment when Michelangelo meticulously carves the statue of David, channeling his inner vision into a masterpiece. His profound vision and unwavering belief in his artistic abilities propelled his meticulous endeavors, transforming a marble block into a true masterpiece. This intentional endeavor, propelled by a well-defined belief system, illustrates the profound impact of conviction in realizing exceptional outcomes.

Walking Humbly: Groundedness on the Path to Self-Mastery

Humility is an essential component in the journey toward self-mastery. It is a meaningful reminder to approach life with a sense of stability and reverence. A person of humble nature acknowledges their capabilities and limitations, perceives the continuous potential for development, and approaches obstacles with a willingness to learn. This humility acts as a protective barrier against arrogance and overconfidence, allowing us to learn from our mistakes and continuously refine our beliefs and actions in our pursuit of self-mastery.

o **Philosophy: Socratic Humility**

Socrates profoundly claimed that genuine wisdom arises from the awareness of one's lack of knowledge. This approach nurtures an ongoing self-reflection and knowledge acquisition journey, cultivating an attitude that embraces development and personal evolution. Embracing humility allows us to cultivate a balanced perspective, essential for achieving self-mastery.

Final Thoughts

Belief serves as a powerful instrument for achieving self-mastery, requiring intentional efforts, concentrated actions, and a foundation of humility. Through the deliberate structuring of our mental frameworks, the conscious manifestation of our values in our actions, and the fostering of humility, we develop the strength essential for gaining mastery over our thoughts, feelings, and behaviors. Embrace belief as a dynamic instrument for personal mastery, allowing it to steer you toward a life rich in purpose, growth, and fulfillment.

Belief: A Gift and a Responsibility

The Creator's Relic: A Gift of Immeasurable Worth

Belief, often referred to as a "Creator's Relic," represents an extraordinary endowment from a transcendent source intricately woven into the fabric of every individual. This inherent strength allows us to shape our experiences, infuse our existence with meaning, and traverse our paths with unwavering determination.

o **Science: The Power of Belief**

The Influence of Conviction Albert Bandura's theory of self-efficacy illuminates the significance of belief as a crucial factor in achieving one's goals. This intrinsic strength nurtures resilience and a sense of purpose, essential for psychological health. The brain's remarkable capacity for neuroplasticity illustrates the profound impact of belief, demonstrating how it can reconfigure neural pathways and elevate our potential.

o **Philosophy: Existentialism**

Existentialism invites us to confront the fundamental questions of life, freedom, and individuality by exploring the depths of existence and the essence of being. It challenges us to reflect on our choices and the meaning we ascribe to our experiences. Existentialist thinkers, such as Jean-Paul Sartre, highlight the profound capacity of the individual to forge their own meaning in life. This perspective resonates with the notion that belief, viewed as a sacred artifact, empowers individuals to shape their purpose and traverse life with intention.

A Gift for All: The Universal Access to Belief

Belief transcends the boundaries of material wealth and social status, existing as a universal thread that connects us all. This democratization process empowers each person to cultivate a robust belief system, enabling them to forge a fulfilling life.

o **Philosophy: Stoicism**

Exploring the Principles of Stoicism The essence of Stoic philosophy, especially as articulated by Epictetus, emphasizes that although we may not have power over external events, we retain control over our beliefs and perceptions. This resonates with the idea that belief is a universal endowment available to everyone, irrespective of their circumstances.

o **Religion: Islamic Concept of Iman**

The Islamic Concept of Iman in Islam, Iman, or faith, stands as a fundamental principle, emphasizing that belief in Allah is within reach for every individual. This viewpoint highlights the egalitarian essence of belief, stressing the individual's duty to nurture and sustain their faith.

Absolute Authority: The Power of Choice

We possess the power to shape our belief systems, allowing us to intentionally select beliefs that resonate with our values and aspirations. This independence allows us to mold our mental terrains.

o   **Science: Metacognition**

Exploring the intricacies of metacognition reveals profound insights into our cognitive processes. It invites us to reflect on our thinking, enhancing our understanding of how we learn and make decisions. This self-awareness is crucial for personal growth and intellectual development. Metacognition, often described as the process of reflecting on one's own thought patterns, encompasses a profound self-awareness and the ability to regulate cognitive functions. This scientific concept underscores the notion that we possess the ability to consciously assess and mold our beliefs, thus empowering us to navigate our mental landscapes with intention.

Harnessing the Potential: A Call to Action

The concept of belief, regarded as a profound gift, possesses extraordinary potential. Through intentionally cultivating and applying empowering beliefs, we access our inner resilience and enhance our capacity to realize our aspirations and values.

o   **Philosophy: Pragmatism**

Exploring the essence of pragmatism in philosophy. Pragmatist thinkers such as William James champion beliefs that produce tangible advantages. This perspective promotes the nurturing of convictions that enable us to realize our goals and maneuver through life's complexities with skill.

o **Religion: The Bhagavad Gita**

The Bhagavad Gita is a profound exploration of spirituality and duty. It underscores the importance of engaging in righteous action, or Dharma, that resonates with one's beliefs. This profound manuscript encourages the intentional cultivation of beliefs that nurture inner resilience and the realization of one's utmost potential.

The Responsibility of Belief

With the gift of belief comes the duty to wield it with discernment. Fostering uplifting and empowering belief systems enables us to reshape our existence and positively influence the world around us.

o **Religion: The Ethical Use of Belief in Buddhism**

The Ethical Application of Belief in Buddhism: Buddhism's notion of "right belief" emphasizes the importance of adopting beliefs that foster ethical behavior and a sense of compassion toward others. This spiritual viewpoint emphasizes the duty that comes with belief, encouraging individuals to channel their convictions toward constructive results.

Final Thoughts

Belief is a deep and shared endowment that enables us to mold our experiences, discover meaning, and traverse life's challenges with strength. It stands as a testament to our essence, intricately interlaced with the core of our existence, and available to all, irrespective of their situations.

This offering empowers individuals to harness the essence of belief, enabling us to fully embrace our belief systems and select convictions that resonate with our core values and aspirations. We reveal profound potential and inner resilience by intentionally cultivating and embodying our beliefs.

Yet alongside this privilege lies the profound duty to wield our convictions with wisdom and integrity. By nurturing uplifting and empowering belief systems, we have the potential to reshape our lives and influence the world in remarkable ways.

The interplay of belief, informed by scientific understanding, philosophical contemplation, and spiritual wisdom, serves as a profound catalyst that shapes our paths, fostering a sense of purpose and nurturing empathy towards others. Welcome this opportunity and allow it to guide your journey with authenticity and intention.

Independent Thought and Mind Power: The Intrinsic Nature of Belief

Independent Thought and Mind Power

Belief represents a core element of our mental processes, an intrinsic part of how we engage with the world around us. It does not come from outside ourselves; instead, it resides inherently within our being. This inherent aspect of belief empowers us to engage with it autonomously, liberated from the necessity of external affirmation. The interplay of belief with our thoughts and mental faculties creates the essential groundwork for our capacity for independent thought. This empowerment allows us to cultivate a reality that originates from our inner selves, free from the constraints of external influences or limitations.

Science: The Role of Metacognition

The Significance of Metacognition in Scientific Inquiry Metacognition, often described as reflecting on our thinking, highlights our ability to engage in independent thought. This process encompasses understanding oneself and managing one's cognitive activities, enabling a critical assessment and regulation of our beliefs and thought patterns. This reflective capacity underscores the fundamental essence of belief as we consciously navigate our cognitive terrain to mold our perceptions and behaviors.

o **Example: Self-Reflection and Growth**

Reflect on an individual engaging in mindfulness meditation. This practice fosters a deeper understanding of oneself and cultivates the capacity to witness one's thoughts with an open mind, free from judgment. This reflective process allows individuals to thoughtfully assess and enhance their beliefs, fostering personal development and mental clarity.

The Power of Independent Thought

The ability to think independently grants us the power to form our own conclusions, choose our beliefs, and navigate our paths based on those choices. Our inner conscience remains unshackled by external pressures, societal norms, or the judgments of those we hold dear. This autonomy serves as a profound opportunity for personal growth and the exploration of one's true self.

Philosophy: Existentialism and Individual Freedom

Exploring the depths of existence and the essence of personal liberty. Existentialist thinkers such as Jean-Paul Sartre and Friedrich Nietzsche highlighted the significance of personal freedom and the weight of individual responsibility. Sartre's notion of "radical freedom" suggests that we possess complete autonomy in selecting our beliefs and actions, liberated from external limitations. This viewpoint emphasizes the liberating essence of autonomous thinking and the obligation that comes with it.

o **Example: Personal Decision-Making**

Envision an artist who boldly embraces a distinctive style, undeterred by the critiques of their contemporaries. Their autonomous thinking and conviction in their artistic vision propel them to produce unique work, illustrating the strength of self-directed creativity and the bravery to resist external influences.

The Weight of Our Convictions

With this autonomy arises a profound sense of accountability. We exist within a dynamic framework where the interplay of cause and effect, particularly concerning our belief systems, is of paramount importance. We must approach our beliefs with a sense of responsibility for our well-being and the benefit of those around us. This duty invites us to harness the strength of conviction with insight and empathy.

The Ethical Dimensions of Belief Systems

Numerous spiritual practices highlight the importance of employing belief in a manner that aligns with ethical principles. For instance, the notion of "right belief" within Buddhism emphasizes the importance of beliefs that foster ethical behavior, compassion, and the overall well-being of both oneself and others. This ethical framework emphasizes the importance of belief, encouraging individuals to harness their convictions for constructive influence.

o   **Example: Collective Accountability**

Reflect on a business leader who embodies the principles of corporate social responsibility. Their conviction compels them to engage in ethical practices, champion community initiatives, and advocate for sustainability. The mindful application of belief enhances both the organization and the broader community, showcasing the constructive ripple effect of principled values.

Final Thoughts

Belief, an essential component of our cognitive processes, grants us the ability to think autonomously and shape our reality. This autonomy, nonetheless, carries the duty to wield our convictions with wisdom and empathy. By cultivating autonomous thinking and the moral application of our convictions, we can traverse existence with authenticity, intention, and constructive influence. Allow your convictions to steer you in creating a purposeful and enriching path fueled by personal growth and empathy toward those around you.

Key Takeaways

- **Belief as a Foundational Human Capacity:** Belief serves as the cornerstone of our human experience, molding our perceptions and guiding our actions with unwavering conviction.

- **Transcending Scientific Boundaries:** As we move beyond the confines of scientific inquiry, it becomes evident that in moments when empirical understanding wanes, belief emerges as a profound psychological experience—a beacon of hope amidst the uncertainties of existence.

- **Discipline and Freedom:** A mind anchored in a robust belief system serves as the crucible that purifies the spirit, freeing it from the shackles of fear and discord.

- **Selective Cultivation:** Intentional cultivation of our thoughts and discerning information intake empower us to construct belief systems that are formidable instruments for pursuing our aspirations.

- **Action and Validation:** The interplay of action and validation shapes our beliefs, acting as a transformative force that hones our convictions and drives us toward achievement.

- **Self-Mastery:** A cultivated belief system embodies self-mastery, steering us to traverse life with purpose and grace.

- **Humanity's Gift:** The essence of belief stands as a remarkable legacy of our species, granting us the ability to mold our convictions and access vast opportunities for individual development.

- **Inherent Property:** The essence of belief systems lies deeply embedded within the human mind, providing us with the freedom to think independently and the power to mold our realities.

- **The Power of the Unseen:** The framework of belief CgX exemplifies the profound impact of belief—an elusive energy that shapes our existence in ways frequently transcending objective examination. This energy acts as a transformative force, deeply influencing the essence of our being.

- **The Architect of Your Reality:** By integrating the ADM-GENE theory, the CgX belief system presents a holistic approach to personal growth, empowering individuals to navigate their realities, surmount obstacles, and achieve their utmost potential.

- **Cultivating the Creator's Relic:** The CgX framework perceives belief as an intricate blend of privilege and responsibility. This capacity enables us to mold our own experiences, encouraging a thoughtful approach as we embark on a journey of introspection and personal growth.

These essential insights invite you to contemplate the profound influence of belief and its fundamental significance in molding our existence. By consciously nurturing our belief systems with care and accountability, we can utilize this extraordinary capability to traverse life with intention, authenticity, and significant influence. Allow your convictions to illuminate your path, guiding you toward personal mastery and a deeply rewarding experience.

At the Last: Nurture the Relic of the Creator as You Build Your Own Reality

It is essential to acknowledge the individual's significant position in shaping their existence, thoughtfully nurturing the core of the Creator's heritage. The framework, deeply intertwined with the CgX-ADM-GENE theory, offers a fascinating exploration of the psychological phenomenon we refer to as belief. It goes beyond the boundaries of mere science; it serves as an extraordinary "engine of miracles" capable of molding our reality in ways we can scarcely conceive. The essence of that influence presents a captivating mystery, yet CgX enables individuals to shape their realities by fostering a strong belief system.

The Power of Belief: A Gift and a Responsibility

The belief system in CgX possesses a dual nature. Belief is a profound endowment for humanity, granting us the unparalleled liberty to determine our convictions and the boundaries of our acceptance. This privilege carries with it significant responsibility. Our beliefs shape how we see the world, influence our choices, and play a crucial role in creating the realities we experience. Through the thoughtful embrace of the Creator's Relic, we unveil our true potential and advance along this remarkable path of self-exploration and personal fulfillment.

Harnessing the Power for Growth

As articulated in CgX, the essence of belief empowers us to engage with and harness our convictions for transformative progress and self-improvement. This is accomplished by structuring one's thoughts, curating the information we engage with, and taking intentional actions that align with our core beliefs. Through introspection and understanding, we can nurture belief systems that propel us toward remarkable achievements. A focused mind, aligned with steadfast convictions, liberates us from anxiety and turmoil, empowering us to confront life's obstacles with assurance.

The Intrigue Continues: An Endless Journey

The exploration of the belief system within CgX, as it relates to the ADM-GENE hypotheses, captivates the mind with its rich tapestry of secrets yet to be unveiled, quietly shaping the essence of our existence. Though the full scope of this belief remains partially obscured, CgX serves as a beacon, sparking an enduring journey of exploration and understanding. Gaining a deeper understanding of the psychological foundations of belief empowers us to cultivate a meaningful and fulfilling life. This insight empowers us to embody the essence of the Creator in our existence, crafting journeys that lead to a life rich in significance and satisfaction.

Ultimately, cultivating the Relic of the Creator while shaping your reality requires a deep understanding of the significant influence of belief and the importance of wielding it thoughtfully. Embrace this opportunity and duty to consciously craft your existence with purpose and empathy, persistently pursuing development and satisfaction. Allow this insight to illuminate your path as you embark on an enduring quest for self-awareness and growth.

꿼꿼꿼

HARMONIC INHERITANCE: SHAPING THE CGX SYSTEM'S CORE AND INFLUENCING FACTORS

꿼꿼꿼

Orchestrating Mindscapes: The Symphony of CgX System s Evolution and Influence

The Maestro Within: Conducting the Orchestra of Thought

The human mind, a remarkable instrument surpassing the intricacy of any big symphony, is not a static object but a dynamic composition in constant change. Envision yourself as the conductor of this splendid mental landscape, directing the baton of awareness to compose a symphony of ideas. Several instruments influence the music that arises, each fulfilling a certain function in the overarching performance of your existence.

- **The Instrumental Ensemble: Effectors Shaping the CgX System**

  The resounding brass part of this internal orchestra symbolizes environmental forces. These profound experiences make a lasting impression on our comprehension of the world. Social variables intricately shape cultural norms and collective ideas, forming a cohesive context for our narratives. Ingrained in our essence is the subtle yet enduring influence of heredity, reflecting the legacies of previous generations. The forces, referred to as effectors, merge to form the essence of our cognitive processes - the enigmatic Cognitexis (CgX) system.

- **A Subtle Balance: The Dual Nature of Effectors**

  The interaction of effectors is a complicated process characterized by both elegance and potential risk. Although these influences significantly influence the distinctive melody of our cognition, they may also unintentionally alter our established CgX system. Unfiltered or naively accepted information might introduce discordant elements into our cognitive framework, potentially resulting in erroneous perceptions of reality. Consequently, we aim to comprehend these effectors and cultivate the talents required to manage their impact.

- **The Road Ahead: Comprehending and Strengthening the CgX System**

  In the subsequent sections, we shall explore the mechanisms of this remarkable internal orchestra. We will examine each ensemble component, including the environmental, social, and genetic factors and their impact on the CgX system. Our objective is to provide you, the maestro, with the knowledge and tools to:

o **Recognize** the diverse instruments operating within your mental landscape.

o **Evaluate** the caliber of the notes they generate.

o **Integrate** the varied melodies into a cohesive and robust symphony of thoughts.

By comprehending the CgX system and the influences that mold it, we acquire the ability to develop our intellects actively. We can orchestrate our remarkable lives, creating a symphony of thinking that directs us toward insight, fulfillment, and success.

The Immutable Score: The Two Laws Governing Thinking Disposition

Two cardinal laws intertwined in the fabric of creation have massive repercussions on people's thinking. These laws constitute the baton of the invisible conductor who orchestrates the flow of information that shapes our CgX system.

a. **The Law of Physical Heredity: The Immutable Seed**

Our genetic heritage is a fixed world into which we are built, beautifully and precisely written in our DNA. We inherit various characteristics, including eye color and height, and even traits that predispose us to certain qualities or illnesses, just as instruction is given for a rosebud to open into a perfect bloom. This biological inheritance roots us in the past, echoing stories about our ancestors and connecting us to a gigantic lineage. It is genetic threads that we cannot change. But we can respect and honor them by nurturing our physical welfare. The body then becomes an ancient estate, carrying echoes of generations past in every corpuscle, where the law of physical heredity and genetics is the seed for the core equations of the CgX system. From this base, the characteristics of the thinking machinery -our thought pattern -start to sprout and take shape; these two are the predeterminant factors.

b. Law of Social Heredity: The Alchemical Modifier

The human mind is not like a script written in advance: it is very plastic. The law of social heredity acts as the alchemical modifier in this lifelong thought experiment, leading to limitless abilities. This law symbolizes the symphony of influences on the outside that mold and modifies the CgX system throughout our lifetime. Our thinking processes are constantly changed and improved through education, experiences, and a constant bombardment of stimuli. Think of a good alchemist who produces gold from base metal. The same power lies in the law of social heredity; we have to change our genetic makeup through the enrichment that we prefer to undergo. Social heredity, as an essential factor of derivatization of the CgX system, allows us to go beyond, guide, control, and modify the influence of our genetic support. It is the symphony of external influences, education, experiences, and impulses of thought produced by external impulses, especially those received through the following major processes of the environment.

The Grand Orchestra of Experience: Shaping the CgX System

The law of social heredity acts like the conductor's baton in leading the grand symphony of outer influences in and through our CgX system during our lifetime. Like different instruments, each playing a different tune, they all contribute to the incessant stream of information that polishes our core thinking processes.

1. **Education:** Schools are crucibles for knowledge, where neural pathways are hammered, almost like a sculptor slowly molding clay. We absorb wisdom and learn the art of critical

thinking. Practical Application: Every day, make it a point to raise questions about information. Perhaps after reading an article or watching a documentary, one may ask, "What assumptions do they make here? How does this align or conflict with what I already know?

2. **Cultural Immersion:** The cultural norms and customs we experience are like interlaced threads in a complex tapestry, forming a distinctive pattern in our worldview. Every exposure, a clandestine revelation transmitted through history, influences our comprehension of the universe and stimulates a need to elucidate its enigmas.

3. **Religion:** Temples, mosques, and cathedrals all stand in holy testament to faith, building the inner sanctuaries of our minds. Religious rituals and scriptures can guide our moral compass and encourage a search for something greater than what can be experienced through the senses. Personal Application Reflect on your central beliefs and how these guide you in your choices. You may wish to write in your journal about how your beliefs influence what actions you take each day or how they get you through times of challenge.

4. **Social Interactions:** The busy marketplace, with mutual confidence and laughter, is in the weave of society. Social interactions among persons allow us to absorb norms, biases, and collective dreams that shape our reality. Practical Application: Try to consciously interact more with people with different perspectives than you do through community groups, online forums, or simply striking up a conversation with a neighbor. You might learn about some things you don't know.

5. **Traditions:** Ancestral whispers carried through generations— grandmother's recipes, folklore, vibrant festivals—comfort us with the reassurance of continuity. These traditions unlock the treasure chest of our heritage. In a more practical application,

preserving and celebrating family traditions is fine as long as you also consider how they might be adapted in today's world. Perhaps you start a new family tradition or take an old one and fit it into more modern values. It is this balance that will help you connect with your heritage.

6. **Media Consumption:** Information and entertainment to ring in our ears with the vast symphony of noise. Yet, even as conductors must make informed decisions about which instruments to highlight and which to mute, we should be critical information consumers. Now Try It: Take some time each week to review what you have watched, read, and listened to. Consider stopping subscriptions or unfollowing any source that contributes to your negativity or spreading misinformation, and find something that educates, inspires, or positively challenges you.

7. **Technological Progressions:** Technology, an ever-evolving force, upsets the status quo and brings novel instruments into the symphony of experience. These innovations, from the printing press to the internet, revolutionize our access to knowledge, interpersonal connections, and worldview. Similar to the introduction of a new tune in a symphony, we must adjust our cognitive frameworks to align with this ever-evolving environment.

8. **Political Economy:** The rhythm of administration and trade resonates like a commanding drumming amid the big ensemble. The repercussions of debates, uprisings, and persistent quests for justice permeate history, influencing our civic awareness. Engagement with other policies, ideologies, and economic systems enhances our comprehension of the world and our role within it, simultaneously fostering our curiosity in the complexities of power and societal frameworks.

9. **Business, Professional, and Occupational Habits:** Productivity is a strange form of music in the world; it is more or less a symphony of productivity. By occupation, we inherit the traditions of labor, creativity, and attainment. Application: Take some time to reflect on the arc of your career. Are you building habits and competencies that align with the future work for which you are aiming? Maybe you need more learning time, a call to your professional network, or more time to mentor others. This proactive stance would make great strides in assuring your professional life has a full share in the great symphony of human accomplishment.

Remember!

Taking charge of your CgX system, if you are now better equipped to understand the instruments and their melodies, you can once again become an active contributor to creating your own CgX system. Call to Action: Think about your own life's orchestra. What have been the influences at play in your melody, and how do you control the play of this melody? Choose one area of your life, whether education, your use of media, or your social environment, and make one - just one - change consciously.

Whether learning any new skill, curating your media diet, or seeking out diverse perspectives, you are creating a beautiful, harmonious symphony of thought that guides your life through all these actions.

Illustrations and Anecdotes: Weaving the Tapestry of Thought

Consider life a magnificent tapestry in which the threads of genetic inheritance cross with the rich patterns formed by social influences. We are all artists adding colors to the ancestral sketches passed down through generations. Look closely, and you might see in your entrepreneurial drive the pioneering spirit of an ancestor reflected or the storytelling talent of the bard echoing in creative writing.

- **Defying the Script: A Symphony of Willpower**

  Our history has, and will always be, replete with individuals who break through the constraints of their genetic scripts to compose their personal symphonies of accomplishment. Consider Ludwig van Beethoven, an artist who lost his hearing and yet continued to generate heart-ripping music. The musical genius within him, from the threads of his genetic endowment, found refinement in the cultural inputs of his era. The product? A career of innovation that altered classical music forever.

  The immobility wrought by ALS on Stephen Hawking is another testimony to what the human spirit can do. His awesome mind gift from his genes was honed further by education and steeping in scientific thought. Such a combination of nature and nurture enabled him to uncover some secrets of black holes and give us insights into the universe that few have.

- **Exploring Your Symphonic Legacy: A Conductor's Invitation**

  Each of us has a unique symphony of inheritance, a tapestry interwoven by the threads of nature and nurture. Through such understanding, we can each play the role of a conductor in guiding our CgX systems with purpose and intention.

- **Embrace the Echoes of the Past**

  Consider what the influences that vibrate within you are. Maybe you are innately curious about the world around you- a murmur from some ancestor, the explorer. Or perhaps your artistic abilities reflect the talents of some long-ago craftsperson. These ancestral notes form the basis of your personal symphony.

- **Harmonize with the Future Crescendo**

  Think about cultural influences, educational experiences, and social interactions that formed your distinctive point of view. These are the instruments currently playing in the orchestra of experience, which is you. How can you learn from them? How might you challenge them?

By tuning your CgX system to the echoes of the past and the crescendos of the future, one can compose a life symphony that informs and inspires the steps one takes toward fulfillment and achievement. Now, take a minute to listen to the music within. What instruments do you hear, and what melody are they playing? The awareness of the conductor and the composer's creativity- the power lies within you to create a symphony of thought that can change the world.

Unveiling the Hidden Orchestra: Heredity and Social Effectors in the CgX System

The human mind is an intriguing arena where personal beliefs blossom like a magnificent symphony within the sanctified realms of awareness. Every conviction we possess resembles a unique note, resonating with the collective human experience. However, a nuanced inquiry persists inside this orchestral magnificence: Are these melodies indeed our own creations, or are they simply reverberations from our forebears, educators, and the culture we reside in?[6]

---

[6] Refer to "Reality Transurfing" by Vadim Zelan, Book number 4: about herd thinking and overcoming their collective process.

The Symphony of Belief: Echoes and Originality

In the depths of our minds, beliefs vibrate like a symphony within a cathedral. Each belief resonates with a deliberate note aligning with the extensive symphony of human experience. Amidst this grand crescendo, a poignant inquiry arises: Are the melodies we assert as our own genuinely original, or are they simply echoes — refrains appropriated from our families, mentors, and the culture surrounding us?

While shimmering with the illusion of uniqueness, our individual beliefs often find their roots in the vast tapestry of human thought woven by those who came before us. They are reflections, sometimes distorted, of the convictions held by those who walk beside us and those who paved the path we tread. As we navigate life's intricate labyrinth, the true challenge lies in discerning the authenticity of our beliefs. Which notes resonate from the wellspring of our own soul, and which are echoes borrowed from the grand symphony of humanity?

Unearthing the Authentic Self

This necessitates a nuanced balance between introspection and attentiveness. We must value the insights derived from the community while fostering autonomous thought. It is during tranquil periods, apart from the cacophony of the crowd, that we may genuinely heed the murmurs of our inner voice. In isolation, we may uncover ideas that align with our fundamental essence, free from extraneous pressures.

It is essential to recognize the unsettling reality that a significant portion of what we assert as our own beliefs may, in fact, mirror the genuine and, at times, disingenuous perspectives of those closest to us. This reflection compels us to delve into the depths of our inherited convictions, uncovering the fundamental nature of our authentic selves.

Composer and Archaeologist: A Journey of Self-Creation

In this path of self-discovery, we serve as both composers and archaeologists. We create a distinctive melody while concurrently uncovering the genuine principles that shape our identity. This endeavor necessitates bravery, as it compels us to depart from the echo chamber and join the domain of original creation, where our personal convictions may prominently resonate with clarity and intent.

Harmony Unveiled: Navigating the Young Mind's CgX Orchestra[7]

Recent advancements in neuroscience provide intriguing insight into the functioning of the human brain. Imagine a symphony, rather than a straight tune, whereby visual experience emerges through a multifaceted interaction of processing cycles. Like repetitive musical motifs, these loops interlace the essence of our conscious experience. Forward processing, which involves the preliminary interpretation of information, is interwoven with horizontal connections that facilitate the association of similar concepts. Feedback loops, like a conductor returning a composition segment, enhance our comprehension.

World of Perceptual Development

A group of researchers has reported in recent research on the world of perceptual development, particularly focusing on the dynamic process of recurrent processing in visual perception. The phenomenon to be studied is called "backward masking," where a brief visual stimulus—a fleeting perceptual process in vision—is

---

[7] For further information, refer to "Perception of invisible masked objects in early infancy" - https://www.ncbi.nlm.nih.gov/pmc/articles/PMC8271636/

obscured by a successive image called a mask. Disruption of feedback loops presents a strong sensory illusion: under such conditions, an initial stimulus becomes nearly invisible.

The test subjects were infants, all less than seven months old. Like novice composers trying to navigate a complex new score, their young minds confronted a different challenge: immature visual masking processes. These infants could see objects being masked from adult perception—that is, their perceptual "hidden harmonies" were uncovered—whereas older children and adults could not. Because their feedback loops were underdeveloped, the masking effect did not blind them to invisible details to more mature visual processing systems.

A Cautionary Crescendo: The Imprint of Social Heredity

Yet, this early perception advantage has challenges of its own. The development of the CgX system filters information all day and night in these little minds. So, they absorb the world around them bit by bit, while self-reflection is that faint introspective melody still developing. The world waits for a blank white canvas upon which the strokes of external influence paint upon it, guided by a small star called curiosity.

Herein lies the crucial warning: the stamp of social heredity. Just as a conductor decides on the character of the symphony, the environment plays its leading role in shaping the developmental symphony of these tender young minds. As caretakers and teachers, we must ensure that this developmental symphony rings out in harmony, not discord. Early experience and social influence will play a big role in these children's future cognitive and emotional development.

By thoughtfully leading them on that perceptual journey, we can nurture their potential into a future symphony rich in wisdom, curiosity, and a lifelong pursuit of truth.

The Curious Case of the Fledgling Composers:

Envision a young infant as an emerging composer, avidly assimilating every note and detail of the immense symphony of existence. Their CgX technology operates with exceptional efficiency, assimilating all surrounding elements. However, the capacity to introspect on their ideas and experiences—a vital talent for maneuvering through the intricacies of the world—has not yet completely matured. Curiosity, the catalyst for autonomous learning, remains in its nascent phase. Their experience of the world is sober and unembellished, reflecting their purity. Nonetheless, this openness renders children vulnerable to external influences, especially the significant social factors that impact their early development. As caretakers, we must ensure that these external effects foster a harmonious and well-developed CgX system.

The Enigma of Indigo: A Different Melody in the Symphony of the Mind[8]

In the vast research of cognitive development, one theory is as captivating as it is controversial: the Indigo Children. Through the hallowed imagination of their proponents, the young minds possess one variant, let's call it CgX' system: a mental fortress standing aloof and impervious to the influences of the ambient environment in shaping our subconscious mind.

Picture a group of children described to radiate an aura of deep indigo. Wrapped in the veneer of New Age mystique, these kids are said to possess an armamentarium of traits defying easy explanation, including an intuition heightened to near-telepathic ability and profound empathy bordering on an almost supernatural connection to the universe. Or is it that their CgX' systems march to a different tune, in some hidden inner sanctum protected from

---

[8] For further information, refer to "Indigo children" -
https://en.wikipedia.org/wiki/Indigo_children

the expectations of the world and the pressures their communities put upon them, enabling them to dance through life in rhythm to some different conductor's baton?

The story of the Indigo Children was first articulated during the 1970s and then through books and films, one of being the frontrunners in human evolution: empathetic, creative, and one stride further than the rest. The story, if it may be called that, of Indigo Children, first articulated in the 1970s and popularized through books and films, was that they were the forerunners in human evolution: sensitive, creative, and a step ahead of the rest. But this again comes under the ambit of pseudoscience since there is a lack of empirical data to prove the existence of such idiosyncratic capability.

Critics say it has become a convenient label for some parents to explain away their children's learning differences without seeking professional help. They say the purported traits of the Indigo Children are so vague and general that they could apply to a wide array of personalities, a kind of Forer effect, in which general descriptions generate a high degree of self-identification.

Integrating Fact and Fascination

The Indigo phenomenon can only be approached with a mixture of disbelief and fascination, considering the complexity of consciousness and CgX development involved. This alone reminds us of our human tendency toward pattern-seeking, seeking order in chaos, and moving toward the extraordinary. Whether Indigo Children are truly harbingers of a new cognitive dawn or simply one more reflection of our own urges toward something different, their story beckons us to look at latent potentials buried inside the human mind.

In doing so, we must also navigate these intriguing waters with a critical eye, steering our quest for knowledge onto scientific grounds.

After all, the journey is as important as the answers we seek, stirred by this constant hum of curiosity that guides us to the destination of truth. Thus, the symphony of human development continues to be composed, note by note, with every question adding one more layer of complexity to this grand exploration of the human mind.

Can Indigo Children Process Information Differently?

- **The question continues:** do Indigo children have a distinct CgX' system, impervious to external factors? Possibly one that provides them with remarkable control over external subconscious influences?

- **Beyond the Designation:** The notion of Indigo Children presents the compelling prospect of an alternate CgX' system — a cognitive stronghold possibly resistant to external influences. This mechanism may give people remarkable control over their surroundings' subconscious influences.

- **A Spark of Wonder:** Indigo children are intriguing beings spoken of in subdued tones and enveloped in an aura of mystery. Myths describe their enhanced intuition, deep empathy, and intrinsic bond with the universe. Can their CgX systems genuinely challenge established norms? Envision an inner sanctum resistant to cultural influences and communal tides. They may possess a metaphorical baton, orchestrating a distinctive symphony outside the world of the commonplace. If such extraordinary intellects exist, they possess the capability to release latent human potential.

Genetic Resilience: The CgX System s Suitability and the Fabric of Free Thought

The Tapestry of Thought: Weaving Resilience and Free Will

Consider the intricate tapestry of human cognition, wherein genetic resilience comes alive through brilliant golden threads. These threads are interwoven within the very fabric of our being, determining the CgX system, the internal loom upon which we weave our perceptions of the world. Stop and consider for a moment: How resilient do you perceive your own mental loom to be? Is there something in your genetic makeup that has granted you an added armor of resilience buffer between you and those forces form without compelling you to fit into the molds of belief and perception?

Bastions of Free Thought:

Consider the CgX system as a kind of loom upon which the intricate tapestry of the mind is woven. To them, this loom is made of threads unyielding and strong: CgX seems to come off as a bulwark of resistance against storms of tradition, peer pressure, and dogmas of society. Now, take a minute to ponder: Have you ever felt your mind stand firm against the gales of conformity, deeply rooted, indeed, within bedrock free thinkers? These resilient minds are the mavericks, the trailblazers who take charge of their mental journeys, navigating challenges with unwavering determination. Their CgX systems, much like ancient oaks, bend under the winds of influence but remain unbroken.

These rare individuals challenge established norms that have told the melodies of thought for so long. They write new harmonies that ring across time and inspire change. Consider your own experiences: Have you ever challenged conventional thinking and felt empowered? Genetic resilience could give you that unique perspective to see the world through a lens unclouded by external control.

Not All Looms Are Created Equal:

Equally important is to be in a position and realize the difference in human experience. Not everyone is cut from the same cloth of resiliency. Many minds are shaped and molded by the prevailing winds of their surroundings: religion, culture, and societal burdens. Do you not notice how these influences have shaped your cognitive canvas? Yet, once in a while, that kid or the individual who simply cannot be explained comes along: one who brushes off all influences applied to them from outside and decides to take control of their own mind and set their course. That individual would be the epitome of free thought, a shining star for the future of free thinking.

Reflect upon your life journey and how your CgX system has been sculpted through the dance between genetic resilience and environmental influences. Now it's your turn: How will you marshal your strengths to keep free thinking alive and find your way through the challenges of contemporary life? As you ponder this, you continue to develop a sense of your own mental tapestry and weave a story of your resilience in striving for independence of thought.

Celebrating the Symphony of Individuality

As we explore the complexities of the CgX system and its influence on our cognitive framework, we must acknowledge the genetic resilience that promotes the capacity for independent thought. This reflects the remarkable diversity of human experience and the inherent capacity for creativity and advancement inside our DNA. We must cultivate these seeds of freedom since they embody the potential for a future where the harmony of human thinking consists not of echoes but of original, lively songs that honor the distinctiveness of each individual mind.

Cultivating the Symphony of Independent Thought

- **Threads of Strength:** Genetic inheritance significantly influences the CgX system. Certain individuals possess a resilient "loom" — a CgX system that remarkably tolerates environmental stressors. These tenacious individuals remain steadfast against tradition, peer influence, and societal norms.

- **A Spectrum of Susceptibility:** It is crucial to acknowledge that children exhibit varying degrees of susceptibility to environmental stimuli. Although most people are influenced by their surroundings, a select minority emerge as genuine free thinkers—those who take command of their own intellectual paths. Their CgX systems have a remarkable capacity to flex without fracturing under external pressures. These remarkable people challenge conventional standards, creating evocative compositions that echo through centuries.

- **The Power of Genetic Diversity:** The CgX system exemplifies the significance of genetic variation. By acknowledging and cultivating the distinct differences within our people, we access a substantial pool of resilience and ingenuity. Examine how varying genetic compositions might affect our reactions to illnesses, environmental adversities, or economic recessions. This intrinsic variety is not alone a biological reality but a cultural advantage, igniting the creative impetus that propels human advancement.[9]

The CgX system enhances comprehension of genetic variety, enabling cultivating a culture that celebrates individual differences instead of fearing them. This cultivates an environment of autonomous thinking, where varied viewpoints amalgamate to form a more profound and robust

---

[9] More information about the concept of Genetic Diversity can be found in this article: Genetic Diversity: Sources, Threats, and Conservation
https://link.springer.com/referenceworkentry/10.1007/978-3-319-95981-8_53

tapestry of human experience. The CgX system functions as a conductor, orchestrating the diverse elements of our genetic variety into a cohesive representation of human potential.

The Tapestry of Resilience: Threads of Strength Woven Within

A Gallery of Potential: Imagine a huge gallery, its walls full of children's portraits, each canvas pulsating with a vibrant indigo hue. Their large and luminous eyes would mirror a universe of possibilities; with every stare, the resiliency stitched intrinsically into their genetic makeup would be revealed. Like budding artists, these children can paint their masterpieces on life's canvas.

The Child's Wonder: Consider the narrative of a small child seated on a verdant hill beneath the celestial expanse of the night sky. The child, filled with pure curiosity, delineates patterns among the stars—constellations invisible to the average observer. This child, endowed with a CgX system resistant to conformity, discerns an unspoken cosmic tale. The Child's intellect, liberated from cultural constraints, can distinctively navigate the cosmos.

Echoes of Rebellion: Reflect on the sagas of historical renegades-Galileo peering up to the stars with his telescope, Hypatia trying to piece together the mechanisms of the universe from the libraries of Alexandria, Malala-a solid soldier facing the winds of oppression. All had a CgX system unwilling to be burdened by its weight that soared into history. Free thought personified, their voices rose above the chorus of sameness in powerful melodies composed.

An Expedition of Self-Discovery: I encourage you, readers, to engage in an exploration of self-discovery and investigate the intricacies of your own genetic composition. Examine the extensive collection here, identifying the notes of perseverance that connect with you. Heed the faint reverberations of insurrection that have influenced your ancestry. Within human DNA resides a composition awaiting performance—a distinctive tune of cognition and perception. Awaken the latent capacity for independent thought inside you.

The Spark of Curiosity: Imagine a classroom where a teacher introduces a highly difficult problem. Most children would view this problem with apprehension, while the eyes of this particular child light up. This child's CgX does not bear the weight of possible defeat and thus is free to spark curiosity and creativity. Their resilient mind is free to travel to uncharted territories, seeking solutions beyond what is commonly seen.

A Variety of Voices: Consider a society where the cumulative echo of beliefs and convictions ripples down the lane of time. But then, coming through this chorus, there is the distinct sound of a voice that sings another tune- a voice that speaks for the rare individual whose beliefs are not an echo but an original composition. Consider a society that celebrates this tapestry of voices, where every different perspective adds depth to human thought's grand symphony.

᠅᠅᠅

HARMONY IN SOCIETY AND INDIVIDUAL LIBERTY

᠅᠅᠅

This section effectively establishes the foundation for a discourse on free thinking and individual agency within the framework of the CgX system. The human mind, an extraordinary apparatus, is at the core of an enduring discourse. Should it resemble a free-flowing river, carving its own course through varied intellectual terrains? Or should it be a precisely designed canal directed by a singular, comprehensive vision? This conflict is central to social heredity and its impact on the "human cognitive apparatus," as you observed.

Introduction: The Symphony of Freedom and Constraint

One interesting debate has played out on the great stage of human cognition: should our thinking machinery be like a free-flowing river, its course through varied landscapes, self-carving, or a precisely engineered canal, its course determined by a single directing mind? The following study attempts to investigate that symphony of thought where individual notes fall into harmony with the collective melodies that shape our notion of the world.

Underpinning this debate is the question of how to develop human thinking machinery that supports freedom and alignment. Should thought processes be completely unfettered to go where no one has gone before, even if the risk is that individuals become misled away from societal values? Alternatively, should they be tempered by a set of guiding principles that result in a level of conformity but at the risk of individual creativity?

One must strive for a golden mean between these two extremes. Suppose the machinery of thought were to run riot and without control. On the one hand, this may be advantageous in as much as a diversity of views and diverse ways of looking at things may flourish in such an atmosphere; on the other hand, it may result in a maze of beliefs conflicting with one another and disrupting social cohesion. On the other hand, thought machinery that is strictly controlled would have its share of stability and uniformity in society, but progress and individual creativity would also be sacrificed.

Finding Harmony in the Symphony

The solution may reside in identifying the optimal balance within this metaphorical symphony. It is essential to develop a cognitive framework that embodies both adaptability and knowledge. This entails fostering an environment where individuals are motivated to engage with various ideas and viewpoints while simultaneously providing them with the necessary tools to critically assess the information they come across. By cultivating an environment that encourages open inquiry and critical thinking, we can shape a society in which individuals are empowered to think independently, all the while appreciating the significance of shared values and the collective good.

The Role of Social Heredity

Social heredity refers to passing cultural norms and beliefs from generation to generation, shaping even the very mechanism of our thinking. Since childhood, the values, traditions, and beliefs inculcated into our brains work as initial programming. This guides our perceptions concerning how we view the world and our thought processes. While social heredity no doubt furnishes a very useful foundation on which to start the struggle with life's difficulties, it is well to remember that such heredity has serious limitations. Just as a river, if its banks are too rigid, it loses the power to flow, so our thinking machinery may become ossified if we indiscriminatingly follow the grooves with which social thought has been molded.

The Path to Liberation

The liberation of human cognitive processes does not stem from total autonomy from societal influences; instead, it is rooted in the cultivation of critical thinking skills. By questioning, analyzing, and synthesizing the information at our disposal, we can liberate ourselves from the constraints of uncritical conformity and carve out our distinct trajectories within the expansive landscape of human intellect.

The path to liberation necessitates a dedication to continuous learning and an openness to intellectual humility. Recognizing the limitations inherent in our knowledge and perspectives allows us to embrace the enriching possibilities that diverse viewpoints offer. Ultimately, the genuine emancipation of human cognitive processes resides not in solitude but in the synergistic interaction between personal inquiry and communal knowledge.

Part 1 - Engineering the CgX System for Liberation and Effectiveness

This section delves into the critical task of building a liberated and effective CgX system – the internal machinery that shapes our thoughts and perceptions. We begin by examining the dangers of a single, dominant mode of thinking and then explore the importance of fostering free will to unlock the full potential of the human mind.

1. The Tyranny of the Monolithic Mind: A Symphony Stifled

Envision a magnificent concert hall, where the stage, once teeming with life and energy, now stands as a stark and empty void. The room has ceased to resonate with the harmonious blend of instruments, each adding its distinctive voice to the overarching composition. In contrast, the atmosphere is permeated by a continuous, unvarying sound, a singular tone resonating without cessation. This restrictive intellectual environment exemplifies the perils of a "monolithic mind," a singular mode of thought that undermines the fundamental nature of human cognition: its remarkable diversity.

A Tapestry Unraveled: The Cost of Conformity

A reality dominated by a singular ideology, where a specific set of beliefs, cultural practices, and artifacts is imposed as the sole truth, would inevitably lead to the disintegration of the diverse and intricate fabric of human existence. The essence of independent thought, a catalyst for personal exploration that ignites the flames of creativity, diminishes in the face of enforced uniformity. Individuals are reduced to mere tools within a predetermined composition, their distinct harmonies muted by the burdensome authority of an imposed arrangement. The ensuing mental stagnation resembles a symphony in which all musicians are confined to a singular note—devoid of life, flat, and lacking the dramatic tension that has the power to awaken the spirit.

History's Echoes: A Cautionary Tale

Reflect on the events that befell different civilizations throughout history when a tendency for intellectual conformity took hold. An overarching and excessively authoritative ideology stifled discourse and opposition, consequently hindering innovation and progress. The limitation of diverse thinking led to a stagnation in scientific progress, while the arts devolved into mere imitations of their dominant forms. The essence of humanity, yearning for exploration and discovery, ultimately revealed itself as constrained by the inflexible confines of a singular perspective.

The Kaleidoscope Mind: A Symphony of Perspectives

The human mind embodies a rich tapestry of experiences and ideas, reflecting a vibrant spectrum rather than a singular note; it is a complex entity capable of an endless array of thoughts and perspectives. Arrange these concepts into a captivating symphony, where each instrument—distinct in its tone and viewpoint—merges together in perfect harmony. Amidst this symphony of rivalry, within the rich tapestry of perspectives where thoughts collide and refine one another, we uncover the profound potential of human intellect. Similar to the delicate harmony among various instruments in a grand orchestra, this intricate dance of ideas unveils new realms, ignites creative expressions, and ultimately contributes to the very evolution of what it means to be human.

2. The Divine Gift of Free Will

Indeed, there exists no greater tragedy than the loss of the inherent right to govern one's own thoughts. The profound Creator of existence bestowed upon us a remarkable endowment: the capacity for autonomous reflection. Within the depths of our consciousness exist expansive, uncharted realms and dimensions that await our exploration. This intrinsic capacity for exploration, this fundamental drive to seek knowledge and understanding, empowers us to take control of our own fate.

Think of the giant canvas, which is a representation of our life. Each thought our brains develop would be one stroke on the canvas of our lives. Let us yield this divine palette not as conducted by one mind but with the freedom to create symphonies of thought that would echo through the ages. Freeing the CgX system lets the human journey unfold as each person chooses their own direction in an expression that is peculiarly their own.

The Symphony of Self-Authorship

Every thought we decide to engage with, every path we opt to investigate, contributes a distinct note to the singular melody that defines our existence. Through the cultivation of free will and critical thinking, we enable ourselves to create symphonies that echo throughout history. The essence of the human experience lies not in unquestioning compliance but in the empowerment to investigate, innovate, and forge our own destinies.

In essence, this section argues for a CgX system that is both:

- **Free:** Unburdened by the constraints of a singular thought process, empowered to explore diverse ideas and perspectives.

- **Effective:** Equipped with the critical faculties necessary to analyze information, form independent judgments, and navigate the complexities of the world.

3. Shattering the Chains: A Call to Unchain the Mind

The journey towards a robust CgX system requires a pivotal action: liberating oneself from the constraints of mental limitations. The concept of social heredity, which refers to the transmission of ideas and beliefs through generations, can occasionally manifest as a nuanced form of mental servitude. The inherited cognitive frameworks we adopt, when not critically examined, may transform into unseen constraints that hinder our capacity for autonomous reasoning.

The Inherent Yearning for Freedom

Nevertheless, the essence of humanity is fundamentally characterized by a spirit of rebellion. The intricate web of connections within our brains, often referred to as neural constellations, seeks a form of liberation. There exists a profound desire for the autonomy to navigate unexplored realms, to create innovative avenues of intellectual inquiry, and to question the prevailing paradigms. It is through this profound desire that we discover the motivation to liberate our constrained thoughts.

Embracing the Power of Inquiry

Through the cultivation of critical thinking and the encouragement of an inquisitive mindset, we initiate the journey toward emancipation. By liberating ourselves from the

mental constraints of social norms and inherited dogma, we
can truly harness the potential of our CgX systems. This
liberation transcends individual aspirations; it represents a
collective effort that lays the groundwork for a more
enlightened and progressive society.

A Symphony of Liberated Minds

Envision a society characterized by intellectual liberation,
where individuals are empowered to investigate, challenge
norms, and carve out their distinct trajectories. This represents
the symphony of liberated minds – a beautiful harmony crafted
from diverse perspectives, each enriching the grand orchestra
of human thought. Much like a river that, when freed from its
constraints, forges its own course and enriches the
environment around it, liberated minds possess the remarkable
capacity to cultivate innovative concepts and advance societal
progress.

4. The Man-Made Shackles: Dismantling Social Heredity

One major obstacle greets anyone who desires to free the CgX
system: social heredity. Social heredity describes how culture,
beliefs, and ideas are passed between generations. It is a kind
of bond that provides a grounding by which humans may
comprehend much about life, but it can easily be used to
suppress critical thinking.

A Distortion of Nature's Harmony

It is in flagrant violation of natural law to take away, through
social heredity, this prerogative of independent thought from
individuals. The violation constitutes a man-made tragedy, for
it dissolves the harmonious symphony that characterizes
human thought into chaotic discord. Imagine a beautiful

garden where each flower blossoms into its variety, adding its distinctive vibrancy in color and fragrance. Heredity in society is used as a means of control, forcing each plant to grow into the self-same sterile shape, monotony, and uniformity-never permitting anything beautiful coming from such diversity to pop through.

The Inherent Rebel

Our innate curiosity, a born drive to question and investigate, rebels against this artificially imposed constraint. We are cosmic revolutionaries who will never stop pushing the frontiers of conventional thinking. Social programming can try to shape us into predetermined forms, but each of us is kindled by the spark of free-ranging investigation.

Restoring the Symphony's Melody

Through the deconstruction of the fabricated limitations imposed by social heredity, we have the opportunity to reintegrate the genuine elements into the harmonious composition of human cognition. The distinct experiences and perspectives of each individual mind contribute a valuable layer of complexity to the broader tapestry of understanding. Envision the symphony enriched by the dynamic harmonies of autonomous reasoning. Every voice and perspective plays a crucial role in creating a richer and more intricate harmony. [10]

5. Decentralization: A Symphony of Diverse Thought

The investigation into the preservation of cognitive diversity presents an intriguing perspective when considering the principle of decentralization. This section emphasizes the

---

[10] Social thinking is not a natural process of human thinking development. In fact, it is a man-made tragedy against nature to control a mass of humanity.

potential function of public school systems as a safeguard against the perils of a singular, monolithic perspective.

A Marketplace of Ideas

The strength of decentralization lies in its very structure. Whereas in a centralized system, a single entity can stipulate what is taught, a decentralized system makes it virtually impossible for any single group to exert control over information flow. This actually creates a quite dynamic marketplace of ideas in which a variety of perspectives can more easily engage each other. This can be done by turning a lecture hall into an interactive marketplace where students are challenged with various perspectives. The result is intellectual cross-pollination, where they can arrive at a more profound and complex realization of the issues involved.

The Conductor-less Symphony

In a decentralized learning environment, one observes the absence of a singular "conductor" exerting absolute authority over the collective symphony of ideas. Each individual student contributes their unique voice, much like a distinct instrument within an orchestra. This collaborative approach cultivates a more harmonious and dynamic intellectual exchange. Each viewpoint and every detail holds significance, enhancing the collective depth of the work.

A Celebration of Diversity

This is in utter contrast to any system where one set of beliefs would be imposed on all minds. In such a system, the CgX system is greatly reduced and impeded from exploring a wide range of possibilities and thoughts independently. Decentralization, instead, rejoices in this orchestra of thought in all its complexity. It provides a platform where the CgX system will flourish in all its diversity and nurture a generation of critical thinkers and independent minds.

6. The Crucible of Reason: Forging Universal Truths

The path to a truly empowered CgX system undergoes a significant metamorphosis—shifting from externally imposed beliefs to the natural development of universal ideas. This final section advocates for establishing an educational environment that fosters the development of enduring truths, utilizing the powers of rational thought and critical examination.

Beyond Imposition: The Alchemy of the Mind

This critiques the enforcement of universal concepts—those essential truths that surpass cultural and generational boundaries. Rather, it envisions a world where intellects transform unrefined understanding into the precious essence of insight. The CgX system emerges as a transformative crucible where concepts are subjected to intense scrutiny and harmonized with our unique cognitive frameworks. Within that framework, rational thought holds the highest authority. Ideas are permitted to circulate and establish themselves in the rich soil of reflective thought and unrestrained exploration.

The Power of Organic Discovery

The essence of the message is clear: the imposition of universality is unwarranted. When the developing intellect is given the opportunity to discern general truths through personal exploration, these truths transform from mere abstract concepts into integral components of one's inner cognitive framework. This natural progression fosters a deeper understanding and a more genuine commitment to these fundamental concepts. By permitting the natural unfolding of our thoughts, we nurture a harmonious expression that resonates more profoundly in its genuineness.

The Fruits of Independent Thought

Envision a classroom transformed into a dynamic laboratory, where the pursuit of knowledge unfolds through active intellectual exploration rather than mere transmission of information. Students engage with intricate concepts, utilizing critical thinking skills to discern fact from fiction and truth from dogma. By engaging in independent thought, individuals cultivate their own comprehension of the world, assimilating universal truths not as dictated doctrines but as the outcomes of their own intellectual endeavors.

7. Untrammeled Thinkers: Managing Information Sources

We must thoughtfully curate all primary sources of intellectual inspiration—including newspapers, radio, educational institutions, and literature—so that individuals are equipped to critically engage with and either accept or reject the ideas presented through these channels. As a result, every community member is granted the chance to participate as independent thinkers, employing their intellects in alignment with the Creator's design, and this freedom must be preserved.

Information sources embody a cohesive integration of varied viewpoints. Foster an environment that promotes individual expression while preserving decision-making autonomy. As active contributors to the auditory landscape, we consciously navigate the spectrum between harmonious melodies and dissonant sounds. Let us celebrate the liberation of our intellect, shaping our distinct stories, as the Creator grants us the privilege of cognitive independence.

8. The Sculptor Within: Fault and the CgX System

The notion of "fault" presents an intriguing perspective when examined through the lens of the innovative CgX system. This passage critiques the inclination to attribute shortcomings in personal cognition to external systems.

Beyond the Tools: The Sculptor's Responsibility

Envision a sculptor diligently shaping a remarkable statue with precision and care. The selected stone may exhibit certain imperfections, and the chisel serves merely as a tool in the creative process. However, should the ultimate creation fail to meet the anticipated ideal, the responsibility rests not with external factors but rather with the sculptor's expertise and conceptualization. In a parallel manner, the excerpt indicates that when an individual's reasoning displays deficiencies, it stems from self-imposed constraints within their CgX system rather than an external influence enforcing erroneous logic.

The Chisel of Critical Thinking

Attributing faulty thinking to social heredity or any external system that may have influenced our initial perspectives is misguided. It is imperative for individuals to actively engage in the process of cultivating their own mental environment. This aligns with the concept of the CgX system as a fluid and continuously developing construct. We do not simply absorb information; we possess the metaphorical chisel of critical thinking, empowering us to actively refine our understanding by dismantling the biases and fallacies that can obscure our judgment. By adopting critical analysis, we can enhance our CgX system, evolving it from a mechanism constrained by external factors into a robust vehicle for independent thought.

The Mystery of the Unfinished Masterpiece

The investigation into the faults present within the CgX system unveils an intriguing layer of complexity. Much like a sculptor wrestling with the vision of the final form concealed within a block of stone, we find ourselves contending with the constraints of our present comprehension. The potential of the CgX system is an area of continuous investigation, akin to the evolving nature of a sculptor's masterpiece. As we cultivate our critical thinking abilities and interrogate our assumptions, we progressively enhance this internal framework, guiding us toward realizing its complete potential.

9. The Alchemist's Forge: Unearthing the Self

The foray into the CgX system raises one important question above all the rest: What does self-determination really consist of? True self-determination is neither place nor state but a process—a process of transformation. It is an inner search—an attempt to find out who we really are.

The Mirror of Self-Awareness

Not as one looking into a mirror just to see physical likeness, but to the edge of the mind. This is the kind of introspection true self-determination needs: intense investigation of the very roots of all our thoughts and their motives. Self-awareness lets us look through superficial reflections and face multi-layered influences that form our identity.

The Cacophony of Social Heredity

Here, the noises of social heredity can be viewed as a metaphor to denote how norms and expectations, deeply ingrained, veil our real selves. Smothering our unique thoughts and aspirations with all these socially inherited influences from generation to generation, we find ourselves often working toward goals or beliefs that are not our own but echoes of what has been demanded by this century or that of our lives.

Discerning the Inner Voice

This notion encourages us to engage deeply with our internal dialogues, navigate through the cacophony of external influences, and discern the subtle expressions of our true identities. By enhancing our capacity for critical self-reflection, we can effectively differentiate between the entrenched beliefs shaped by social heredity and the authentic desires that remain latent within us. Through this discernment process, we embark on the journey of exercising our self-determination.

Beyond Socially Constructed Achievement

True self-determination is not about seeking external validation or attaining socially recognized milestones. It is rather an understanding of the origins of our own thoughts, aligning our actions with core values and personal aspirations. Real achievement ensues from this genuine self-awareness, in which our goals and actions emanate from our true self. If this level is missing, the notion of individual achievement will remain superficial. We become genuinely self-determined only when societal conditioning and its constraints are recognized and challenged.

Coda: The Unfinished Symphony – A Chorus of Eternal Inquiry[11]

Though the last echoes of this movement may have dimmed, the majestic symphony of freeing the mind endures, resonating through the corridors of time.

---

[11] Composed with assistance from Google Gemini AI

This is not a tale with a conclusive finale but instead an endless melody, a harmony of perpetual questioning.

Our minds are expansive realms, untouched landscapes – realms of thought overflowing with the promise of revelation. In these realms, sparks of thought arise, defying the norms and guiding us toward a profound grasp of our essence and the cosmos we dwell within.

In this realm, the CgX system emerges as the vessel through which we articulate our ceaseless journey of discovery. A liberated CgX system, infused with the essence of free will and the dance of critical thought, invites us to weave a timeless symphony of ideas that resonates through the corridors of eternity.

This symphony is not a gentle lullaby, but a mighty and ceaselessly transforming masterpiece. It dances between discord and melody – a tribute to the unyielding essence of human exploration. It honors the essence of our boundless wonder, the ceaseless quest for understanding, and the vibrant collisions of thoughts that ignite the flames of creation.

The last note may remain unstruck, for the melody of human contemplation is an endless voyage of revelation. With every generation, a new stanza unfolds in this majestic symphony, layering upon the groundwork crafted by the hands of our ancestors. This ceaseless journey weaves the fabric of our existence, a tribute to our relentless pursuit of wisdom.

Part 2 - Critical Insights: Charting the Course Through the CgX System s Labyrinth

1. Fallacy-Proof CgX Systems: Striking a Balance

Uncharted Territory: The Challenge of Freedom

Envision a grand vessel, its sails fully extended and gracefully catching the breeze. It holds the capacity to traverse expansive seas and arrive at uncharted territories. However, in the absence of a proficient leader and a meticulously planned trajectory, this same freedom has the potential to veer off course, adrift in an infinite sea. Comparably, a CgX system exhibiting complete autonomy encounters the risks associated with unexplored domains. The concept of unrestricted freedom, while enticing, has the potential to induce disorder within the CgX system, ultimately impairing its capacity for efficient information processing.

The Engine of Thought: Inherent Potential and the Need for Guidance

Our intrinsic CgX systems, akin to formidable cosmic engines, are teeming with potential. These elements serve as the basis for the framework through which we develop our comprehension of the world. Nonetheless, akin to how a robust engine necessitates skilled oversight for peak performance, the inherent capabilities of the CgX system thrive under knowledgeable guidance. The challenge resides in achieving equilibrium: offering crucial guidance while preserving the innate spark of curiosity and the capacity for autonomous exploration.

The Art of Resilience: A Blend of Inherited Wisdom and Self-Directed Exploration

The answer to this challenge may lie in cultivating resilience within the CgX system. This resilience should ideally be a harmonious blend of two key elements:

a. **Inherited Processing:** This involves the information and experiences of our ancestors coming into our lives at birth with some sort of preliminary tools to interact with the physical world, including cultural, educational, and family influences upon our first cognitive frameworks.

    Example: Consider traditional values learned in the family, such as holding on to perseverance and hard work. In this case, it would form part of the inherited processing, which at some point forms a baseline from which everyone approaches specific challenges. A student who has grown up in a family that values education might approach obstacles with some built-in resiliency, drawing on their family's emphasis on perseverance to get them over difficult times.

b. **Self-Guided Enhancement:** This involves proactively exploring and developing unique thought patterns. It allows individuals to question established norms, challenge assumptions, and create their own intellectual pathways.

    Example: In an educational setting, self-directed improvement would mean that instead of merely accepting information, the student learns how to think. For instance, a student may research controversial topics not covered in class, debate the issue, and make a judgment call. This helps him develop more critical thinking and deeper insights into various issues.

Remember!

By developing a CgX system characterized by resilience and adaptability, we can enhance individuals' abilities to engage in critical thinking, facilitate effective learning, and approach the complexities of the world with a well-rounded perspective.

2. The Indigo Enigma: Balancing Rebellion with Harmony

The notion of Indigo children embodies a captivating paradox. Imagined as cosmic insurgents equipped with CgX systems that resonate with a challenge to conventional norms, they are perceived as prospective stewards of a delicate equilibrium. Nonetheless, the journey toward attaining this balance is anything but simple.

The Stifling Grip of Conformity: Social Sarcophagi

Social conformity often emerges as a detrimental influence, resembling social sarcophagi that jeopardize our unique identities. The imposition of rigid structures, driven by an aspiration for uniformity, can potentially suppress the fundamental essence of human thought: its remarkable diversity. In such environments, the vitality of independent thought diminishes, yielding to the pervasive influence of groupthink, which emerges as a uniform cadence that overshadows the distinctive symphony of individual cognition.

The Disruptive Symphony: Indigo Children and the Call for Change

The potential role of Indigo children is explored herein. Their intrinsic defiance of conformity and disruptive harmony could be the essential catalyst for questioning the prevailing norms. This disruptiveness, however, transcends mere destruction; it has the potential to catalyze positive transformation. Through the act of challenging conventional norms and promoting autonomous thinking, Indigo children have the potential to guide society toward a more vibrant balance.

Restoring the Balance: A Delicate Dance

Achieving a harmonious interplay between the evolving processes of the CgX system and the social structures that provide a sense of order and stability is crucial. Individuals identified as indigo children, possessing distinct viewpoints, may significantly contribute to this intricate interplay. It is essential to acknowledge that genuine advancement seldom emerges from unchecked insurrection. The optimal situation does not entail the total disassembly of social frameworks; instead, it involves an ongoing process of enhancement, wherein existing conventions are scrutinized and modified to meet the dynamic requirements of a society enriched by many perspectives.

3. Teachers: Cultivating the Symphony of Thought

This concept highlights educators' essential influence in molding the youth's intellect. It challenges educators' perception as simple transmitters designed to convey knowledge in a predetermined fashion. Rather, it positions them as architects of thought, orchestrating the symphony of learning that unfolds within the confines of the classroom.

Beyond the Conduit: Shaping the Melody of Young Minds

Educators' character, integrity, and judgment profoundly shape their students, impacting the essential framework of their evolving CgX systems. This metaphor underscores the significant influence educators exert on their students' cognitive development and information-processing skills. An educator's commitment intricately influences the development of a young intellect, steering it toward the realms of critical analysis, inquisitiveness, and an enduring passion for knowledge acquisition.

The Paradox of the Programmed Teacher

The excerpt recognizes a possible inconsistency. The existing educational frameworks might unintentionally constrain the intellectual autonomy of those responsible for fostering it within their students. Envision a symphony conductor, bound by a strict score, devoid of the freedom to improvise or weave in new melodies. A genuinely resilient CgX system necessitates educators with expertise and individuals who possess critical thinking skills, challenge prevailing assumptions, and motivate their students to engage in similar intellectual pursuits.

The Ideal Conservatory: A Chorus of Values

The optimal educational framework would take the form of a dynamic conservatory, serving as a space where a harmonious blend of values reverberates through its corridors. This collective effort would encompass individuals ranging from board members to classroom educators, all aligned in their dedication to nurturing the following:

- **Character:** Integrity and equity are essential in the quest for understanding and enlightenment.

- **Integrity:** Integrity involves steadfast adherence to one's values and principles, particularly when facing external pressures to conform.

- **Commitment to the Advancement of Humanity:** Embracing the transformative power of education as a catalyst for a brighter future for everyone.

- **a vigorous pursuit of knowledge:** an enduring commitment to lifelong learning and exploration.

- **Autonomous Evaluation:** The capacity to think critically, challenge prevailing assumptions, and derive personal, well-reasoned conclusions.

Remember!

It is only through the acquisition of these essential tools that educators can truly emerge as architects of thought. By creating a dynamic learning environment and nurturing their own intellectual autonomy, educators enable the upcoming generation to develop robust and cohesive CgX systems.

Coda: The Unfinished Symphony - A Chorus of Stardust[12]

As the last echoes of this passage wane, the majestic symphony of freedom in thought endures ever-resounding. This is not a tale with a conclusive finale but instead an eternal melody, a harmony of celestial whispers.

Flaws, akin to celestial dust, are intricately interlaced within the essence of our existence. These flaws, these unforeseen shifts, bestow upon our distinct CgX systems their singular harmonies. Social heredity stands as the bedrock, the canvas upon which our lives are artfully inscribed. Yet, it is the innate wonder, the flicker of defiance, the yearning for understanding that drives us to weave our unique melodies into the celestial symphony.

Let our musings resonate across the ages, a tribute to the timeless essence of humanity. Let us wander through the vast, uncharted realms of thought, eternally yearning to grasp the essence of our being and the cosmos that cradles us. The last note may remain unstruck, for the melody of human contemplation is an endless voyage of revelation. With every generation, a new

---

[12] Composed with assistance from Google Gemini AI

line is woven into this majestic tapestry, a tribute to our relentless pursuit of wisdom and a profound bond with the enigmas of life.

Part 3 - The Crossroads of Inheritance: Disentangling Social Heredity from the CgX System s Evolution

In Part 2, we thoroughly explore the intricate dynamics between social heredity and the evolution of the CgX system. The narrative here engages in a critical examination, analyzing the possible obstacles that social inheritance may present to independent thought.

The Labyrinth of Conformity: Where Paths Converge

The passage commences with an intriguing metaphor, comparing the mind to a complex labyrinth of thought. In this complex network, neural pathways intersect, establishing the essential basis of our convictions. Yet, embedded within these trajectories is the subtle influence of social heredity. Envision it as a spider diligently crafting its web, with each delicate thread intricately molding the nuances of our cognitive terrain.

This imagery highlights the conflict between groupthink, characterized by the uncritical acceptance of dominant ideas, and the indigo souls, who represent independent thinkers forging their own paths. From this analytical standpoint, social heredity impedes the organic development and progression of the CgX system. The imposition of prefabricated belief structures significantly constrains the evolution of a diverse array of thoughts, leading to a homogenization of the human experience landscape.

1. Echoes of Youth: The Labyrinth of Political Heredity

Political allegiances can be likened to intricate tapestries carefully crafted by the threads of social inheritance. The family and close associates, serving as the weavers, imbue their beliefs into these tapestries' complex patterns and vivid hues. As individuals, we often find ourselves absorbing various perspectives akin to sponges, and in this process, we may unintentionally internalize biases and fallacies alongside fundamental principles.

For example, a child brought up in an environment where political discussions are dominated by fear and xenophobic attitudes may unintentionally adopt these beliefs. In a comparable vein, being raised in an environment that emphasizes conformity rather than critical analysis can hinder the cultivation of nuanced viewpoints. Once interlaced within the fabric of our convictions, intricate patterns of prejudice and misinformation hold substantial sway over our political decisions.

Acknowledging that social heredity does not operate as a deterministic force is crucial. Although it may influence our foundational perspective, personal experiences, education, and critical analysis have the potential to question and redefine these pre-existing convictions. The CgX system, renowned for its capacity to analyze and manipulate genetic information, presents an intriguing lens through which we can explore the complex relationship between biological factors and environmental influences in forming our political perspectives.

The Labyrinth of Conformity: A Symphony of Influences

Early conditioning of this sort typically aligns a sense of group identity with a particular political stance. Consider, for a moment, a grand symphony of political thought in which each instrument plays a distinct melody. Social heredity dictates which melodies we first learn from this instrument and perhaps entraps us into the one already set.

For example, a person brought up in a conservative society may be more likely to have traditional political values without attempting to fathom the other way of thinking. Similarly, people who have been conditionally programmed with progressive ideologies since their younger years will find it hard to question or even challenge those concepts. In this regard, conditioning at younger ages creates some sort of cognitive dissonance in the mind, so any other opposing ideas are hard to put into the bigger picture regarding a complex political issue.

Yet, the symphony is not without its realm of improvisation and dissonance. These could be revised through experience, education, and critical thinking, which build a wider portfolio of political cognition. The built-in genetic information provides the bedrock on which the CgX system is established—a very interesting view on the interaction between biological and environmental influences shaping our politics.

Beyond the Swaying Saplings: The CgX System's Quest for Autonomy

The quote aptly likens the CgX systems in youth to saplings blowing in the winds of social heredity. The developing minds are susceptible to external influences, much like these saplings in the breeze. The metaphor, however, may be carried one step further: just as a sapling develops its root system, can the CgX system develop its intellectual foundation? Then, critical thinking is added to it, which calls into question assumptions and processes the information with a critical eye. Let this light of independent analysis fall upon it- like sunlight- not trapped in conventional melodies but dancing freely as the CgX system grows.

Breaking Free from the Echo Chamber: The Mystery of the CgX System's Potential

We must know how to break free from the echo chamber of inherited beliefs. If the real potential of the CgX system is to be realized, we must nurture an attitude that helps us synthesize various viewpoints and weigh the information critically that comes before us. This process is similar to that of a musician continuously adding new instruments and styles to his symphony so that the overall symphony becomes more enriching.

- **Include Diverse Perspectives:** A musician would want to keep adding instruments to enrich the sound. In our lives, too, we need to actively seek and engage with diverse perspectives through reading diverse books, attending talks and discussion forums, and holding conversations with people from different backgrounds and ideologies. For example, joining community forums or discussion groups may expose us to opinions different from our own.

- **Critical Thinking:** This requires us to reconsider, a little more critically, the things that come our way lest we echo our inherited beliefs alone. It is like the conductor who has to make sure every instrument is in concert tune. One can employ critical thinking by questioning sources, considering alternative explanations, and weighing evidence before drawing conclusions. One can work on this ability through practices related to reflection, writing in a journal, or discussing ideas with others.

- **Develop Intellectual Curiosity:** Just like musicians experiment with new sounds and techniques, we should develop a sort of intellectual curiosity within ourselves. This would entail researching topics outside our comfort zones, taking on new hobbies or courses, and staying open to continuous learning. For instance, subscribing to online courses in subjects unrelated to our expertise will improve our knowledge and cause an influx of ideas.

With these practices combined in our cognitive approach, the echo chamber of inheritance is overcome, and we find our way holistically in political and social thought. The CgX system's full capability is to change and adapt; it unravels the intriguing mystery of independent thought and intellectual exploration.

2. Religious Echoes: Can We Compose Our Hymns of Faith?

Religious Echoes: Can We Compose Our Hymns of Faith?

Many religious beliefs resemble complex tapestries woven from strands passed down through generations of cultural legacy. The complex patterns we encounter reflect the beliefs that have been passed down through the ages, deeply shaping our convictions from a young age. We welcome these traditions with a familiarity and comfort akin to engaging with a beloved, calming tune. However, this feeling of solace may come at a cost, as it might lead us to overlook the opportunity to forge our interpretations of belief.

The Question of Authenticity: Echoing Chants or Personal Anthems?

A pivotal inquiry arises: have we genuinely grasped the
fundamental nature of our convictions? Are we merely
reverberating the chants that have been transmitted through
the ages? The excerpt indicates a possible divergence between
traditional practices passed down through generations and an
authentic comprehension of their significance. Envision the
CgX systems of adherents resonating with echoes, producing
a haunting melody that may elude genuine understanding.

Beyond Blind Conviction: A Journey of Exploration

The disconnection becomes even more pronounced when one
considers the challenges in articulating the nuanced
distinctions among various denominations. While many hold
robust convictions, it is often the case that a comprehensive
understanding of the foundational principles is not fully
realized. The imperative is evident: we must pursue
an understanding that transcends rigid beliefs. This process
may require dissecting the complexities of inherited beliefs
while initiating a personal quest for understanding and
discovery. Envision the careful analysis of each individual
thread, probing into its origins and intentions before
interlacing them into a tapestry that embodies our collective
comprehension.

A Symphony of Faith: Respecting Tradition, Embracing Individuality

The fundamental question persists: Can we transcend the
melodic patterns dictated by social heredity to create our own
anthems of belief? The solution resides in cultivating a CgX
system that honors tradition while simultaneously possessing
the capacity for critical self-examination of its own beliefs.
Only through this process can we compose a harmonious
blend of beliefs that echoes not only the traditions passed
down to us but also our individual interpretations of the

cosmos. This symphony represents a harmonious fusion of tradition and individual exploration, serving as a testament to faith's dynamic and evolving essence.

3. Campfires of Thought: Examining the Embers of Belief

We are inherently attracted to the comforting glow of collective ideologies, congregating around symbolic campfires of contemplation alongside those dear to us. Their convictions, transmitted across generations and exchanged within the community, become deeply embedded in our belief systems. However, before becoming too complacent in the comforting familiarity, an essential inquiry emerges: On what basis do these convictions rest?

The Strength of Our Bridges: Examining Inherited Beliefs

This concept employs striking metaphors to illustrate the possible dangers of accepting ideas without scrutiny. Do the beliefs we acquire from our social environments serve as robust structures that can uphold the demands of independent reasoning? Or are they, in fact, delicate constructs that may falter under the rigorous lens of critical analysis? Envision evaluating the capacity of each belief – will it remain steadfast or yield under pressure?

Beyond Passive Acceptance: A Call to Critical Thinking

Social heredity has the potential to lead us into a condition of passive acceptance. We find ourselves in agreement with well-known narratives, gently swayed by the reassuring murmurs of the collective. We must take a moment to carefully scrutinize every fragment of our beliefs. Does it serve as a guiding light,

revealing authentic insights for our journey, or is it merely a
deceptive illusion, diverting us from reality?

The Double-Edged Sword of Social Heredity

Social heredity is a two-edged sword: on one side, it
constitutes the spark that sets fire to our belief system, much
like a campfire that would warm and give light; on the other
hand, it can cast long shadows that obscure the possibility of
independent exploration within our CgX systems. The task is
how to harness the warmth of community and shared values
while developing the facility with reason that
enables navigation beyond these shadows.

Real-World Examples of the Consequences of Social Heredity

Examining cultural traditions and beliefs necessitates a
thoughtful consideration of various elements, including food
intake. Numerous cultures have embraced traditional
perspectives on food, exemplified by vegetarianism within
Hindu practices and halal dietary laws in Islam. Although these
traditions foster a sense of identity and belonging, they can also
constrain exploration and critical engagement with emerging
scientific evidence regarding dietary practices. Individuals who
critically examine these practices in pursuit of fresh insights
into dietary habits contribute to a nuanced comprehension of
nutrition, harmonizing established traditions with
advancements in scientific research.

- **Examining Historical Biases and Social Norms: A
  case study of racial segregation in the United States**

  The concept of social heredity perpetuates racial
  prejudices and norms, ensuring their transmission across
  generations. Individuals like Martin Luther King Jr.

actively challenged this longstanding tradition of pursuing civil rights and equality. Change is facilitated through inquiries that challenge the status quo; individuals who pose such questions foster critical thinking, pave the way for social progress, and demonstrate that revising one's own beliefs can lead to significant social transformation.

- **Economic Perceptions and Entrepreneurship**

  Economic perceptions play a pivotal role in shaping career trajectories within families, often guiding individuals toward traditional paths in entrepreneurship. For instance, aspirations related to entrepreneurship may be obscured by societal expectations prioritizing careers perceived as more stable, such as those in medicine or law. Visionaries such as Steve Jobs, Bill Gates, and Elon Musk opted to diverge from conventional career paths, actively challenging the established norms of their industries. Their success can be attributed to these groundbreaking innovations, highlighting the significance of critical thinking and exploring new avenues, irrespective of prevailing social beliefs.

Operating in the Shadows

Remember!

Harmonizing the nurturing aspects of communal values with the quest for autonomous thinking is essential to avoiding the limitations imposed by social inheritance. This necessitates intentionally pursuing varied viewpoints, introspective examination, and the courage to question established beliefs when appropriate. We would find ourselves capable of forging our paths and contributing to creating a more intricate and nuanced tapestry of human thought.

In conclusion, while social heredity provides a fundamental basis for our beliefs and identities, it is imperative to cultivate critical thinking and an openness to diverse perspectives. This equilibrium allows us to honor our cultural heritage while simultaneously guiding ourselves toward a more enlightened and inclusive future.

4. The Alchemy of Familiarity: Transforming Strangers into Beliefs

The human mind is an inquisitive laboratory, efficient in the alchemy of familiarity. Indeed, those ideas that come to our minds at first as strangers knocking on the door gradually mold into our dearly loved beliefs. Suppose those ideas are some foreign guests who come to our door. At first, we would not open the door, perhaps for fear of their unfamiliar presence.

From Resistance to Acceptance: The Power of Proximity

The following passage considers the interesting way in which novel ideas take root in our CgX systems- uninvited visitors at the threshold; they somehow find their way into our homes through repeated exposure and proximity. Indeed, we may eventually invite such notions in and offer it a figurative cup of tea- a symbolic indication of intellectual hospitality. Suppose these conceptions are left to persist, getting allowed into our cognitive living room for a stimulating discussion.

The Reshaping of Beliefs: It's a Slow, Subtle Process of Change

This passage is a cautionary note about a potential consequence that may arise under these circumstances. As individuals find their footing, these ideas start to reorganize the mental environment, leading to a reconfiguration of core values that were once considered firmly established and are now subject to nuanced transformation. It transcends mere debate; rather, it transforms our perception of reality, reshaping the very arrangement of thoughts within the confines of our consciousness. The transformation is subtle and gradual; it unfolds over an extended period. This is how familiarity gradually shifts understanding into belief, demonstrating such a process's profound and often unnoticed influence.

Tracing the Roots of Belief: A Journey of Discovery

The core assertion of the narrative revolves around the necessity for individuals to reflect on the origins of their beliefs. We follow their origins, seeking a profound comprehension of their impact, to the genesis within the expansive realm of contemplation. Did these concepts emerge from a place of genuine originality stemming from personal inquiry, or were they simply appropriated and absorbed through the influential mechanism of social inheritance that shapes our understanding? Imagine venturing into this expansive nebula, actively pursuing new ideas rather than merely accepting those that arrive at our threshold. Exploring the origins of our beliefs can be a profound journey of introspection, revealing the myriad influences that have molded our cognitive frameworks.

The Discerning Mind: Recognizing the Alchemist's Touch

The excerpt indicates that regular exposure can potentially convert ideas that may initially appear objectionable into fundamental elements of our CgX system. In this context, social heredity serves as a significant mechanism for transmitting beliefs and forming cognitive frameworks. Nevertheless, the essence of intellectual development resides in acknowledging the intricate process at work – the nuanced metamorphosis of unfamiliar individuals into firmly established beliefs. Only through this lens can we engage with new ideas critically, inviting them into a meaningful dialogue instead of relinquishing control over our cognitive frameworks. By acknowledging the profound impact of familiarity, we can cultivate intellectual development and ascertain that our beliefs genuinely reflect our individuality, contributing a distinct note to the expansive symphony of human thought.

5. The Indigo Spirit: A Discordant Melody in the Symphony of Thought

The Tyranny of the Herd: Following Well-Worn Paths

The passage presents the fascinating notion of the Indigo personality, which contrasts sharply with the conventional thinker who uncritically adheres to established norms of conformity. Like sheep, many individuals tend to forage within the confines of familiar cognitive landscapes. Their CgX systems, shaped by social heredity, resemble established pathways, guiding them toward collective beliefs and uniform modes of thought. These individuals, satisfied within the collective's boundaries, assimilate information passively, their ideas reflecting the prevailing narratives instead of crafting their own distinctive harmonies.

The Indigo Enigma: A Spark of Originality

The Indigo soul, in contrast, emerges as a distinctive cosmic anomaly. These individuals embody a spirit of defiance, with their CgX systems radiating the vibrancy of innovation. They refuse to simply follow the crowd; instead, they are the innovators who create new harmonies within the vast orchestra of human intellect. Their distinctive viewpoints, akin to constellations brightening the nocturnal expanse, question the conventional paradigms and provide novel understandings. The passage encourages us to actively pursue these Indigo minds, as they possess the capacity to transform the established frameworks of conventional thought.

The Unique Treasures: An Ode to Autonomous Thinking

The narrative culminates in a poignant contemplation regarding the rarity of genuine individuality. Encountering an individual who possesses the courage to engage in independent thought and forge their path is often characterized as a remarkable experience. The passage posits that these Indigo thinkers represent invaluable gems within the expansive landscape of human thought. Their audacity to question established norms and commitment to autonomous inquiry significantly enhance the fabric of human knowledge.

6. The Social Tapestry of Professions: Tradition, Doubt, and the Indigo Thread

Social heredity occupies a prominent position in the intricate landscape of professions and research, where numerous intellects don the attire of established norms. A captivating dynamic emerges at the intersection of tradition and skepticism as the Indigo thinkers actively question and redefine the established narrative.

Professions: The Symphony of Expertise

The overarching impact of social heredity is evident in various professions, especially in esteemed fields such as law and medicine, which fundamentally depend on precedent as a foundational element. Professionals such as lawyers and doctors refine their expertise through the diligent study and application of the extensive knowledge amassed by their predecessors. Their actions resonate as notes within an expansive symphony of knowledge, reverberating across generations. Precedents function as sheet music, directing their decisions in a manner reminiscent of ancient manuscripts.

Nonetheless, this concept prompts an essential inquiry: Where does innovation reside within this strictly organized framework of performance? Social heredity resonates with a well-known melody, and numerous professionals align themselves with its cadence. The imperative is unmistakable: we must actively engage with the Indigo lawyers and doctors—those who boldly innovate and create new harmonies within their disciplines. By critically examining established practices and delving into innovative solutions, these individuals play a pivotal role in the progression of their respective fields.

Exploring the Landscape of Scientific Inquiry

- **Selective Bias: An Outcome of Social Heredity.** While scientific research is frequently celebrated for its objectivity, it remains susceptible to the impacts of social heredity. The discussion posits that social heredity may emerge as a form of selective bias, wherein researchers may inadvertently prioritize findings that resonate with established theories.

- **Laboratories: Epicenters of Exploration.** Envision laboratories as transformative spaces where researchers, much like modern-day alchemists, diligently seek to uncover the essence of truth. Nonetheless, the passage serves as a reminder that social heredity can exert a nuanced influence, subtly guiding even the most astute intellects. Their hypotheses, reminiscent of constellations mapped across the night sky, may adhere to recognized investigation patterns.

Remember!

The imperative here is to interrogate that which lies beyond the realm of the known. In a manner akin to how astronomers diligently scrutinize celestial bodies to uncover irregularities, it is imperative that we rigorously assess the dominant scientific frameworks of our time. The pursuit of intellectual curiosity, emblematic of the Indigo spirit, promises to guide us toward unexplored realms of knowledge and discovery.

7. Unbelief: The Chilling Frost that Stifles Innovation

This notion delves into a significant obstacle to human progress: unbelief. Unbelief emerges as a quiet yet formidable force capable of extinguishing the flickers of creativity and innovation before they have the chance to flourish. This discussion explores different approaches to tackle the current challenge.

The Chilling Embrace of Doubt

As trailblazers in aviation, the Wright Brothers exemplify remarkable innovation and determination. Their groundbreaking idea of a flying machine encountered a stark reception—the cold skepticism of individuals unwilling to accept its feasibility. This preconceived disdain, as articulated by Herbert Spencer, represents a dangerous trap within the landscape of intellectual discourse. Unbelief is a significant obstacle, obstructing our capacity to explore new possibilities and stifling innovation.

Fostering an Environment Rich in Inquiry

This concept encourages us to nurture the antithesis of skepticism: a belief rooted in the rich terrain of curiosity. Embracing new ideas with curiosity and a willingness to learn fosters an atmosphere conducive to innovation and creativity. Nonetheless, the discourse advances a compelling argument, positing that unbelief transcends a mere passive existence. It serves as a fundamental basis through which social heredity dismisses innovative concepts.

Safeguarding the Established Order: The Oppression of the Known

In this context, social heredity pertains to entrenched modes of thought that are transmitted across generations. The phenomenon of unbelief, often sustained by the allure of the familiar, may serve as a protective mechanism for perpetuating social heredity. Dismissing innovative concepts protects the current framework and hinders adopting potentially transformative thought processes.

Remember!

The imperative is unmistakable: we must confront the dominance of the known and cultivate a spirit of curiosity. By nurturing a culture of inquiry and receptiveness, we can cultivate an atmosphere where innovative concepts can flourish, challenging the stifling constraints of skepticism.

8. Guardians of Stagnation: How Pseudo-Thinkers Hinder Progress

This subsequent section will critically examine the so-called watchwords of tradition, focusing on the pseudo-thinkers. Rather than serving as a robust foundation for intellectual inquiry, they present a hindrance to advancement through their limited skepticism.

Fortress of Social Heredity

History has repeated this process in the case of the invention of the telephone. Just take a glance at the arrogance of these pseudo-thinkers. Confronted with the grand idea of transmitting the voice over long distances, it was only logical that they would reason themselves into disbelief. But they became victims of their rather faulty reasoning and an almost slavish adherence to social heredity, which promptly made such an achievement impossible. This form of weaponized skepticism is a kind of dogma that is common throughout history. Every great creator has faced the barricades thrown up by people terrified of anything threatening to derail the status quo.

Fear of the Unexplored: The Enemy of Progress

This section argues that pseudo-thinkers are the shock troops of social heredity, fiercely defending it against the enlightenment contributed by genuine thought. Their fear of change emanates from a fundamental distrust of whatever is proposed that moves one footpath off the well-worn paths of tradition. These people, it would seem, are sworn enemies of the future since they stand actively in the way of progress and improvement.

The Indigo Key: Unlocking the Gates of Possibility

Standing in radical contrast to the pseudo-thinkers are the minds of Indigo. These intrepid individuals are armed with the intellectual keys of curiosity and open-mindedness that will unlock the gates of exploration. While the pseudo-thinkers slammed shut the iron gates of tradition, the Indigo spirit pushes relentlessly forward, hammering at barriers that limit humanity's potential.

Their fearlessness can afford to swing open the doors to new, unexplored dimensions of knowledge and understanding. The paper now concludes by celebrating these Indigo pioneers as the real heroes who rise beyond the shackles laid by the pseudo-thinkers and lead the way into a brighter tomorrow.

9. The Symphony of Exceptions: Indigo Melodies Defying the Score

Social heredity frequently shapes our cognitive frameworks, compelling us to depend on established precedents – the familiar melodies of conventional wisdom. This inherent inclination may lead us to intellectual complacency, where we are satisfied with accepting information at face value, neglecting the essential process of firsthand inquiry. Nonetheless, history is embellished with anomalies, the cosmic nonconformists who challenge the established norms and create their intellectual masterpieces.

Exploring the Boundaries: A New Perspective on Melody

In contrast to the majority who are satisfied with adhering to conventional norms, these individuals emerge as the trailblazers of human advancement. For them, precedents serve as mere footnotes, subtle hints nestled within the margins of the grand symphony of knowledge. Their genuine enthusiasm is rooted in the pursuit of firsthand knowledge, the fundamental elements from which they construct innovative frameworks of understanding. Envisioning the careful collection of data, the execution of experiments, and the rigorous examination of established beliefs represent the essential initial phases in creating an innovative melody.

Indigo Melodies: Echoing Through the Ages

The Indigo thinkers, often referred to in scholarly circles, represent the virtuosos of this intellectual orchestra. They create melodies that echo not only in their contemporary context but also transcend through various historical periods.

Their innovative concepts disrupt conventional norms and advance the trajectory of human progress. Envision the profound impact of a singular, resonant melody; it possesses the capacity to motivate countless individuals to engage with their instruments, thereby enriching the continuous evolution of the collective human narrative.

Coda: Symphony of Rebels – A Farewell Note[13]

As the curtain descends upon this scene, may the whispers remain: Our CgX systems, akin to boundless galaxies, twirl within the swirling nebula of possibility. Social heredity may sing a relentless melody, yet we are the celestial renegades, eternally in pursuit of uncharted realms of contemplation. Let the melodies of our thoughts echo through time, blending with the heavenly song of the stars above.

This final movement, named "Symphony of Rebels," unveils a vivid tapestry of human contemplation. We are not mere shadows aboard the vessel of social lineage; we are the stewards, charting our course through the swirling mists of possibility, with our CgX systems illuminating the path like distant constellations. The gentle strains of social heredity linger, a whispering tune in the shadows, yet we stand as celestial maestros, crafting our own harmonies of reflection and dream.

Once more, the significance of singular reflection emerges, painted vividly through the enchanting metaphor of an orchestra. Our crafts and inquiries weave the singular melodies we offer to the majestic orchestra of human understanding. Social heredity may offer a gentle, underlying cadence, yet we are the artisans, crafting our own harmonies into the rich fabric of existence. The mingling melodies of our varied musings weave a tapestry that echoes through time, a tribute to the infinite possibilities of the human spirit.

The final vision, where our musings dance with the celestial bodies, deepens the

---

[13] Composed with assistance from Google Gemini AI

notion that our dreams possess the strength to transcend the boundaries of the now. We are not mere shadows in the vast tapestry of human discourse; we are vibrant voices, each adding a distinct melody to the celestial symphony of wisdom that resonates across the cosmos.

Thoughts and Reflections on The Maestro of Nature: Managing Diversity with Dexterity[14]

Nature is the greatest conductor, orchestrating a grand symphony of variation with her powerful genetic tools. This extends into the fascinating realm of human handedness, where coexistence within humankind plays a vital role in the species' ever-unfolding story.

The Counterpoint of Lefties: A Symphony of Asymmetry

Left-handed thinkers are the instruments of an orchestra playing a different tune; they provide a necessary counterpoint to overall harmony. The brains, sculpted by different genetic patterns, show intriguing asymmetry that fosters a dissimilar mode in solving problems and processing thoughts. This, in turn, creates conflict with established right-handed dominance, pushing the envelope on human cognition.

The Harmonious Right Hand: A Foundation for Shared Understanding

With their more common cerebral structure, the right-handed form a basis for efficient communication and shared understanding. Their thinking might easily be more comparable to guidelines that guarantee a level of coherence in human experience. Try to contemplate a world where everybody thinks and behaves the same way. That would be no less than boring until left-handedness breaks

---

[14] For further information refer to "Handedness and its genetic influences are associated with structural asymmetries of the cerebral cortex in 31,864 individuals" - https://www.pnas.org/doi/10.1073/pnas.2113095118

the monotone unison with an essential share of variance. It obliges us to consider other outlooks and inspires innovation and progress. On the other hand, if there were a fully left-handed population, they would never find common ground to understand each other or be able to work together in synchrony.

The Beauty of Duality: A Symphony Enriched by Complementary Melodies

Now, envision a world where all people thought and acted exactly alike. The beauty of left-handedness brings into this terrible harmony an essential element that breeds diversity. It enlightens us to seek other ways, a means to progress and innovation. On the other hand, if the population were purely left-handed, it could find many difficulties in common grounds of understanding for communication and collaboration.

The beauty actually lies in how left and right complement each other. Each side contributes its rhythm to the symphony of human thoughts. Coexistence, pressed by the underlying code of genetics and the presented CgX system, will continue to evolve without any stagnation, nurturing a dynamic intellectual landscape.

Handedness: A Neutral Exploration of Nature's Blueprint

Humanity's narrative is intricately woven with threads of genetic diversity, and the phenomenon of handedness presents a compelling subject for exploration. Research such as "Handedness and its genetic influences are associated with structural asymmetries of the cerebral cortex in 31,864 individuals" uncovers the intricate relationship between genetic factors and the brain's architecture.

The Cerebral Canvas: Unveiling Asymmetries of Left and Right

The cerebral cortex, known for its role in higher cognitive functions, displays nuanced yet important structural differences between left-handed and right-handed individuals. The observed variations, especially in language and motor control areas, could be shaped by genetic factors such as NME7. This gene functions as a conductor within the developmental orchestra, coordinating not only the organization of the brain but also potentially influencing the positioning of visceral organs.

Nature's Guiding Hand: A Signature of Evolution

The Complex Interplay of Genetic and Environmental Influences: Exploring Heritable and Non-Heritable Asymmetries. The fascinating element resides in the interplay between heritable and non-heritable asymmetries. Genetic predispositions may influence certain structural variations within the brain, while others can emerge due to environmental factors and individual hand preference. This distinction is essential, as it underscores the dynamic relationship between nature and nurture in influencing human development.

The Non-Random Influence: Handedness and the Evolution of CgX

The notable prevalence of left-handed individuals indicates a potentially non-random factor at play in human evolution. The observed influence, presumably stemming from genetic diversity, could have facilitated the emergence of a wider array of cognitive capabilities and methodologies for addressing challenges within the CgX system. The diverse spectrum of thought patterns and behaviors enhances the human experience, fostering ongoing intellectual and societal evolution.

Embracing a neutral perspective allows us to delve into the intriguing narrative of handedness, free from the constraints of value judgments regarding left or right. The interplay between both sides enriches the intricate tapestry of human existence, fostering a dynamic and continuously evolving CgX system.

Conclusion: The Human Symphony: Balancing Freedom and Societal Harmony

The Human Symphony: A Tapestry of Freedom and Harmony

The human carries an emergent tension between the individual's freedom and the bond with society. This tension is embedded in the CgX system, which is the internal means through which thoughts and beliefs are digested. Herein lies the challenge: whether it should be a river, flowing free and forging its own paths, or whether it should be guided through a canal formed with pristine ideals.

The Symphony of Thought: Harmony Through Individually Expressed Notes

It may well be that the solution lies in viewing our thinking as a symphony—a symphony in which every differing type of instrument can add its voice so that together, they form one harmonious whole. In that manner, our thought processes should function: divergent visions inextricably linked, affording thereby a deeper and more subtle insight.

The Importance of Balance: Freedom and Constraint

Yet, just as a symphony requires structure, untrammeled thought can devolve into chaos. A directionless orchestra produces dissonance, and the same would be true for unshackled thought at the social level, which might devolve into disintegration. The important thing is balance: a system fostering exploration and diversity while retaining a framework within which collaboration and shared meaning are possible.

Avoiding the Extremes: A System that Encourages Exploration

Of course, there is social heredity, the transmission of cultural
norms and beliefs across generations. This makes for a very
complex balance, which greatly influences our CgX systems with a
foundation of ideas already inherited. It should not limit us,
however, but merely serve to support the development of our
unique thought processes.

Social Heredity and the Shaping of Thought

The challenge remains in maintaining this diversity of thought while
reaping from generations of wisdom. Social heredity is supposed to
enrich and not belittle our way of thinking. On this platform, the
thought processes we fashion can surely be new yet with valuable
historical insights.

The Challenge: Preserving Diversity While Learning from the Past

The task at hand involves navigating the delicate equilibrium
between honoring the richness of diverse perspectives and drawing
insights from the accumulated knowledge of previous generations.
Our social heredity mustn't be a restrictive framework, limiting our
engagement with contemporary ideas. Rather, it should serve as a
foundational platform to cultivate our distinct cognitive
frameworks.

The Path Forward: Fostering Critical Thinking and Open Dialogue

The path forward lies in fostering critical thinking skills and
encouraging open dialogue. By critically evaluating our ideas and
those passed down to us, we can ensure that our CgX systems
remain flexible and responsive to a changing world. Open dialogue
allows us to share our diverse perspectives and learn from one
another, enriching the overall symphony of human thought.

In other words, freedom and social harmony can be balanced by systematically combining and introducing multiple perspectives. We can use social heredity as the ground for growth, develop critical thinking, and encourage open opinion exchange to navigate the uncharted landscapes in our minds and society with ease. Thus, we will build a more harmonious and enlightened future.

SECTION 5: HARMONY IN SOCIETY AND INDIVIDUAL LIBERTY

᪥᪥᪥

SHAPING OUR DESTINY: CONTROLLED HABITS AND SOCIAL TRANSCENDENCE

᪥᪥᪥

The Theatre of Thought: Habits as Lenses on Reality

The human mind is a great theatre of thought, with each playing one's own role. There are interestingly controlled habits playing the main role in that theatre. These habits act as specialized lenses that have focused the cameras in our minds and framed the way to take the photo of thought. Think of how different a landscape appears when framed through a wide-angle lens compared with a telephoto one. Our habits similarly modulate how we perceive and interact with our surroundings. In this chapter, we will discuss the transformative potential of habits- the process through which behaviors start as impulses and are redesigned to make our destinies.

From Impulses to Destiny: The Power of Regulated Habits

The power of transcending social inheritance through regulated habits is the ability to transcend those societal norms and expectations passed down through generations. We can break down this whole process of turning habits into the architects of our destiny into manageable steps.

Social Heredity: A Challenge and an Opportunity

Perhaps the greatest obstacle to reshaping our destinies is the dominating influence of our environment in the form of what might be termed as social heredity. Hardwired into the very core of nature is the law that every living thing is greatly influenced by its surroundings. Of all our surroundings, social relations have a chief role in our heredity derived from sociability. While it is difficult to change, social heredity is greatly facilitated by combining the principle of controlled habits as a powerful tool for change. The key to this will be remembering that while our environment may not be completely under our control, certainly our habits are.

The Mind s Maestro: Orchestrating the Symphony of Self-Mastery

1. Thought Impulses: The Miracles of Creative Thought

Our exploration begins with examining one of humanity's most remarkable achievements: the phenomenon of creative thought. This remarkable process enables us to convert ephemeral thought impulses into concrete realities, whether they manifest as physical objects, financial success, or spiritual enrichment.

Envision the mind as a celestial instrument, skillfully crafting the tapestry of existence with the rich hues of our cognition. How can we convert these intangible strokes into tangible entities we can possess, engage with, or truly experience? The solution resides within the realm of creative thought, an influential and transformative process. In this context, our ephemeral reflections are transformed into concrete "gold" – whether in the form of physical artifacts, economic stability, or a profound spiritual bond. It is essential to approach this remarkable phenomenon with deliberate intention and concentrated focus.

The Spark of Inspiration: Igniting the Flame of Creation

Creative thought frequently initiates as a fleeting spark of inspiration, a transient impulse illuminating the expansive landscape of the mind. This initial inspiration can arise from a challenge needing resolution, an awe-inspiring natural landscape, or even a seemingly ordinary daily occurrence. Capturing this fleeting impulse is paramount; it requires nurturing with focused attention to prevent it from fading into oblivion.

The Alchemy of Creative Thought: From Idea to Reality

Upon being captured, the impulse is directed into the transformative realm of creative cognition. In this context, the mind operates as a proficient alchemist, carefully converting the raw material of the initial spark into a concrete result. This transformation could encompass the generation of innovative solutions, the careful creation of a work of art, or the development of a comprehensive financial strategy. The essential component in this endeavor is the deliberate harnessing of our cognitive abilities and skills, carefully shaping the original idea into a tangible manifestation that can thrive in reality.

2. The Mind as a Sensitive Recording Plate

Now, take this further and consider the mind a sensitive recording plate. Think of your mind as one great photographic plate, exposed and sensitive, ready to receive and record the impressions you make upon it. The controlled habits are the lens, focusing, sharpening, and directing the light of your thoughts upon this mental canvas. Like a photo, these concentrated thoughts paint bright images on the plate, forming the mold of our destiny. Therefore, we must select our subjects judiciously, as they become the blueprint for the formation of our future.

The Lens of Habit: Directing the Mind's Impressionable Canvas

The human mind is a vast and sensitive plate in its pristine state. Like a photographic plate ready to be exposed, it is susceptible to many stimuli and experiences. However, through the filter of our controlled habits, we define which images are placed onto this mental canvas. Our habits act as filters, guiding the direction of our attention and influencing our perception and interaction with the world.

The Law of Attraction: Aligning Our Thoughts with Our Desires

The notion of the mind functioning as a recording plate resonates with the principles of the Law of Attraction. This principle posits that our prevailing thoughts and beliefs possess the capacity to draw analogous experiences into our existence. Through intentionally developing constructive and purpose-driven habits, we direct our mental focus toward the reality we aspire to manifest. The clarity of these thoughts, akin to vibrant brushstrokes on a canvas, constructs a vision of our aspirational future, shaping the trajectory of our lives.

Empowering Ourselves: Taking Control of the Mental Camera

By conceptualizing the mind as a recording medium and understanding controlled habits as the lens through which we view our experiences, we cultivate a profound sense of empowerment. We do not merely stand by as spectators in the grand performance of existence; rather, we engage as dynamic contributors equipped with the power to mold our own futures. By intentionally choosing and nurturing our habits, we position ourselves as the architects of our realities, skillfully guiding the focus of our minds to frame the visions of the future we aspire to achieve. This intentional perspective enables us to move beyond the constraints of social inheritance and cultivate a life that resonates with our most profound aspirations.

3. Universal Acquisition: The Law of the Mind

The human mind, in its primitive state, functions according to a principle referred to as universal acquisition. Envision a camera that captures all elements within its frame, irrespective of their characteristics. In a comparable manner, the mind, when devoid of conscious oversight, effortlessly records each thought, experience, and sensation that it encounters, regardless of whether they are positive or negative. The relentless stream of information can indeed be overwhelming, obscuring the clarity of our cognitive perceptions.

The Art of Focusing: Mastering the Mental Lens

Just as a distinct photograph demands an accurately focused lens, focusing the mind also requires the art of harnessing one's powers. Our controlled habits are that essential lens that orients our attention and screens out the irrelevant noise constantly impinging on our consciousness. As one practices habits that further mindfulness and intentionality, one sharpens the focus of one's mental lens, ensuring clarity and distinctness are present in the impressions etched on the canvas of the mind.

Illuminating the Subject: The Role of Subconscious and Emotions

Sitting in the back of our minds, along with our emotions, is like lighting in photography. Just as proper lighting enhances clarity and detail in a photograph, so do the emotional state and subconscious beliefs we bring to an experience, which greatly influences how our minds register it. For example, an optimistic attitude may illuminate a circumstance so that we can see its intricacies and possibilities. A negative and fearful attitude throws a shadow on it, which keeps the details from us and our ability to learn and grow.

The Law of Mind in Action: Selective Registration Through Habit

We deal with selective registration when working with the law of mind in action. Although our mind can, in reality, record everything, it's the habits that serve as a lens to bring this or that aspect into sharp focus for registration on the mental canvas. Subconscious programming and our emotional state determine how sharp and detailed these impressions are in our minds.

The Power of Intention: Flooding Our Subjects with Light

Through a comprehensive understanding of the Law of Mind, we empower ourselves to illuminate our subjects with clarity of intention. By intentionally fostering positive habits and emotional states, we bring to light the facets of life that resonate with our aspirations and objectives. This deliberate methodology enables us to assume the role of photographers in our own lives, framing the visuals that lay the foundation for a rewarding and significant future.

4. Controllable Attributes: The Art of Mental Photography

The notion of controllable attributes presents a compelling analogy, envisioning the mind as a mental camera. Our habits serve as the adjustable settings of a camera, influencing how we document experiences and construct our realities. Let us explore this analogy further to comprehend how we might leverage these attributes for our benefit.

Focusing the Lens: Selecting the Subject of Our Mental Photographs

The initial controllable attribute resembles the lens of a camera, allowing for precise focus and clarity. Much like a lens that sharpens a camera's focus on a particular subject, our habits curate the themes inscribed upon the canvas of our cognition. Within this framework, the "subjects" refer to our clearly defined major purposes – the objectives, ambitions, and principles that steer our existence. By intentionally cultivating habits that reinforce these foundational principles, we enhance the clarity of our cognitive perspective, thereby aligning our thoughts and experiences with our aspirational goals.

Exposure and the Emotional Landscape: Illuminating the Subject

The second attribute that can be controlled is exposure, reflecting the camera's exposure modifier. Exposure governs the quantity of light interacting with the film, influencing the captured image's clarity and intricacy. In a comparable manner, our emotions, efforts, and intentions are the variables that adjust the lens through which we perceive our mental landscape. These elements illuminate the subject, shaping our understanding and connection to it. The complexities and possibilities become clear when encountering a predicament with a positive mindset and considerable effort. Conversely, a negative outlook and absence of energy create confusion and hinder the journey toward success.

The Picture of Our Destiny: A Product of Skillful Control

The final picture that our mental camera clicks, the picture of our destiny, is the result of how skillfully we can control all these attributes. As a photographer's skill determines the quality of an image, our ability to 'focus' on managing our habits, emotions, and concentration shapes the trajectory of our lives. We are conscious photographers who can skillfully capture experiences and nurture habits that will launch us into our aspired future.

The Power of Selective Focus: Framing Our Lives with Purpose

As the mental camera analogy shows, selective focus is crucial. Our habits, acting as the lens, permit the choice of subjects to be brought into sharp focus within the camera of our mind. The choice of subjects, our definite major purposes, gives such a life its framing principles. By paying conscious attention to these core values, we align our thoughts, feelings, and activities to create a purposeful and satisfying life.

The Role of the Operator: Cultivating Conscious Control

This analogy further emphasizes the significance of the operator – which is, in fact, ourselves. The intricate internal mechanisms of the camera execute the final act of image capture; however, the photographer selects the subject, modifies the exposure settings, and ultimately influences the resulting outcome. Comparably, we serve as the operators of our cognitive lenses. The habits we cultivate grant us the agency to determine our focal points, modify our emotional environments, and ultimately influence the trajectories we pursue. This comprehension enables us to actively construct our lives, surpassing the constraints set by social inheritance and collaboratively crafting a reality that resonates with our innermost aspirations.

5. The Art of Controlled Habits: Focusing and Exposure

In the expansive realm of intellectual exploration, where the landscape of our cognition extends boundlessly, the genuine thinker manifests as a creator, skillfully employing the tools of purpose and insight. These brushes represent our cultivated habits, serving as instruments that enable us to concentrate on and reveal the mental images we gather over the course of our lives. Let us explore the intricate process of creation, where the unwavering commitment to disciplined practices kindles the flames of imagination.

The Alchemy of Focused Exposure: Imprinting Thoughts in the Mental Darkroom

The processes of focusing and exposure are the true thinker's principal tools. Through these processes, fleeting thoughts become lasting impressions in our conscious minds as the photographer stamps his image on the sensitive film. For the latter process, repetition of the lensing process—which controlled habit provides—assures that our desired thought is brought into sharp focus. But this is not all that is required. Just as a photograph requires the right exposure to come out clearly, so do our mental impressions, which require the right emotional charge.

The emotional feelings are the light in the mental darkroom, and unless properly done, the brain cannot register a clear outline of the thought. Patience and practice are the two most important features of mastering this process. We must be prepared to return to our mental images, re-expose them in the light of focused habits, and allow the emotional landscape to carry them into full light. Through this artistry of intention, we may sculpt our thoughts and, ultimately, our destinies.

The Four Pillars of Focused Action: Building the Scaffolding of Our Dreams

Having delved into the intricacies of focused exposure, we shall now shift our attention to the pragmatic implementation of controlled habits in the pursuit of our objectives. This framework is comprised of four essential pillars:

a) A Clear and Specific Objective: The North Star, A Beacon for Our Journey

Establishing a clear and defined major purpose marks the initiation of this journey. This purpose serves as our guiding principle, a beacon that clarifies the direction we must take moving forward. Much like a compass that aligns with the North Star, our cultivated habits serve as the guiding rudder, meticulously directing us toward realizing our intended goals. Thus, the initial step involves recognizing this fundamental principle, the guiding star that directs the trajectory of our existence.

b) A Practical Approach: The Framework for Our Aspirations

The second pillar encompasses the formulation of a pragmatic strategy. These plans are foundational frameworks that convert our ambitions into tangible actions. Much like an architect carefully designs blueprints before breaking ground, we must also outline a strategic pathway toward achieving our objectives. Subsequently, intentional habits transform into the instruments we employ to build this vision, molding the frameworks underpinning our aspirations' realization. By carefully formulating our strategies, we create the foundational framework that enables our aspirations to materialize.

c) **The Intellectual Synergy Alliance: A Harmonious Convergence of Collective Knowledge**

The third pillar underscores the significance of cultivating an alliance centered on intellectual synergy. Envision a magnificent orchestral composition in which diverse instruments converge to produce a unified and impactful melody. Comparably, by cultivating partnerships with individuals who bring forth significant experience, education, skills, and influence, we enhance our own repository of knowledge and acquire invaluable insights. The habits we cultivate serve as the foundational musical notes, harmonizing with the efforts of our collaborators to compose a compelling melody that drives our progress. Ultimately, we are in pursuit of those exceptional individuals who can join us in our endeavors, enhancing our experiences with their distinct viewpoints.

d) **Immediate Action: The Artistry of Innovation**

The concluding pillar emphasizes the imperative for prompt action. Action serves as the essential brushstroke, converting the abstract canvas of thought into a dynamic and vivid tapestry of reality. Driven by purpose and shaped by our deliberate practices, these behaviors form the intricate hue layers that create our existence's exquisite tapestry. By intentionally using these brushes, we convert ephemeral ideas into concrete manifestations, positioning ourselves as the creators who infuse vitality into our aspirations.

Remember!

By embracing the art of controlled habits and harnessing the power of focused exposure, we gain the ability to transform the fleeting impulses of thought into the permanent imprints of our minds. Furthermore, by establishing a definite purpose, crafting a practical plan, cultivating intellectual alliances, and taking immediate action, we translate these mental imprints into the vibrant reality of our choosing. In this way, we transcend the limitations imposed by social inheritance and become the architects of our destinies.

6. The Engine of Action: Controlled Habits and the Four Pillars of Success

The efficacy of regulated habits is fundamentally rooted in their capacity to serve as the pivotal mechanism propelling individuals through the four essential stages necessary for realizing any specific objective. Establishing a clear purpose, devising a strategic plan, fostering collaborative relationships, and executing actions are entirely within our sphere of influence. Nonetheless, the cornerstone of achievement resides in the unwavering implementation of these strategies. This is the point at which regulated habits become significant.

The Consistent Conductor: Habits Orchestrate Our Destiny

Envision a splendid orchestral ensemble. Every musician, embodying a distinct phase, showcases the artistry and expertise required to produce a captivating melody. Nonetheless, without a conductor to harmonize their endeavors, the outcome would inevitably be a dissonant cacophony. In this analogy, controlled habits serve as the conductor. Maintaining a steadfast approach guarantees that each of the four steps is afforded the requisite focus and attention, steering us toward the harmonious realization of our objectives. The consistent application of this principle is essential; we must maintain a disciplined approach to our habits with steadfast concentration until we reach our intended goals.

7. Social Heredity and the Symphony of Success

The impact of social heredity on the subconscious mind can be understood as the transmission of tradition, values, and expectations across generations. We refer to social heredity as the legacy of these inherited elements. In a comparative sense, social heredity can be viewed as an ancestral echo that softly resonates within us; however, it is ultimately our response that holds the true significance. In this regard, regulated habits function as a guiding force. As individuals, we actively shape our futures by deliberately selecting habits that will ultimately define our experiences and realities.

The Subconscious: The Silent Maestro

Not every note, however, is orchestrated by this ensemble conductor. Our conscious awareness does not consistently monitor our habitual behaviors. This is the realm in which the subconscious operates as the unseen conductor. When practiced consistently, the application fosters the development of a disciplined habit, enabling the subconscious to assume control and execute the action effortlessly, thereby steering us in our endeavors. The depths of our subconscious mind skillfully arrange our actions, creating a harmonious interplay that reflects the intentions set forth by our conscious thoughts. By mirroring the actions of the subconscious as our quiet ally, we can access and harness its power to guide us in our desired path.

Controlled Habits: Attenuating Social Heredity and Shaping Destiny

Take a dimmer switch that controls the volume of the echoes of our ancestors' voices. Controlled habits are that dimmer switch. Building habits into a future we want, rather than one that society and others may want or expect, softens the limiting influences of social norms and expectations. Tapping into the subconscious mind through the enlightenment of the imagination, controlled habits ensure that our chosen actions are brought to their natural conclusion. In that sense, the controlled habits unshackle us from the constraints of social inheritance and grant destiny fabricated in conformity with our more profound urges.

8. Self-Determination: Charting Our Course with the Subconscious as Ally

Clarifying the role of the subconscious mind is of paramount importance. Although it serves an essential function, we must not relinquish all accountability and depend exclusively on its direction. The principle of self-determination continues to be a fundamental concept in contemporary discourse. Envision ourselves as captains steering through an expansive oceanic expanse. Our self-determination serves as a guiding compass, offering us a clear sense of direction and purpose in our endeavors. While we look to the stars for direction, it is imperative that we take an active role in navigating our course.

Controlled Habits: Harnessing the Winds of Intention

Regulated habits serve as our vessel's navigational sails. These mechanisms enable us to channel the winds of intention, guiding us toward our desired outcomes. We can embed these habits into our daily routines by consistently applying them, effectively converting our intentions into concrete actions.

The Subconscious: A Celestial Map of Inspiration

The subconscious mind plays an active role rather than serving as a mere passive observer. It evolves into our celestial navigation guide, steering us through concealed realms of creativity and illuminating possible routes to achievement. By cultivating positive and goal-oriented habits, we provide the subconscious with essential resources to generate innovative ideas, strategies, and solutions to facilitate our journey. It is crucial to recognize at this juncture that we regard the subconscious as a valuable partner in our endeavors rather than a substitute for our efforts.

The Power of Imprinting: Shaping the Subconscious Mind

The concept of self-determination is significantly enhanced when one comprehends the influence of imprinting on the subconscious mind. The knowledge, skills, and positive habits we cultivate and consistently apply through deliberate practices become deeply embedded in our subconscious. This internalized knowledge subsequently emerges as a rich source of ideas, strategies, and motivation, enabling us to realize our aspirations. By intentionally cultivating our habits, we fundamentally influence the architecture of our subconscious mind, thereby transforming it into a formidable instrument for achieving success.

9. Breaking Free from the Labyrinth: Overcoming the Fallacy of Assumption

Grasping these foundational principles represents merely the initial phase of a more comprehensive journey. Genuine transformation requires the implementation of these concepts into practice. Persistence is of utmost importance. We must diligently integrate these principles into our routines until they are firmly established as foundational habits in our everyday existence. Repetition serves as a fundamental principle, given that deeply embedded social patterns often resist change. By consistently nurturing our selected habits, we systematically displace the constraining factors of our surroundings and substitute them with empowering frameworks that drive us toward our objectives.

The Fallacy of Social Heredity: Breaking Free from Silent Sculptors

In the intricate maze of our cognition, where the repercussions of ancestral wisdom persist, we confront the misconception of assumption. Social heredity encompasses the traditions and expectations transmitted across generations, functioning as a subtle yet powerful force that molds our behaviors and habits, often without our conscious awareness. The peril resides in conflating these unregulated habits with deliberate decisions. These forces resemble invisible chains, subtly constraining us to patterns we have not consciously chosen.

Envision these chains as the unseen influences that steer our behaviors, frequently beyond our conscious recognition. These factors can significantly influence our dietary preferences, professional trajectories, and interpersonal connections. Escaping these constraints necessitates a purposeful engagement in self-reflection and an intentional decision-making process. By cultivating an awareness of these unseen influences, we can start to critically examine our behaviors and engage in more deliberate decision-making.

Achieving self-mastery fundamentally involves critically examining the misconceptions surrounding social heredity and making the conscious decision to forge our own unique trajectory. Much like a conductor meticulously guides an orchestra, we can take charge of our own lives, skillfully arranging our habits and decisions to compose a harmonious symphony of self-mastery.

Remember!

Through the embrace of self-determination and the strategic harnessing of controlled habits, we have the potential to convert the subtle influences of social heredity from mere limitations into significant stepping stones for personal growth. When regarded as a collaborator and enhanced through affirmative conditioning, the subconscious mind emerges as a wellspring of inspiration and creativity. By engaging in consistent efforts and deliberately dismissing the misconception of social heredity, we can liberate ourselves from the intricate web of restrictive patterns and take on the role of creators of our futures, steering through the expansive sea of existence with intention and clarity.

10. Action: The Spark that Ignites the Furnace

The path to crafting our future is fundamentally anchored in one essential principle: action. Action serves as the catalyst that ignites the fire of disciplined habits. Without establishing these habits, the essential mental imprints—the foundational blueprints for our future—cannot be inscribed within the subconscious mind. Fundamentally, action serves as the catalyst that fuels the process of transformation.

The Alchemy of Action: From Thought to Reality

Envision a blacksmith's forge, where raw materials are transformed through skill and artistry. Action is a formidable tool that converts ephemeral ideas into concrete reality. Disciplined habits are the foundational framework that molds and enhances our cognitive processes. However, much like a solitary spark cannot shape a blade, ephemeral thoughts alone do not possess the capacity to instigate enduring transformation. Thoughts, akin to fleeting sparks, dissipate and diminish without the enduring intensity that action provides.

Fueling the Transformation: The Chain Reaction of Action

To foster enduring transformation, it is essential to stoke the flames through unwavering commitment to action. This action initiates a significant chain reaction. Initially, the process of thought generation takes place, driven by our intrinsic desires and aspirations. Furthermore, the establishment of controlled habits guarantees that these thoughts are consistently highlighted, thereby creating a profound and enduring impact on the brain. Ultimately, the subconscious mind, fortified by this ongoing input, assumes control, effortlessly steering our actions and driving us toward our objectives. The ongoing interplay of action, cognitive reinforcement, and subconscious involvement serves as a fundamental mechanism for actualizing our aspirations.

Remember!

Simply possessing good intentions does not suffice in the endeavor to effectively shape our destiny. It demands a steadfast dedication to active involvement. Through the regular practice of disciplined habits, we can meaningfully convert fleeting thoughts into lasting mental impressions. We cultivate the depths of our subconscious, allowing it to guide us in manifesting the future we aspire to create. Embrace action, the essential force that propels the journey of transformation, and assume responsibility for shaping your own destiny.

11. The Power Within: Unveiling the Sources of Achievement

Having examined the significant impact of regulated habits, let us further investigate the sources of power that propel us on our quest to attain our aspirations. We will further explore the essential cognitive faculties engaged in the four previously delineated steps.

a. The Subconscious Mind: The Alchemical Crucible of Creation

The subconscious mind presents itself as a formidable reservoir of creative potential. It can be compared to an alchemical crucible, a container in which the transformative process of creation takes place. In this realm, our profound aspirations intertwine with the boundless essence of universal wisdom. Envision this boundless intelligence as a concealed elixir, a formidable reservoir of universal energy. By exploring our desires, the subconscious mind formulates powerful constructs of thought. These reflections circulate within a conceptual mixing chamber, poised for transformation into concrete realities. It is essential to leverage the creative potential of the subconscious mind by deliberately articulating our desires and aspirations. In this process, we assume the role of alchemists, crafting the elixirs that will ultimately influence our destinies.

The subconscious mind serves as a portal to the vast realm of infinite intelligence. It represents the intersection of our intrinsic human aspirations and the universe's boundless possibilities. This powerful combination generates significant creative potential, which we can subsequently channel and realize in the tangible realm. In this process, we witness the evolution of our thoughts and aspirations into actionable steps and measurable outcomes.

b. Willpower: The Forge Bellows that Shape Destiny

Another significant source of energy resides in the will. Envision a blacksmith's workshop, where the rhythmic clanging of metal against metal resonates, shaping not just iron but the very essence of creation itself. Our will serves as the bellows, the force that sustains the flames of our intentions, ensuring they continue to burn brightly. By harnessing unwavering determination, we cultivate disciplined habits, the raw material that will be shaped into the tools necessary for achieving our aspirations. However, without the steadfast exercise of our will, we risk becoming mere spectators in the unfolding narrative of our existence. Habits, shaped by our circumstances, create entrenched pathways that can lead us astray from the intentions we have established for ourselves. It is essential to understand that we are the architects of our own existence. We must wield the force of our determination to continuously sculpt and refine our habits and actions in alignment with our principles.

Remember!

The dynamic relationship between the subconscious mind, a reservoir of creative potential, and willpower, the catalyst that influences our behaviors, enables individuals to transcend the constraints of social heredity and carve out their unique journey toward success.

12. Willpower: The Artist's Brush that Paints Our Desires

The faculty of will is an important means of shaping our destiny. Willpower may be thought of as the brush with which the artist paints within our conscious mind a clear, vivid picture of what we desire. This is accomplished by repeated presentation. We engrave upon our mentality the things we desire by continually bringing those desired results before our minds.

The Palette of Controlled Habits: Blending Colors of Intention

Controlled habits are like an artist's palette, containing all the colors needed to paint life with desired things. Each controlled habit is like one color or another, representing an action or behavior executed in a manner that contributes to some sort of overall achievement. By strategically merging these habits with one another, we will allow the dynamic and intricate blend of intention to evolve our first vision into a masterpiece of achievement.

The Power of Repetition: Refining the Masterpiece

Nevertheless, one solitary brushstroke alone cannot suffice in creating a true masterpiece. Comparably, transient thought is unlikely to create a durable impact on our cognitive landscape. This is the point at which repetition becomes significant. Envision the artist diligently applying successive layers of brushstrokes, intricately enhancing details, and meticulously refining the composition on the canvas. Much like an artist meticulously applies strokes to attain clarity in their work, we, too, must consistently articulate our desired outcomes to our conscious mind for optimal understanding and manifestation. By engaging in this iterative process, we enhance our cognitive representation, fortifying its presence in our subconscious and amplifying the probability of its realization in the tangible realm.

Remember!

Painting Our Dreams into Reality. The essential point is to regard the individual's will as the artist's brush, shaping the canvas of their existence. Embrace it with unwavering intention and a relentless mindset that continuously, in his thoughts, illustrates a compelling vision of his aspirations. When mixing, it is essential to employ deliberate techniques on your palette, strategically combining elements to enhance the depth and dimension of your artistic vision. Ultimately, it is essential to reiterate: the application process over time hones your cognitive creation, transforming that vision into a vivid reality, as vibrant as one envisions.

Coda: The Enduring Exhibition[15]

As the gallery lights fade, a serene silence envelops the expansive realm where the creations of our souls gleam in the soft glow. May this moment echo with profound significance: Our thoughts, the delicate brushstrokes of our being, weave the timeless tapestry we leave in our wake. Though social heredity may softly murmur its sway, we stand as the artists of this grand display. Let the mental canvases we weave be rich with purpose, each brushstroke ignited by the vivid shades of disciplined routines.

The dancing glow reveals the fleeting nature of the world beyond. Our musings, like whispers of the eternal, possess the strength to rise above the fleeting moments. Let us recall that we are the creators holding the brush of fate. Let our minds be vibrant tapestries woven with steadfast intent, where every line is drawn by the relentless hand of determination.

---

[15] Composed with assistance from Google Gemini AI

As the last whispers of light dissolve, a profound truth emerges from the shadows. Deeds, not mere musings, are the artisan's tool that carves the path of our fate. The echoes of social heredity may sing their unwavering song, yet we are the artisans who shape the ultimate visage. Let our habits, crafted with purpose and carried out with steadfast resolve, weave the tapestry of our enduring legacy.

Though the gallery's doors may gently shut, the exhibition lingers on, a whisper of art in the air. We are the creators, the weavers, and the chiselers of our own destinies. Let us embrace the art of mindful habits, crafting a tapestry that rises above the bounds of our lineage, resonating with the timeless grace of our most cherished dreams.

The Symphony of the Mind: A Conductor's Guide

Our cognitive processes resemble magnificent theaters, vibrant with the enthralling display of thoughts and emotions. In this space, concepts gracefully dance while underlying motivations quietly brew just out of sight. However, this performance does not consistently exhibit harmony. Disorganized thoughts, reminiscent of whirling dervishes, have the potential to disrupt our cognitive flow, while ingrained habits, serving as echoes from our past, may guide us toward unproductive trajectories.

Willpower's adept direction is essential to orchestrating a harmonious blend of concentrated thought and intentional action. In the subsequent sections, we will explore the intricate interplay between structured cognition and willpower. Our focus will be on strategies to foster concentrated thinking and an analysis of the influence our thoughts exert on our behaviors.

Part 1: Important Notes for Organized Thought and Willpower

Our minds are an interesting stage, the grand theater of cognition. Here, a symphony of thoughts and emotions unravels; some are clear, focused, and driven by refined emotions, and others are light, raw feelings. This section acts as your conductor's guide, offering essential notes on creating a balanced and purposeful symphony of thought guided by the spirit of organized thought and willpower.

1. **Organized Thoughts: The Balanced Symphony**

    Think of your thoughts as being analogous to musical notes. Organized thoughts are the clear, well-articulated melodies that provide the backbone to any beautiful symphony. These results of pointed concentration and unclouded reason come with a harmonious blend of will and emotions. Just as a conductor uses his baton, so will ensure the ideal ratio between emotional energy feeding our thought processes and guiding light, or reason, shaping them. A balance that enables us to write melodies of thought that vibrate with purpose, moving us toward our goals.

2. **Disorganized Thoughts: The Wild Dance**

    Not every thought is a beautiful note in a symphony. At times, emotions take over center stage and introduce us to a wild dance of disorganized thoughts. Whirling dervishes might be chaotic and distracting. Powered by raw emotion-the untamed rhythm- they can lead one astray. But the conductor is not impotent. We will consider methods for harnessing the whirlwind of disorganized thoughts and giving coherent narrative forms to them. By controlling the faculty of reason-the choreographer- we can impose purpose upon our thoughts, take the chaotic ballet, and turn it into an intentional performance.

3. The Faculty of Willpower: The Balancing Act

Will navigates the precarious path, skillfully balancing the turbulent winds of emotion with the steady direction of rational thought. The intense waves of feeling can disrupt our equilibrium, yet rational thought offers the guidance and steadiness necessary to maintain our course toward clarity. Mastery of willpower transforms us into adept practitioners of intention, enabling us to navigate our thoughts, emotions, and, ultimately, the course of our lives.

4. The Motive of Willpower: The North Star of Purpose

Envision the mind as an elaborate orchestra, where each thought represents a distinct musician contributing to a harmonious symphony. A conductor needs to lead the performance with a well-defined vision to achieve a harmonious symphony. This conductor embodies our willpower, the driving force that channels our thoughts and actions toward a specific objective.

A robust and steadfast purpose serves as our guiding light, illuminating the trajectory toward our objectives. Much like a conductor orchestrates the tempo and direction of a symphony, a clear and defined purpose steers our willpower, cohesively harmonizing our thoughts and actions; this purpose invigorates our determination, acting as the guiding force that directs us toward our intended goals.

Envision willpower as a tightrope walker, skillfully navigating the delicate balance between our desires and aspirations. A clear and defined purpose serves as a foundational safety net, offering both stability and direction in our endeavors. By strategically applying a clear and defined purpose, we position ourselves as navigators of our own fate, meticulously plotting a trajectory toward our envisioned goals.

5. **Navigating the Landscape of Habits**

a. **Voluntary Habits: The Explorers of Habit**

Voluntary habits are like footprints in the sand. They develop when a desire has been repeatedly expressed, whether with a well-defined motive or not. Just as explorers work their way through unfamiliar terrain, we can develop these habits by willfully choosing the thoughts and actions appropriate to reaching our goals. Willpower may be necessary to force this repetition initially, but the action becomes automatic after a while. The motive acts as our compass to keep us in the direction of travel toward our wanted goal. In this chapter, we shall consider methods of forming and maintaining voluntary habits.

b. **Involuntary Habits: The Currents of Social Heredity**

Involuntary habits constitute the currents that may sweep us far from our chosen course. These character habits instilled by social heredity- the river- drag us toward apathy and the lack of purpose. Consider for a moment being in a rapid current: the power of the current is like the power of involuntary habits. And just as a strong captain tames the wild waters to land his ship unharmed, our will can master such currents of habit. Observing the rapids of involuntary habits allows one to set a new course so as not to be taken by the tide of social conformity. It is to recognize and override involuntary habits that we now turn to in this section.

Remember!

The Perils of Unchecked Involuntary Habits. When left to their own devices, involuntary habits can guide us toward the path of least resistance, culminating in procrastination, apathy, and an overwhelming feeling of stagnation. By comprehending these habits and their associated risks, we can implement proactive measures to liberate ourselves from their impact.

Coda: The Everlasting Melody[16]

As the curtain descends upon this scene in the vast stage of our thoughts, may we remember the deep spectacle that reveals itself to us with each passing day. Our thoughts, akin to elegant dancers, twirl upon the stage, crafting our experiences and etching an everlasting impression upon the world. Willpower, the vigilant maestro, orchestrates their movements, weaving purpose and direction into each graceful step.

The melody of our musings is not a transient act but a ceaseless creation that resonates through the ages. Let us endeavor to weave a melody that resonates with the universe, a creation born of concentrated intention, steadfast resolve, and uplifting deeds. In mastering the delicate dance of this symphony, we weave not just our own legacy but also add our notes to the vast, resounding harmony of the cosmos.

Part 2: The Role of Thoughts in Shaping Behavior

The Architects of Our Reality. Our minds are like fertile grounds where the seeds of our thoughts take root and, after some time, grow into the fruits of our actions. This section elaborates on how our internal narrative significantly shapes the way we function in society and provides actionable means of tapping into that for results.

1.   The Footprints of Habit

Habits are the footprints etched into the soil of our existence. They come into being through the repetition of actions guided

---

[16] Composed with assistance from Google Gemini AI

by the blueprints our thoughts have created. While designing our behavior and lives, we need to create positive thought patterns and rehearse them consciously.

Actionable Strategy: Techniques of Habit Formation

Identify the key habits: First, identify the things you want to work on in developing or breaking a habit. For example, if you want to instill in yourself a daily exercise habit, know this as one of your key growth areas.

Thought Map: Visualize positive thoughts and motivations associated with this particular habit. For instance, imagine how great improved health and an increase in energy will feel.

Plan and Perform: Where does this fit in your schedule? You need to program your workouts and create a system of reminders that will make you responsible.

2. The Quality Control Check: Monitoring Thought Habits

Everything one thinks into being has the potential to be projected forward into a physical reality. Thus, becoming aware of and managing thought habits becomes an important factor in avoiding negative consequences.

3. From Seeds to Harvest: The Power of Action

The thoughts are like seeds that lie in the fertile soil's womb; continuous action makes them grow. Successful people know how important it is to nurture their thoughts with serious effort.

4. The Peril of Uncontrolled Habits

Habits function as influential forces, possessing the potential to either advance our progress or hinder our momentum. Uncontrolled habits resemble whirlpools, drawing us into a vortex of negativity that may culminate in misery, poverty, and

THE EVOLUTION OF THOUGHT

failure. Much like a proficient captain adeptly maneuvers through dangerous waters, we must cultivate the ability to avoid these mental whirlpools. The seductive call of mediocrity, embodying the appeal of unrestrained habits, can potentially divert us from our intended path. By acknowledging the perils associated with unchecked habits, we position ourselves as the architects of our destiny, navigating a pathway toward achievement and personal satisfaction.

Actionable Strategy: Controlling Habits

- **Recognize Detrimental Habits:** It is essential to pinpoint behaviors that impede your progress. Procrastination is a significant barrier to achieving any goal you set for yourself.

- **Establishing Replacement Habits:** Identify constructive alternatives to detrimental behaviors. For those who struggle with procrastination, it is advisable to implement short, focused work intervals complemented by breaks between sessions.

- **Seek Support:** Identify the individuals—friends, accountability partners, or mentors—who can provide the most effective support and encouragement as you work towards transforming these habits.

5. Escaping the Canyons of Stagnant Thought

The human mind can be likened to an expansive riverbed, wherein the continuous stream of thoughts etches distinct patterns over time. Repetition, akin to the flowing water, significantly deepens these channels. Nevertheless, unregulated repetition may result in the establishment of cognitive canyons, confining us within a loop of unproductive thinking. Such stagnant thought processes can potentially undermine our cognitive engagement and impede our advancement.

We must assume the role of architects of our cognition, consistently redirecting the trajectory of our thoughts to avert the emergence of these cognitive voids. By acknowledging the perils of unchanging perspectives, we position ourselves as the designers of our freedom. We have the capacity to construct connections across these mental divides, facilitating a seamless exchange of ideas and nurturing a vibrant and inventive cognitive process.

Actionable Strategy: Enhancing Cognitive Flexibility

- **Embrace Novel Experiences:** Cultivate a mindset actively receptive to new challenges and opportunities that can stimulate your cognitive processes. It may encompass a range of experiences, from acquiring a novel skill to adopting an alternative viewpoint.

- **Engage in reflective thinking** by consistently examining the processes that shape your thoughts. Critically examine your thought processes to approach running from a novel perspective. Engage in self-reflection by posing inquiries like, "What underlying assumptions are I making?" or "In what alternative ways can I approach this issue?"

- **Broaden Your Horizons:** Intentionally immerse yourself in various knowledge and perspectives. Read, participate in seminars, and converse with individuals from diverse backgrounds.

Coda: The Artisan of Existence[17]

As the curtain descends upon this journey of reflection and action, let us embrace this deep revelation: Our musings are the architects of our existence. Every thought, every ephemeral whisper, weaves into the magnificent tapestry that is our existence.

Willpower dances as the maestro, guiding with a wand of unwavering focus. It orchestrates the rhythm of our musings, weaving together a symphony of contemplation and endeavor. In mastering the delicate dance of this inner ensemble, we do not merely mold our actions; we weave a tapestry of experiences that echo with meaning and joy.

Let this melody resonate not only across the ages, but within the hearts we embrace. May the whispers of our musings rise as a gentle tide, weaving together the fabric of existence, nurturing the symphony of evolution, unity, and uplifting transformation.

Endnote: Willpower and the Symphony of Success

Willpower as Passion: The Maestro of the Mind

In the grand concert hall of the mind, it is not just the willpower that conducts; the will is the fiery maestro conducting the orchestra of all our cerebral faculties. Visualize the will as some wild maestro, standing firm upon the podium as he conducts an ensemble of faculties playing fervently. Every faculty plays its role- from focused precision to the wilds of creativity- to harmonize into the grand symphony of achievement.

---

[17] Composed with assistance from Google Gemini AI

The secret to using and perfecting these mental processes is to focus our willpower as strongly as passion will. When we project that willpower into something valuable to be done, it becomes an irrepressible powerhouse, guiding and controlling the mind, emotions, and activities up the ladder of success.

The Maestro s Baton: Willpower in Action

Imagine our intellects as expansive venues where the harmonious echoes of success reverberate. A diverse ensemble of faculties stands poised, anticipating the guiding influence of a passionate maestro—willpower. Driven by enthusiasm, determination ignites the collective ensemble, guaranteeing that every element plays its distinct role in the magnificent symphony of achievement.

1. **The Emotional Fiasco: Willpower Conducts the Heart**

   With its wand in hand, the will exerts influence over our emotions. Each emotion—be it fear, joy, or determination—stands tall and contributes to the intricate symphony of our experiences. The emotional resonance is palpable; the orchestra crescendos embody the depth of sentiment within. The intensity of emotions, ignited by sheer determination, propels us into fervent endeavors.

2. **Reason's Measured Melody: Willpower and Logic in Harmony**

   Reason, the composed soloist, strides forward with assurance as willpower offers a subtle affirmation. Reason stands at the center, conducting a seamless integration of logic, analysis, and insight. This meticulously crafted symphony vibrates with emotional intensity, guaranteeing that our choices are guided by both passion and clear understanding. Willpower does not dominate reason; instead, it nurtures collaborative interaction.

3. **Imagination's Dazzling Display: Willpower Paints the Canvas of Dreams**

    Imagination serves as the central force in the grand symphony of the cosmos. The call of the will resonates, igniting the imagination in a vibrant display of kaleidoscopic hues and illumination. The interplay of aspirations and imaginative potential unfolds on the stage, crafting a cosmos of opportunities through the lens of cognition. The will serves as a compass for the imagination, directing it through various pathways to enable a vivid visualization of our intended achievements.

4. **Memory's Ancient Echoes: Willpower Whispers from the Past**

    Memory, the venerable custodian of knowledge, unveils the timeworn volumes of lived experience. The faculties will invite forth lessons, experiences, and knowledge from the depths of our cognitive reservoirs. The echoes of history resonate profoundly, imparting wisdom that informs our actions and enriches our contemporary endeavors. Willpower navigates the vast repository of memory, extracting the knowledge and experiences most pertinent to our present objectives.

5. **The Bridge to the Unconscious: Willpower and the Flow of Inspiration**

    Willpower serves as the crucial link, facilitating the connection between the conscious and subconscious domains. Across this vibrant bridge, one can observe the seamless flow of intuition, inspiration, and insight. The symphony reverberates with the subtle echoes of the unconscious mind, enhancing the performance with a profound depth of comprehension that transcends the limits of mere conscious awareness.

6. Beyond the Ordinary: Willpower and the Sixth Sense

Willpower serves as the alchemist, skillfully blending the elements within the cauldron of our minds. The elixir effervesces, revealing glimpses of insight, anticipation, and prophetic vision. The symphony elevates itself beyond the confines of the mundane, extending its reach into dimensions that surpass the capabilities of the five senses. The concept of willpower has the potential to enhance our intuitive capabilities, enabling us to access a profound reservoir of comprehension and awareness. Nevertheless, this increased awareness emerges solely when driven by a profound desire or a clear objective.

The Power of Positive Habits: A Symphony Unleashed

The Maestro Reveals the Symphony! The orchestra, meticulously tuned and the maestro firmly grasping the baton of determination, orchestrates the symphony of success in all its splendid glory. Effective habits serve as the essential catalyst for each component of this orchestra to fulfill its role, resulting in a powerful and inspiring performance that resonates profoundly.

1. Continuous Enthusiasm: The Timpani of Passion

The enthusiasm serves as the resounding kettledrums that establish the rhythm for the entire symphony. It resonates with the vibrancy of aspirations, objectives, and visions. The expert understands that unrestrained passion serves as the driving force propelling us forward in the journey of success. A well-practiced habit engages a continuous source of enthusiasm—a motivation that flows both consciously and subconsciously within us, propelling us toward achieving our objectives. This enduring enthusiasm has the potential to ignite insights and ideas during our slumber, propelling us further along the trajectory we have selected.

2. The Pleasure of Work: A Virtuoso Performance

The violins commence their performance, intricately crafting a sonata that embodies the essence of labor. The resonance of diligence permeates the hall, anchored by a concentrated intent and mastery—a performance of virtuosity that captivates the audience. Transforming a chore into a fulfilling endeavor is a remarkable outcome of cultivating effective habits. The intricate nuances of our work can captivate us to such an extent that the act of labor transforms into a source of joy, akin to the satisfaction derived from a well-prepared meal.

3. The Anthem of Courage: The Brass Section Takes Center Stage

The brass section resounds with a formidable anthem of bravery. The resonant composition comprises various risks and challenges, embodying the essence of taking leaps of faith. The maestro embodies a sense of pride and stature, acknowledging courage as the vital connection that opens pathways to new and remarkable possibilities. As we cultivate positive habits, we witness the blossoming of courage within ourselves. It becomes increasingly evident that obstacles do not serve as our downfall; rather, they transform into integral components of the pathway toward achieving success. Moreover, the positive momentum of our habits may be fostering cooperation from those around us, thereby enhancing our sense of empowerment.

4. The Harmonious Chorus of Cooperation

The choir collectively elevates its vocal expression in a harmonious display of collaboration. Allies, partners, and collaborators harmonize their voices, producing a cohesive and impactful resonance. The audience participates, contributing to a collective crescendo. Establishing positive habits fosters a collaborative ethos, drawing in individuals who align with our objectives and principles. Individuals are inherently attracted to those who radiate a clear sense of purpose and direction, fostering a desire to engage in the shared journey toward collective success.

5. **Unveiling Opportunities: The Celestial Overture**

The strings elevate the narrative, heralding the emergence of opportunity. The celestial overture arrives, brimming with the potential of new opportunities and pathways, heralding a period ripe for the fulfillment of our destiny. The maestro embodies the role of a gracious host, enticing the audience to step into the spotlight of these remarkable opportunities. As we cultivate positive habits and diligently pursue our objectives, unforeseen opportunities begin to emerge. The cosmos aligns to assist individuals who exhibit unwavering focus and determination, strategically positioning the appropriate individuals and resources along their journey.

6. **Uprising of Intuitive Imagination: The Playful Woodwinds**

The woodwinds produce a playful trill, evoking a whimsical melody that resonates with the emergence of innate imagination. Concepts, innovations, and elaborate choreography now elegantly take center stage. As beneficial practices are established, your imagination sharpens and becomes increasingly dynamic. The symphony dances anew with vibrant energy; novel patterns of potential emerge unexpectedly. Through a steadfast commitment to our goals, we cultivate a fertile ground for innovative problem-solving and creative insights to flourish.

7. Increasing Stamina: The Thunderous Percussion

The percussion enters with an unyielding rhythm, serving as a clear manifestation of increasing endurance. With a rhythmic cadence of progression, qualities such as endurance, resilience, and strength continually move forward. The conductor strikes the baton with unwavering determination, setting the tempo for a journey of achievement. Establishing positive habits cultivates the resilience necessary to sustain prolonged periods of productivity without experiencing fatigue. We have the potential to cultivate both mental and physical endurance, enabling us to navigate obstacles and maintain our determination in the face of challenges.

8. Improved Health Conditions: The Healing Flutes

The flutes emit a soft melody, embodying a profound representation of improved health states. This piece functions as a soothing melody, nurturing energy, harmony, and holistic health. The audience partakes in profound breaths, encountering a rejuvenation of existence's core. Attaining a state of well-being hinges on regular engagement in practices that foster our physical health and enhance our cognitive clarity. As a result, this holistic perspective has fostered improvements in our natural health and overall well-being.

9. Adoption of a More Cheerful View: The Playful Pianos

The pianos produce a delightful melody, creating an atmosphere of joy and vitality. Optimism, hope, and laughter gracefully dance across the stage. The conductor gestures playfully, encouraging all to participate in this exuberant celebration of movement. As effective methodologies are implemented, the oppressive lenses of despair begin to diminish in their influence. We begin to perceive the world through lenses imbued with clarity, optimism, and conviction. Embracing a positive attitude as our default setting enables us to navigate challenges with remarkable cheerfulness and resilience.

10. Positive Charge in Self-Vibration: The Resonant Orchestra

The entire orchestra ascends in a powerful crescendo, akin to a self-vibrational phenomenon. The resonance of the cosmos manifests through frequencies that embody abundance, success, and fulfillment. This symphony resonates through the dimensions of time and space, serving as a testament to the transformative power of positive habits. By aligning our thoughts and actions with our objectives, we transformed the entire frequency of our being. The distinct vibration within the energetic signature attracts positive life experiences, facilitating the realization of desired outcomes.

11. Overcoming Defeats: The Trumpets and the Stepping Stones

The trumpets resound in a commanding fanfare, leading the symphony into a transformative shift. It is the unavoidable tempest of failure. Amidst the chaos, a fresh melody emerges, captivating the senses. The obstacles encountered were, in fact, opportunities for growth all along. The conductor should embrace each setback with a smile, recognizing it as merely another note in the intricate symphony of life. Effective strategies empower us to perceive setbacks not as failures but rather as valuable opportunities for learning and personal development. We have the potential to cultivate resilience, transforming challenges into pivotal stepping stones that propel us forward in our journey.

12. Transmutation of Negative Energy: The Unassailable Fortress

As the symphony approaches its zenith, a profound transformation unfolds. The melody embodies the transformation of negative energy into a positive force. As one navigates through the complexities of emotion, it becomes evident that fear, misgiving, and doubt gradually give way to a profound sense of determination. The symphony ascends to a crescendo, constructing an unyielding fortress—a citadel of unwavering resolve. Effective practice cultivates the skill of transforming adverse influences into a source of dynamic motivation. We come to understand the challenge in its authentic form—an opportunity—where fear is transformed into courage and doubt evolves into resolute decision-making. This transformative process empowers individuals to surmount challenges and realize their aspirations.

Remember!

The Profound Impact of Harmony. As we carve our paths with deliberate wisdom and purpose, we shape the destiny that defines our being. Skillfully utilized, each practice transforms into a potent tool in the elaborate symphony of mental activity. As these tools perform their harmonious ballet, they create a mosaic of victory that resounds throughout every aspect of our existence. Armed with an optimistic heart, steadfast determination, and the guided precision of an adept, we are equipped to overcome any obstacle we encounter.

CODA

⚡⚡⚡

THE ONGOING SYMPHONY OF LIFE

⚡⚡⚡

The Eternal Act[18]

*A*s the majestic curtain descends upon this scene, a resonant whisper lingers: Our musings, the elegant performers, personify the heritage we imprint upon the world. Willpower, the maestro, commands the baton, orchestrating the rhythm and directing each graceful motion. Let the melody of our existence echo endlessly, entwined with the vast orchestration of the universe.

The Dance of Change
In the grand tapestry of existence, each thread weaves a unique melody, crafting a harmonious opus that resonates through time.

The Prelude of Intent: A Journey Awash in Dreams
The violins ascend, their harmonies lifting the burdens of our aspirations. Purpose, a heavenly prelude, unfolds the canvas for our magnificent display. We enter the luminous glow, hearts overflowing with eager dreams, poised to set forth on the odyssey of our existence.

The lively cadence of endeavor: a spirited procession onward

---

[18] Composed with assistance from Google Gemini AI

The drums resound like a tempest, a vibrant rush that propels us onward with a relentless rhythm. Movement unfolds like a dance, each stride a heartbeat in the symphony of progress. We soar and spin, dancing gracefully upon the grand stage of existence, our movements a mesmerizing display that captivates the onlookers of the world surrounding us.

The gentle cadence of contemplation: a moment to delve within

The cellos release a sorrowful lament, their melodies reverberating through the chamber in a tender adagio. In stillness, a gentle pause beckons, urging us to ponder the path we tread. In the loom of time, memories and regrets entwine, crafting a rich tapestry of reflection, whispering the lessons learned and the journeys that mold our very essence.

The Dance of Bonds: A Tribute to Connections

The flutes weave a tapestry of playful notes, conjuring the bliss of unity. This playful dance weaves a tapestry of joy, honoring the connections we nurture with one another. In a dance of smiles and warm embraces, we find ourselves twirling through cherished moments, a gentle reminder of how vital our connections are in weaving the harmonious tapestry of existence.

The Grand Conclusion of Change: A Renewal Born from Flourishing

As we draw near to the grand conclusion, the whole orchestra rises in a splendid surge of sound. Each instrument spills forth its essence into the melody, embodying the tapestry of our journeys. In the theater of existence, a celestial metamorphosis dances into view. In the embrace of our unwavering quest for growth, fear, doubt, and hesitation dissolve like morning mist beneath the sun's warm gaze. From the ashes, we ascend, transformed into stronger, more resilient echoes of our former selves.

The Final Act: A Journey Woven in Unity

As the last whisper lingers in the ether, we offer a reverent bow. We are the artisans of sound, the orchestrators of harmony, and the players who have woven together this splendid tapestry of music. The cosmos, a vast audience, bursts forth in resounding applause, with shimmering stars bearing witness to our triumph.

Let our return be a tapestry of grandeur woven with threads of splendor! Let us transcend the boundaries of the stage and wander into the boundless expanse of being. The melody of our existence weaves on, resonating through the ages, a tribute to the profound magic of virtuous deeds.

.

᪥᪥᪥

THIRD BOOK: THE COGNITEXIS ENIGMA

The Odyssey of Intellect: Navigating the Cognitexis

᪥᪥᪥

Venture forth, intrepid explorer, into the labyrinthine corridors of cognition. Within these twisting passages, the monstrous Minotaur of truth awaits. This is no mere maze of stone and shadow but a complex reasoning web where emotions and societal constructs intertwine with logic and insight.

Prepare for a perilous journey. Beware the whispers of prejudice, the siren song of confirmation bias, and the chilling miasma of unchecked emotion. These guardians of the labyrinth are ready to lead you astray from the path of true understanding.

This chapter equips you with the tools of a seasoned quester. We will map the treacherous landscape of Cognitexis, a term coined within the ADAM-GENE project to encompass the totality of human cognitive processes. You will learn to discern logic's unwavering blade from emotion's fickle flame, unraveling the tangled threads of thought to reach the heart of the Minotaur's lair—the elusive truth itself.

But tread carefully, for the Minotaur is not a creature to be vanquished. It is within this very confrontation, this grappling with our own biases and limitations, that true intellectual growth is found. The journey through the Cognitexis is not merely about finding answers but about forging the very instrument of inquiry – the discerning intellect, a cornerstone of the ADAM-GENE vision.

Embrace the challenge, dear reader. For within the labyrinth lies the potential for a profound transformation of the mind.